T0312231

THE LIVING FROM THE DEAD

# RSA·STR

THE RSA SERIES IN TRANSDISCIPLINARY RHETORIC

Edited by
Michael Bernard-Donals *(University of Wisconsin)* and
Leah Ceccarelli *(University of Washington)*

Editorial Board:
Diane Davis, The University of Texas at Austin
Cara Finnegan, University of Illinois at Urbana-Champaign
Debra Hawhee, The Pennsylvania State University
John Lynch, University of Cincinnati
Steven Mailloux, Loyola Marymount University
Kendall Phillips, Syracuse University
Thomas Rickert, Purdue University

The RSA Series in Transdisciplinary Rhetoric is a collaboration with the Rhetoric Society of America to publish innovative and rigorously argued scholarship on the tremendous disciplinary breadth of rhetoric. Books in the series take a variety of approaches, including theoretical, historical, interpretive, critical, or ethnographic, and examine rhetorical action in a way that appeals, first, to scholars in communication studies and English or writing, and, second, to at least one other discipline or subject area.

*Stuart J. Murray*

# THE LIVING
# FROM THE DEAD

## Disaffirming Biopolitics

THE PENNSYLVANIA STATE UNIVERSITY PRESS
UNIVERSITY PARK, PENNSYLVANIA

This book is freely available in an open access edition with
the generous support of The Pennsylvania State University
Libraries. Digital copies are available for download through
the Penn State University Press website.

Library of Congress Cataloging-in-Publication Data

Names: Murray, Stuart J., author.
Title: The living from the dead : disaffirming biopolitics /
    Stuart J. Murray.
Other titles: RSA series in transdisciplinary rhetoric.
Description: University Park, Pennsylvania : The Pennsylvania
    State University Press, [2022] | Series: The RSA series in
    transdisciplinary rhetoric | Includes bibliographical
    references and index.
Summary: "Presents a rhetorical critique of contemporary
    neoliberal biopolitics through a series of transdisciplinary
    case studies"—Provided by publisher.
Identifiers: LCCN 2022016490 | ISBN 9780271093413
    (hardback) | ISBN 9780271093406 (paper)
Subjects: LCSH: Biopolitics. | Rhetoric.
Classification: LCC JA80 .M86 2022 | DDC 320.01—
    dc23/eng/20220427
LC record available at https://lccn.loc.gov/2022016490

Copyright © 2022 Stuart J. Murray
All rights reserved
Printed in the United States of America
Published by The Pennsylvania State University Press,
University Park, PA 16802–1003

© The Rhetoric Society of America, 2022

The Pennsylvania State University Press is a member
of the Association of University Presses.

It is the policy of The Pennsylvania State University Press to
use acid-free paper. Publications on uncoated stock satisfy the
minimum requirements of American National Standard for
Information Sciences—Permanence of Paper for Printed
Library Material, ANSI z39.48–1992.

For my grandmother,
whose song I hear still.

# Contents

# Acknowledgments

The writer, it is said, gives up saying "I." . . . What speaks in him is the fact that, in one way or another, he is no longer himself; he isn't anyone any more.
—Maurice Blanchot

This work of slow scholarship, begun in 2012, is continuous with countless conversations over the years. My colleagues and graduate students in Carleton University's Department of English Language and Literature have challenged me in the best possible ways. Various parts of this book have informed every graduate seminar I have taught. I thank my students for their patience, for their curiosity, and for sharing their knowledge. The Canada Research Chairs program has afforded me additional research time to write and rewrite, again and again; this book draws on research supported by the Social Sciences and Humanities Research Council of Canada (2012–21), including a Knowledge Mobilization grant (2021) that has helped offset the costs of Open Access. I have been fortunate as well to belong to many empirical research teams across the disciplines: my collaborations with colleagues in nursing, forensic psychiatry, law and legal studies, social work, communication, women's and gender studies, and sociology have informed—and in many respects, have grounded—this theoretical project.

I owe a particular debt of gratitude to Sarah Burgess, who has read and commented on multiple iterations of every chapter. For years, she has been my constant, generous, and brilliant interlocutor. The true friend never flatters by withholding honest criticism. I humbly thank Barbara Biesecker, Alan Blum, Mary K. Bryson, Judith Butler, David L. Clark, Diane Davis, Michael Dorland, Erik Doxtader, Kathryn Ferguson, Marilou Gagnon, Christine Garlough, Twyla Gibson, Lisa Guenther, Adrian Guta, Kelly Happe, Dave Holmes, Hyo Yoon Kang, Sara Kendall, Brian Macaskill, Franny Nudelman, Keramet Reiter, Roger Stahl, Jill Stauffer, my late friend Deborah Lynn Steinberg, Janice Stewart, Vincenzo Susca, and Percy Walton.

Early versions of various chapters have been presented at the Département de sociologie, Université Paul-Valéry Montpellier (September 2019); the Department of Communication Studies, University of Georgia (February 2016 and

October 2017); the program in Peace, Justice, and Human Rights, Haverford College (October 2016); Kent Law School, University of Kent (May 2016); the Rhetoric Society of America Summer Institute (June 2013); multiple conferences convened by the Rhetoric Society of America (2014, 2016, 2018); the Association for the Study of Law, Culture and the Humanities (2013, 2015, 2019); the Critical Legal Conference (2019); and the Conference in Rhetorical Theory at the University of South Carolina (2013, 2015, 2017, 2019). J'aimerais remercier mes collègues du Centre de recherche en éthique (CRÉ) à l'Université de Montréal où j'ai passé une session en sabbatique à l'hiver 2016. C'est au CRÉ que j'ai écrit le premier jet du chapitre 3.

I thank my outstanding research assistants Delphine DiTecco, Alanna Gray, Megan Misztal, and especially Tad Lemieux, whose thinking on death and sovereignty has informed mine in so many ways. For the cover image, I am grateful to Steve Orrison and the International Institute for Restorative Practices for permission to use Si Lewen's artwork, and especially to Art Spiegelman, who so kindly provided me with the image from his personal collection.

Finally, and not least, I am grateful for my loving family, living and dead, and for my dog Finn, who was my faithful companion for thirteen happy years

# Introduction

This is a book that would hearken the voices of the dead, the dying, the dispossessed. But what might it mean to heed those we have let die, those who have been disappeared or disclaimed as the quiet casualties, the collateral damages, the opportunity costs of life today? Under what conditions might we hearken those dead who summon us, and exhort us, perhaps, to reckon with our unspeakable complicity in their deaths? These pages, which arise in care of such summons, exhortations, and calls to reckoning, neither speak *for* nor *as* the dead, the dying, or lives lost; neither as biography nor autobiography, theirs or ours, for it is too late for them (and for us) to take interest in their living. Rather, in its address to the dead this book would hearken voices that precede it, and in writing, imagine something akin to thanatography. Death would speak. And, in that moment, life would no longer stand as the sole and privileged condition of possibility for speech, no longer as a "value" in-and-for-itself, as it is in liberal-humanist thought. Instead, death would lend necessary contour to living, and would be that nonfugitive condition from which speaking and writing irrupt.

This is a book about biopolitics in our time, about a politics ostensibly devoted to life (*bios*). But it is also about the time and timeliness *of* biopolitics today, which seizes on life-times and propels them into counterfactual futures in which we would be immortalized, tomorrow, life vouchsafed and death deferred, defeated. And yet: there can be no politics of life—no politics of *making live*—that does not also *let die*. Biopolitics kills, albeit indirectly and in the passive voice. It lets die in the name of life. This book begins here in the care of deaths disavowed—rather than from life's sacred vows and avowals—to respond to and theorize neoliberal biopolitics over the last two decades: since 9/11 and the global War on Terror; in light of ongoing Contingency Operations that furnish us with the ways and means—both technological and tropological—to visit unconscionable state violence; with the rise and ubiquity of the internet, meme culture, and the alt-white/right; the revivification of nativist nationalisms and racisms; seemingly sacrosanct identities and identity politics; merciless neoliberal governments and burgeoning authoritarianisms; and most recently, a deadly global pandemic. We live and die today on a knife's edge of disaster, and there is something epochal to be discerned, a historic rupture, in our social order.

Looking to Western history, for his part Michel Foucault has theorized our last great epochal rupture: from classical modes of power to biopolitical ones— that is, from sovereignty (with its divine right of kings and queens) to modern liberal democracy (with its increasing emphasis on human rights, reason, and possessive individualism). Foucault places this rupture around the beginning of the nineteenth century. In broad strokes, we might call this the transition from premodern forms of governance to modern state structures, acknowledging that "modernity" is a sloppy term to describe a deeply contradictory condition: "the modern" is not quite synonymous with teleological progress and development. As Foucault notes, the gallows were once an emblem and locus of the sovereign's right to kill, and yet while spectacular public punishments began to wane late in the eighteenth century, this does not mean that power over life altogether disappeared in modernity. This power was displaced into new technologies and has become increasingly abstract, hidden, and secreted in "a new legal or administrative practice."[1] In the liberal democratic state, power's new legal and administrative scaffolding works biopolitically to "incite, reinforce, control, monitor, optimize, and organize the forces under it: a power bent on generating forces, making them grow, and ordering them, rather than one dedicated to impeding them, making them submit, or destroying them."[2]

This is the productive purchase of biopolitics, in which "life" is cultivated and the living are governed by increasingly autonomous efficiencies and economies of scale, through techno-administrative mechanisms that include systems of surveillance, segregation, health and welfare regimes, pro-"life" policies and improvement programs, through education, statistical forecasts, securitization, risk management, law, biomedicine, and popular culture, too. Together, these inform a vast and diffuse global network, from Davos to Darfur, that defines, regulates, counts, exposes, and encloses human life across our planet. Death, however, is not unequivocally deferred or defeated. For some it has been accelerated or mandated. And even as death is so righteously and widely repudiated, this only belies its indispensability and vital utility. Looking to the future, the following questions impose themselves: Are we living and dying today on the threshold of our own great epochal rupture? Are we at the end times of neoliberal biopolitics—of nominally liberal-democratic state forms (now increasingly illiberal)—awaiting a revolution and a reckoning with our dead?

To offer a tentative definition of biopolitics, I turn to Foucault's March 17, 1976, lecture at the Collège de France, which is often cited as a key text. Note here how Foucault falters, repeats himself, and equivocates in his description:

> I think that one of the greatest transformations political right underwent in the nineteenth century was precisely that, I wouldn't say exactly that sovereignty's old right—to take life or let live—was replaced [*substituer*], but it came to be complemented [*compléter*, also "to complete"] by a new right which does not erase the old right but which does penetrate it, permeate it [*le pénétrer, le traverser, le modifier*, "penetrate it, traverse it, modify it"]. This is the right, or rather precisely the opposite right. It is the power to "make" live and "let" die. The right of sovereignty was the right to take life or let live. And then this new right is established: the right to make live and let die.[3]

If this epochal transformation occurred more than two centuries ago, Foucault writes as if we still can't define it or reckon with its constitutive power over us. Language fails us. Foucault is commenting here on the historical discontinuity between sovereign and biopolitical power that took place in Europe across the nineteenth century—a transformation, he reminds us in the next sentence, that "obviously did not occur all at once."[4] I read Foucault's textual vacillations as symptomatic, an equivocation at the heart of biopolitics itself, a politics *of* life whose genitive is itself ambivalent (a politics that *belongs to* or *speaks as* a biological body?). Foucault resorts to the passive voice: political right *underwent* a transformation; sovereign power *came to be complemented, penetrated, permeated, modified*; a new right *is established*—seemingly by no one, or nothing, and yet in the name of an incipient "life itself." The biopolitical referent is radically contingent—for life is always contingent.

If the "life" of biopolitics is the most concrete biological body, it is, paradoxically, also the most disincarnate, sacred, or transcendent notion. This "life" is a rhetorical accomplishment, neither given nor natural, but it is constituted in and by a tropological regime that fabricates a vital "truth" from which all else seems to follow. Foucault's definition, above, does not permit us to establish a point of origin. And if his grammatical subject fails us, if his locutions become intransitive and language falters, it is because ours remains overwhelmingly a grammar of sovereignty ensconced in liberal subjectivity and transitive speech. This "sovereignty"—in the guise of liberal humanism, possessive individualism, autonomy—has become a great biopolitical ruse, that in and through which biopolitical tropes are propagated and popularized. The illusion is that I freely choose and choose the very conditions of my own choosing—a grammatical "I" propped up in its delusional sense of rationality, autonomy, and enlightened agency. An entitled "I" through which "life itself" would speak.

Foucault ends his description of biopolitics by reiterating that sovereign power was the old right to "take life or let live," whereas biopolitical power is the new right to "make live and let die." These are power's distinct historical impresas or mottos. The "old" power was localized in the sovereign by right of divine origin. Once upon a time, sovereignty intervened into the lives of the living *either* to take a subject's life *or* to let that subject live—an imperial decision that was either/or but that nevertheless presumed the prior givenness of the subject's life. The sovereign therefore possessed the divine right to kill, by the rule of the sword, exercised as a "deduction" (*prélèvement*)[5]—"a subtraction mechanism, a right to appropriate a portion of the wealth, a tax of products, goods and services, labor and blood, levied on the subjects."[6] With biopolitics, however, power's new right is neither localized nor entirely vertical: it is decentralized and reticulate, and the object of that power, its site of application, is not a singular body to be disciplined or punished. Biopolitics makes live and lets die en masse. No longer concerned with given individuals, it is applied systemically on—and constitutes—particular "populations."

Today, life is "made" and no longer preexists the powers that make it. Invoking a discursive "set of processes" and "a whole series of related economic and political problems," Foucault says that biopolitics

> will introduce mechanisms with a certain number of functions that are very different from the functions of disciplinary mechanisms.... Forecasts, statistical estimates, and overall measures. And their purpose is not to modify any given phenomenon as such, or to modify a given individual insofar as one is an individual, but, essentially, to intervene at the level at which these general phenomena are determined, to intervene at the level of their generality.... In a word, security mechanisms have to be installed around the random element inherent in a population of living beings so as to optimize a state of life.[7]

The "agency" and allure of biopolitics resides in its systemic processes, its applied techniques and technologies.[8] In neoliberal parlance, biopolitics is a diffuse power that is scalable, nimble, and resilient. Indeed, neoliberalism is not just a metaphor for biopolitics, but an ideological avatar of it, informing and organizing human conduits according to globalizing circuits of desire, death, and capital accumulation. While disciplinary power once "individualized" bodies, biopolitical bodies are now "massified," "regularized," and "replaced by general biological processes."[9] The biopolitical powers that both "make live" and "let die" are conjoined; these combined and differential powers no longer represent a sovereign decision in the mode of either/or. Making live *and* letting die—both/and—have become part of a hydraulic and absolutely co-constitutive relation, a compact, a sacrificial economy in the differential applications of power. They cannot be cleaved. For some, death is as it were called for, recommended, and covertly produced as a biopolitical necessity—as the cost of living. To employ a metaphor from digital technology, we might say that death is life's biopolitical "protocol,"[10] an anonymous algorithmic effect.

Famously, in the closing lines of *The History of Sexuality*, Foucault imagines a future moment in or from which we might at last recognize contemporary "freedom" as that which, paradoxically, makes us most unfree. In this text, Foucault argues that "sex"—as origin, norm, and truth—is radically contingent on "the deployment of sexuality" (*le dispositif de sexualité*), which is not so much a "deployment" as a discursive "apparatus" (*dispositif*) that constitutes "sex" as ultimate freedom and truth. But "sex," Foucault insists, is "an imaginary point determined by the deployment [apparatus] of sexuality—[a discourse] that each individual has to pass through in order to have access to one's own intelligibility . . . , to the whole of one's body . . . , to one's identity."[11] It is not that our tireless discourse works to free "sex" from the shadows, to reveal its truth; rather, our discourse works frenetically to produce "sex" and to make of it both a truth and a freedom to be "discovered" and lived. Simply put, "sex" is the *effect* of that discourse, even as "sex" is fashioned as a secret origin or cause. Gesturing to the future, Foucault writes, "We need to consider the possibility that one day, perhaps, in a different economy of bodies and pleasures, people will no longer quite understand how the ruses of sexuality, and the power that sustains its organization, were able to subject us to that austere monarchy of sex, so that we became dedicated to the endless task of forcing its secret, of exacting the truest of confessions from a shadow." He concludes, "The irony of this deployment [*de ce dispositif*] is in having us believe that our 'liberation' is in the balance."[12] That "austere monarchy of sex," its sovereign power over us, relies on the ruse of liberation, "enlightenment" as mass deception (to borrow from Horkheimer and Adorno). But it is also the critical moment in which the model of sovereign power is exposed as phantasmatic, even libidinal, and another paradigm of power can be seen at play.

It is, then, no surprise to find a robust discussion on biopolitics in the pages of *The History of Sexuality*. There, biopower is conceived as twofold: on the one hand, it operates as an anatomo-politics that relies on disciplinary mechanisms that "individualize" particular (docile) bodies, and on the other, as a biopolitics that seizes on the *bios*—life itself—and intervenes to "massify" a (re)productive population. For every textual instance of "sex" vis-à-vis the apparatus (or deployment) of sexuality, we might instead read "life" in its place. For "life," like "sex," is also discursively constituted as origin, norm, and truth; "life," like "sex," is that discursive formation that governs our knowledge and incites desire: the *effect* of a biopolitical apparatus rather than the cause. As it is for "sex," so too for "life"—the two are biologically coincident and constituted in and through a heterogeneous set of (pre)dispositions, formal and informal institutions, regulatory mechanisms and police functions, beliefs, laws, moral orthodoxies, scientific statements, pedagogies, or, more metaphorically and in a materialist vein, architectures, technologies, circuits. The future time of critique, the one Foucault imagines, is neither quite the time of my sex nor the time of my life. Critique gestures proleptically to my death, to that future in which I will have been.

The study that follows attends (to) death's claim on our livingness. For this, our life, is purchased on death. "Life" is a rhetorical vestige of the fatal exchange in which the lives of some will matter, will flourish, at the expense of others who will not and who will succumb. If our biopolitical grammars name a future "life" held in trust, this promised referent is always fleeting. As Lucretius wrote long ago, "Nor by prolonging life / Take we the least away from death's own time."[13] In my response to the biopolitical disavowal of death, then, and from death's own time: a disaffirmation of letting die in life's name. For death's temporality interrupts both sovereign and biopolitical time, past and future temporizations. Death undermines the transitive grammars of sovereign speech, which is historically steeped in the power of precedent and convention. "Death is outside the power relationship."[14] As for biopolitics, death finds no grammar in its futures: death is demanded, and yet it is voiceless, a non-concept, disavowed. If, then, I am to hearken the dead, there can be no impulse to resurrect or to reclaim death for the living; rather, in hearkening I must listen instead from my own future having-been, for dead voices will be unrecognizable in the timeliness of life's time.

## "Affirmative" Rhetorics

*The Living from the Dead* isn't intended as a comprehensive introduction to bio-politics,[15] but it also doesn't presume a prior knowledge of the vast and valuable scholarship that employs biopolitical theories to critique racial injustice, socio-economic inequality, colonialism and settler-colonialism, globalization and development, "sustainability," transnational migration and climate crisis, the regulation of women's reproductive freedoms, the uses of biotechnology and pharmacology, "securitization," and the surveillance and militarization of public culture, among others. Instead, this book's case studies home in on the distinctly rhetorical conditions that underwrite some of these critiques: on the tropes of biopolitical sacrifice and abandonment, on the differential fungibility of human lives unto death—all business-as-usual, a social compact that everyone more or less already "knows" (in the deniable modalities of an Orwellian doublethink). I seek to demonstrate how the biopolitical interface of making live and letting die is a rhetorical relation, obedient to the tropes in and by which "life" is constituted and informed by political powers and social (pre)dispositions. In the prevailing biopolitical discourse, it is as if life itself *speaks* the political, and even though this "life" is unreconstructed, it increasingly figures as beyond critique—as both value and fact, means and end, in-and-for-itself. These rhetorical forms matter because they have come to drive neoliberal biopolitics almost autogenously.

I focus on biopolitics over the last two decades, suggesting that there is some-thing distinct in the "life" of our millennial neoliberal moment, a rupture in linear models of historical "progress."[16] It is difficult to discern those discourses and discontinuities that are closest to us, constitutive of us. We find that we've been recruited—however "freely"—as teleological conduits, driving "progress" forward in tandem with materialities and markets, technologies and tweets, medicine and law, together with a host of other agentic nodes in these networks. But develop-ments in pharmacotherapies or weapons or media technologies, for example, do not merely represent incremental or "progressive" differences of quantity or degree; often enough they are qualitative differences of kind, with socio-subjective and ontological effects that herald power's new modalities and sites of application. And more than freedom's false-consciousness is at stake. As the liberal political subject effectively wanes, biopolitical grammars become hegemonic, and, indeed, more desirable as the delusory means of securing and asserting one's self-sovereignty, identity, and right to "life."[17] Didier Fassin has argued that a "new language" of common sense has gained ascendency in recent decades, in tandem with a biopolitical "humanitarianism"—a widespread concern for precarious lives and a desire to make them live: "Inequality is replaced by exclusion, domination is transformed into misfortune, injustice is articulated as suffering, violence is expressed in terms of trauma."[18] In this "new lexicon of moral sentiments"—the grammar of identity and identity politics—it is difficult to discern the sinister paradox of neoliberal biopolitics, namely, how making live, even as a humanitarian gesture, with the best of intentions, relies on and often reduplicates relations of inequality, domination, and death-warranting. Despite ourselves, we, too, are agents of this aggressive world order. The new lexicon hobbles the imagination and, ensconcing us in a sham self-sovereignty, preempts a much-needed critique of our wider social (infra)structures and norms.

This biopolitical Newspeak signals a paradigm shift on a larger scale—a shift in the politics of the production of knowledge and in the commonsense rhetorics of "life" we social beings find ourselves compelled to affirm ideologically and to mirror affectively, conspicuously, publicly. Foucault's historical shift from sovereign to biopolitical power yields a clue to our current moment. In *The Order of Things*, Foucault had analyzed this epochal transformation according to the shifting historical conditions of possibility for knowledge, which he plotted along three intersecting axes: labor, life, and language. It is not difficult to see how the first two, the regulation of the economy and biological life, have been biopoliticized—increasingly governed according to the interplay between making live and letting die.[19] And it is in these realms, in the government of economies and biologies, that most studies on biopolitics are situated. Significantly, however, Foucault's epochal rupture also represents a *rhetorical* discontinuity, even as the transformation of our grammars is trickier to discern because they are that *by* which we are *able* to discern. Theorizing the biopolitical language-effect, Foucault writes, "From this event onward, what gives value to the objects of desire is not solely the other objects that desire can represent to itself, but an element that cannot be reduced to that representation."[20] In other words, something escapes the representation of representational systems *in* and *by* that system itself. And so, this book intervenes precisely here, where "the sovereignty of the Name"[21] begins to yield to other forces. If, as Foucault argues, classical language systems implied a rather straightforward representation, this no longer holds in the biopolitical context:

"What makes it possible to define a language is not the way in which it represents representations, but a certain internal architecture, a certain manner of modifying the words themselves in accordance with the grammatical position they take up in relation to one another; in other words, its *inflectional system*."[22] Building on Foucault, we might say that the manner of modifying the very inflectional system—part of a tropological and socio-symbolic regime—has been colonized by biologizing and capitalizing forces, with neoliberal biopolitics as the "internal architecture" of our dominant discourse.

Today, the politics of life itself has become neoliberalized, and political action reconfigured according to the moral orthodoxies of economic administration. The economy is exalted as our new ontology, immunized from critique because it fashions our inflectional system itself. Managing the economies of lives and measured risks constitutes an advance claim and worldview. Particularly since the economic collapse of 2008–9 or the COVID-19 pandemic, it is in the name of the economy that Western, nominally democratic governments have demanded subjugation, sacrifice, and austerity on the part of their citizens, where both labor and life (ultimately coextensive) conform to political economies (themselves vassals to global debt markets)[23] and are reshaped from within, as if by acts of collective will. Human nature is reconfigured as human (bio)capital, the *animal laborans* as *homo oeconomicus*. Neoliberalism, as Foucault has defined it, "involves extending the economic model of supply and demand and investment-costs-profit so as to make it a model of social relations and of existence itself, a form of relationship of the individual to oneself, to time, to those around one, to the group, and to the family."[24] Under neoliberalism, power is unlocalized, there is no longer a sovereign who demands subjugation and threatens by the rule of the sword, no sovereign whose exceptional prerogative it is to take life or to let live. Instead, power is diffuse and anonymous, circuiting through reticulated vectors of control, digital networks, the ebbs and flows of global(izing) capital. If this is correct, and our relationships to ourselves, to time, and to others have been territorialized, then it becomes difficult to imagine how our evasive tactics might gain any revolutionary momentum. Our resistance feels co-opted in advance, commercialized, sold back to us at a discounted price, and a profound cynicism settles in.

Language fails us in our critical understanding of neoliberal biopolitics, and this is no small irony given the torrent of its terms and tropes, loquacious, and vainly parroted in the empty speech of identity and truth. I hold fast to Hans Blumenberg's insight: "We are appearance to ourselves, the secondary synthesis of a primary multiplicity, not the reverse. The substantialism of identity is destroyed; identity must be realized, it becomes a kind of accomplishment, and accordingly there is a pathology of identity."[25] This is a book, then, about pathologies of persuasion, forms-of-life, and identity politics. Our tropes and twitterings are the means and the manner by which we relate to ourselves, to our bodies, to others, to the time of our lives, and to the wider world. They would ensconce us in a warm dialectic of epistemic closure, driving out any self-awareness that our words' work exceeds the bounds of knowledge-claims. And in this, they lack rhetoricity—not just what our language represents or describes for us, constatively, but what it does and does *to* us, its desirous "end-users," performatively. Indeed, as a normative tropological regime, neoliberal biopolitics advances (on) a kingdom of ends: it's a siren's song and a glittering abyss in which we're meant to find ourselves reflected and perfected.

On the other side of this mirror—in a language to infinity, perhaps even a heterotopia[26]—we might hearken the dead and hear in the rhetoricity of their petitions an ontological claim that transits through us, in life and unto death. In this volume, I'm less concerned with epistemological claims that would permit us to pass judgment. Rather, I'm preoccupied by the rhetorical conditions of possibility for voices to speak and to be heard. To hearken is impossible without a sense of rhetoricity; to disaffirm, impossible in sovereign speech or in the grammars of identity and epistemic truth. It's in this context that I offer a distinctly rhetorical critique of biopolitics, its speech/acts and its tropological constitution of subjects, political identities, and lives lived. For me, rhetoric attends to the trope's turns, its supplications, and persuasive effects. My argument is therefore preoccupied with my own language, for our terms are always-already occupied, colonized, overdetermined. This book proceeds self-reflexively across situated case studies or sites that variously disaffirm the rhetorics of making live while refusing to disavow the (infra)structural conditions, and the social norms, through which we conspire to let die. Indeed, I hope to address these conditions, less through established grammars of social critique than by hearkening the dead— those we have let die—whose voices haunt the tropological constitution of "life" as much as they unsettle my own words here.

My rhetorical approach and its contemporary cultural situatedness distinguish this study from the many sometimes contradictory readings and applications of biopolitical theory. Paolo Virno is surely correct when he declares biopolitics an equivocal concept. "The concept," he writes, "has recently become fashionable: it is often, and enthusiastically, invoked in every kind of context."[27] Indeed, in recent years a surge of "biopolitical" scholarship can be found in virtually every discipline across the social sciences and humanities—some with a transhistorical, politico-philosophical, or even metaphysical remit, while others are narrower in sociohistorical scope, or even molecular in their focus. Such a patent diversity of discursive and materialist approaches and repurposings is itself equivocal. Whether conciliatory or critical, these voices are uneven in their enthusiasm or criticism. And admittedly, biopolitics is a very confusing "concept," especially when diametrically opposed camps make biopolitical claims on (or to) life. For example, both the pro-life and pro-choice movements are typically biopolitical, one advancing a political argument that exalts the life of the fetus, while the other is concerned with a woman's life and the political rights that ought to follow from her livingness. (I address the biopolitics of abortion in the book's Refrain.) How might we adjudicate these contesting conceptions of "life"? In one sense, it will depend on whose life is imagined to speak, morally and politically. There are facts of life, surely, but life itself is not a "fact," and it's impossible to say with any epistemic certitude what "life" is for biopolitics, which is one reason its discourse is so easily propagated. "Life" is a floating signifier, simultaneously moral and material, metaphysical and molecular, from the grandest transhistorical scales to the local and temporally situated micropolitics of genomic technologies. A critical rhetorical approach is necessary to understand the conditions under which a claim might be heard, and to parse how the "life" that is made can be claimed, valued, given voice, and come to be mobilized in public discourse.

I therefore aim to transect the polarized positions situated along a continuum that ranges from those who enthusiastically endorse an "affirmative" or even "democratic" biopolitics, at the one end, to those who hold a highly negative or apocalyptic view of biopolitical power, on the other. Scholars who position themselves in the "affirmative" camp might ask, as Timothy Campbell does, if "our current understanding of biopolitics may, in fact, be too indebted to death."[28] (And if his answer is yes, my own view is that biopolitics has disdainfully defaulted on its debt.) For their part, Michael Hardt and Antonio Negri will celebrate the generativity of the multitude, claiming that "the political has to yield to love and desire, and that is to the fundamental forces of biopolitical production."[29] Roberto Esposito, in turn, argues that the shift to biopolitics is "irreversible," but this does not mean, he contends, "that another kind of democracy is impossible, one that is compatible with the biopolitical turn."[30] Esposito would tentatively "trace the initial features of a biopolitics that is finally affirmative. Not over life but of life."[31] (Here, again, the little genitive "of" begs certain questions.) And Nikolas Rose imagines biopolitics, at its best, as providing us with what he calls a "positive eugenics," because "letting die is not making die."[32] Alongside a host of affirmations, the claim to a "democratic" biopolitics is similarly fraught because the representative opinions of a moral majority do not make those opinions ethical or just—but then, this particular line of critique would require a treatise on the very meaning of democracy, or rather, how we might rescue democracy from corporate plutocracy and "post-democracy."[33] There is no doubt that scholars of affirmative or democratic biopolitics offer distinct conceptualizations of biopolitics—of "life," of "politics," and their relation—from what Foucault has bequeathed us. But I do not wish to rehearse or adjudicate among these many and various studies. Not only would it be impossible to do so in a single volume, but the power to pronounce precisely which (or whose) biopolitics is truly "affirmative" would always involve a sovereign violence. Instead, this book remains close to Foucault's original conceptualization of biopolitics and develops it in a rhetorical reading of our present moment.[34] And if we insist on the co-constitutive relation between making live *and* letting die, as Foucault formulates it, it seems to me that we cannot solemnly "affirm" the terms of life-making without also, at least implicitly, affirming its death-warranting.

In this light, proponents of affirmative biopolitics must either commit to severing its co-constitutive powers to make live *and* let die or find ways to mitigate death for a kinder and gentler biopolitics. To affirm biopolitics would also suggest that biopolitics (or some version of it) could be severed from its neoliberal bio-economies or that the ruthlessness of racial capitalism and resource extraction could be meliorated or contained, again, for a kinder and gentler biopolitics. This strikes me as a rhetoric of secular salvation—akin to humanitarian reason,[35] or white saviorism, perhaps—that invokes transcendental principles, such as universal and inalienable human rights, while nonetheless yielding to a nexus of particular means and mechanisms that are ultimately both neoliberal and biopolitical in their differential alienations. Here, it strikes me that the onto-logic of affirmative biopolitics is obscured by its liberal utilitarian mien: maximizing life and minimizing loss, or, in neoliberal jargon, maximizing production and minimizing costs—all the while knowing that those losses and costs are lethal and incalculable. Said another way, *to affirm* is the performative speech/act of a (neo)liberal political subject and iteratively both relies on and shores up a problematic underlying ontology. Nancy Fraser's use of "affirmative" in the context of distributive justice applies equally for affirmative biopolitics: "Affirmative strategies for redressing injustice aim to correct inequitable outcomes of social arrangements without disturbing the underlying social structures that generate them."[36]

Proponents of affirmative biopolitics therefore have little sense for its tropological dimensions, its rhetorics; their discourse redounds on the purported interiority, and good intentions, of a liberal subject empowered to sovereignly ensure, as Rose phrases it, that "letting die is not making die." But who polices this murky border?

This study has little faith in the liberal subject. And it cuts across the antinomies of negative and "affirmative" biopolitics to disturb the generativity of their underlying social structures. But I'm neither "for" nor "against" biopolitics as such. I've taken inspiration from scholars on both ends of the continuum and cite them where it seemed appropriate. To position me as either "for" or "against" biopolitics, whether in an affirmative or negative voice, misses the point of what it might mean to *disaffirm* its tropes through a rhetorical critique. To critique is not to judge the truths or lies of biopolitics (it proclaims both), or whether it is good or evil (it can be both); rather, critique would pursue rhetorical questions concerning the conditions in and by which such statements could be voiced, circulate, and recruit desiring subjects as agents of the biopolitical apparatus. Here, Blumenberg offers a pithy definition of rhetoric that I find apropos: "Rhetoric is form as means."[37] Rhetoric is, by these lights, a method and an argumentative form that must reckon with its provisional status. It is neither a *mere* means nor is it *the* means employed by self-evident truths (imagined to speak "for themselves"); instead, we might say that rhetoric is the *seeking* of appropriate means precisely when evidence for the ethical distinction between what is appropriate and inappropriate is sorely lacking, and where horizons of interpretation are not necessarily held in common. It grapples, as I do, in a certain humility; it listens for strife and suffering; it obsesses about its form; and it proceeds with the understanding that what is appropriate, ethically, is not necessarily legitimate or sanctioned. To speak is to risk. As Blumenberg continues, "To see oneself in the perspective of rhetoric means to be conscious both of being compelled to act and of the lack of norms in a finite situation."[38] The rhetorical task, in our own finite situation, is not to propose new norms, however "provisional": it is to interrogate our compulsions.

## Disaffirmations

Biopolitics furnishes us with innumerable tropes—the modalities, the means, the manner in and by which an unreconstructed "life itself" is taken up as an ethos, a lived truth, spoken in the grammars of a sham popular sovereignty. The communication is hardly direct. As Blumenberg states, "The human relation to reality is indirect, circumstantial, delayed, selective, and above all 'metaphorical.'"[39] This is true of "life itself"—a technological production, a rhetoric of realism, no matter how "direct," "natural," or nondiscursive it may appear. And indeed, "the deeper the crisis of legitimacy"—today the legitimacy of multiple and clashing forms-of-life and identities—"the more pronounced the recourse to rhetorical metaphor becomes."[40] This book hopes to surface some of these metaphorizations, the tropes of "life itself," and responds not by positing new natures, norms, foundations, or ontologies, but obliquely—and with rhetorical "form as means"— by addressing the normative ways that life has been lojacked by terms that facilitate a flattened conception of "life" easily managed, administered, and normalized according to neoliberal "values" and "identities."

With respect to death, the biopolitical subject remains fugitive. Its devotion to making live is at once a disavowal of death—both its own and the deaths of those others it lets die in the silent bargain of its continued livingness. This subject would flee and prefers not to see that these deaths cannot be uncoupled, mine and theirs. "I" flee from the deaths of those I let die, not only because I might hope to disavow and uncouple myself from this sacrificial exchange, its violence and injustice, but also because I would hear in their voices, if I hearkened them, my own violence and death echoed there, and the deaths of those I love and (will) have lost. The structural, impersonal, and ritual violence of biopolitics is not just a transactional economy; it is intrapsychic and existential. And despite my frenzied biopolitical investments, my livingness will never be secured in time. Foreclosure is certain.

The language of this book is inescapably hostage to—and yet deeply suspicious of—sovereign grammars and "master" tropes. How might we speak in care of death when ours is the unreconstructed language of life? Writing must grapple with its constitutive violence, its purported powers to name and to know, its powers to appropriate and to colonize. In response, my style is at times lyrical and apostrophic, swerving in *form* from the normative and teleological assumptions of logical "content" and epistemic closure; aesthetically, it seeks to make of compositional form both an open question and an occasion for voices other than the one I call mine. Any purple passages are meant to resemble a bad bruise more than airy flights into gratuitous prose. These are sites of struggle in the stubborn effort to say what, in polite company, remains unsaid. I do not rush to summative statements in which readers will "cash out" my argument. Rather, the pace is more ponderous, solitary, as might befit an ethics of listening. Dead voices would speak in and from these pages.

The stakes of this book are rhetorically performative. I hope for plural voices to arise and to perform—in writing, as speech—a disaffirmation of biopolitics that does not merely "resist," whether by attempts to negate or invert, the "affirmative" tropes in and by which biopolitics is propagated. Disaffirmation is vigil, it keeps watch, and it hearkens another kind of speech/act that is irreducible to the tactics of resistance. And indeed, few would deny that there is widespread and diversiform "resistance" in our Age of Identity—a resistance that oftentimes silently shores up and reproduces the powers against which it purports to position itself. To disaffirm is to refuse this dialectic, in another voice. I remain critical throughout of the hypocrisies of liberalism and modernity, and I would disaffirm the normative valences of their tropes as well (even as I'm tangled in their webs). But in no way do I advocate a return to some pre-liberal or pre-modern past. In fact, I'm most anxious that so many, in their oftentimes righteous or fearful rebuke of globalized modernity and (neo)liberalism, have been tempted to hail purist mythologemes and a nostalgic "return" to state structures that predate modern forms of liberal democratic power. They, too, seem to have sensed that we are on the threshold of epochal rupture, maybe even war, and many seek liberation from our fraught commitments to equality, multiculturalism, and human rights—commitments that I'm unwilling to abandon, even as I believe they must be radically rethought.

We might recall the animus of Donald Trump's 2016 presidential campaign, masterminded by Stephen K. Bannon, who would later serve as Trump's White House chief strategist. More recently, Bannon has run a popular (and populist) multiplatform online "information" program called *War Room: Pandemic*.[41] Bannon reflects one face of our current Zeitgeist, where "American freedom fighters" and a far-right "resistance" movement are incited to reclaim the "traditional" values of America's Judeo-Christian past (however phantasmatic), to fight globalists, to destroy the fakestream media, and to protect civilization from a new Communist threat whose vectors are as invisible as the novel coronavirus itself. (Bannon is one of the few on the far right who from the early days took the COVID-19 pandemic seriously, and yet in his imaginary all roads lead to China.) In his recent book on Bannon, Benjamin R. Teitelbaum details Bannon's commitment to the philosophy (or rather, ideology) of Traditionalism—a movement that takes issue with modernity and foments a kind of spiritual awakening, even a "crusade," based on pre-modern values that include religious beliefs, transcendent truths, and homespun values.[42] Traditionalists, like Bannon, position themselves against modernity—now, at this moment, when modernity and liberalism are in crisis. This, too, is a biopolitical project and a claim to lives and livelihoods, and as much as we might deplore the dystopian "life" that such a movement would portend, we ignore it at our peril. I take this animus seriously. If it is not quite mainstream (yet), it is its powerful undercurrent. Its posture of moral innocence, indeed, its victimhood, only belies its ecocidal and genocidal reflexes.

I argue that we must disaffirm biopolitics and advance a critique of (neo)liberal modernity without capitulating to a retrogressive Traditionalism. In other words, my position is neither nostalgic nor does it embrace the teleological "progress" that characterizes an "affirmative" or "democratic" biopolitics. Neither a sovereign past nor a biopolitical future, then, because both variously leave intact the very systems and (infra)structures that generate their normative violence and injustice. The "resistance" of the religious Right, of fundamentalist homeschoolers, anti-vaxxers, radicalized libertarians, and other self-anointed "sovereigntists," ends up—almost despite itself—propagating and rhetorically reenacting the tropes of "life itself" furnished by biopolitics. But much the same could also be said of the "progressive" Left, whose "resistant" postures of moral indignation and identity politics recycle familiar tropes already co-opted in advance, short-circuited by memes and ready-made moralities, to become wounded parodies of themselves. While their intentions are dissimilar, Right and Left, and while I would not wish to collapse these tendentious movements, their rearguard effects converge because they ultimately recirculate similar biopolitical tropes. In their competing claims on Constitutional rights to life and liberty, the radicalized faces of both a Right and Left politics do not belong to fringe movements but represent, in many respects, the apotheosis of a mainstream liberalism driven to its extreme neoliberal-biopolitical conclusions.

My approach, instead, relies on the rhetoricity of disaffirmation, which is not quite a "resistance" to biopolitics. Here, I have imagined death, rather than life, as a productive rhetorical and political force—a thanatopolitics. In my response, I would hearken the dead, whose voices might disaffirm a power that lets die in the name of making live. It is in their address, their prior and abiding call, that we, the grim living, might be gathered in resounding refusal. My case studies diversely problematize the notion of tactical "resistance" under neoliberal bio-politics. What, after all, do we resist? A hydra-headed monster, and no longer quite the strategies and stratifications of a repressive sovereign power that is top-down. Today, power is less a matter of strategy than an amorphous and satirical "strategery." And if we ask, Who resists? it is difficult to locate a coherent subject whose personal actions or devices have not always already been co-opted in advance. Despite this, we still tend to imagine "tactics" as counter-hegemonic forms of resistance that would be appropriate in our moment. I'm trying to think and write beyond the tactic/strategy binary, which is widespread and continues to inform political activism and resistance movements.[43]

To hearken death's rhetorical agency in response to (infra)structural and systemic violence is more than to politicize death: it is to situate an aesthetics of existence, the living of (a) life, within the resonant, rhythmic, and temporizing horizons of death. Mine is not an ethics that impulsively affirms the positive value or content of life itself, or even of lives in their singularity and materiality (as much as each life is both singular and material)—and it is not simply an ethics of resistance, *against* killing and *against* injustice (as much as these should be painfully obvious). I cannot embrace an exalted animism or vitalism. For, an abstract "life itself" is the ultimate biopolitical ruse, the disguise, the meme, that obscures the fact that some lives do not matter, that some lives will be exposed to death, that some lives will be ritually dispossessed, disappeared, shot, suffocated, and systematically cannibalized. I gesture instead toward a shared agony that would hearken death, hold it and hear it, and refuse the productive terms by which some lives are lived, valued, and exalted, while for others it is death that is forcibly lived and lived-out. No redress or salvation, then, but something of a paratactical practice of hearkening those we have let die in silent ignominy.

Mindful that rhetoric is "form as means," the trope I have in mind here is parataxis, which the *Oxford English Dictionary* defines as follows: "The placing of propositions or clauses one after another, without indicating by connecting words the relation (of coordination or subordination) between them, as in *Tell me, how are you?*" Significantly, the *OED*'s example is in the form of a direct address, where it is the addressee's responsibility to join the clauses significatively. In a recent essay reflecting on the (im)possibility of reasoned debate today, Tad Lemieux and I elaborated on this definition of parataxis: "In between, in its lacunae, caesuras, the parataxis unsettles the common current of the text, its topography and durational field, whose movements and metrics become more fluid; sequence and coherence yield to anacoluthia; grammatical conjunctions are unavowed or unavowable, anagrammatical; metaphysical relations of ordination and subordination are ruptured, *dérangées*, neutral-ized; and we become uncertain of the relation of (presumably heteroclite) parts to the (presumable) whole."[44] As a disaffirmation, any tactic of "resistance" must become a para-tactic or para-site, untimely and displaced by parataxis—(a) life, then, not in the productive politics of making live or making work, but alongside, and as a reckoning with, mortality, illness, and human finitude. As a paratactical irruption, such an unworking would interrupt our spatiotemporal and grammatical regimes, the planned and "progressive" livingness of neoliberal biopolitics, and would grasp instead, however tentatively, the times and places of (a) life, set of necessity within the horizons of the inexorable: my death. Here, and in this manner, we might hearken the strange, paratactical lives—and the rhetorical agency—of the biopolitical dead, disappeared, decaying, and delinquent. For they are not simply the waste products or byproducts of neoliberal biopolitics, but foremost its condition of possibility, its raw materials, its inclusive-exclusion. My own parataxes are open wounds. They defy syntactical closure, logical or chronological connection—and if readers "hear" themselves called into this caesura, then in some small way their reading will have performed the kind of "listening" demanded by hearkening. This prior and enabling call is the condition for any response, any speech or writing.

To disaffirm is a devastating undertaking. It is not self-righteously censorious, neither a disapprobation nor a condemnation issued from a posture of moral superiority or a secure sense-of-self. Disaffirmation would spurn the affective affordances of identity, whether compliant with the Right or the Left. Instead, it would turn its gaze inward to reckon with *my* collusion and complicity in systems that let die in the name of my own livingness. And it would not purblindly affirm the virtues of free expression, the "free exchange of information and ideas, the lifeblood of a liberal society."[45] Nothing could be more anodyne (both innocuous and a pain-reliever—but, for whose pain?). It will no longer suffice to seek recourse in these fundamentalist tenets of liberal politics and human rights discourse, which propel the moral censures of what I can only describe as a spurious Left, an alt-left. Many on the Left, half-sleeping yet "woke," make vain display of their affective orthodoxies. How, then, shall we address our "good liberal" complicity—whether as perpetrators or "mere" beneficiaries— in long-standing colonial, racist, misogynist, homophobic, transphobic, and ableist violence and dispossession? For, *these* dead and dying have always been the true "lifeblood" of our "liberal society," fodder for our free-world economies, our cannibalizing machines. My livingness is contingent on the deaths of others, my wealth on their poverty, my security on their precarity. It's not as if we don't *know*. And yet, our rote liberal "acknowledgments"—of unceded lands, of violent histories, of injustices, of self-identity or "positionality"—can neither absolve us nor grant our speech.

These pages may well wish to suggest a heterotopic space, a paratactical in-between, another world. I offer no roadmap, no manifesto, no epistemic closure. None could originate from a single human being writing in lonely isolation from a tiny corner of our plagued planet. Disaffirmation turns first on my own grievous fugitivity. Reluctantly, fearfully, the writing of this book has changed me. Across its chapters, it gains momentum as a mortification of *this* subject, "I," who writes—here, from the sad givenness of my own tenuous identities "gifted" by an accursed social order—and now, from a (neo)liberal subjecthood I would gladly renounce if I could. In my words' work, in care of the dead, I tentatively reach toward a fragile "we," curses notwithstanding. These subjects come undone—first-person, singular, plural—as much as they stubbornly perdure—in the long moment of hearkening: the project becomes one of holding and rendering remains.

## Book Outline

This book's stakes are rhetorical, but by rhetoric I don't have in mind a singular methodological or theoretical approach to the study of persuasive discourse. My argument presumes the transdisciplinarity of rhetoric, just as the case studies themselves are "undisciplined" sites of critical contestation and travel across often divergent communities of reception. I'm in conversation with—but by no means expert in—the many distinct fields of study that have variously informed my rhetorical critique of neoliberal biopolitics: Military and Terrorism Studies, Critical Race Studies, Critical Public Health, Human Rights and Prison Studies, Legal Studies, Philosophy, Sociology, and Media Studies, to name a few. I would add, as well, that these disciplines—much like Rhetoric—are not monolithic. They are rich in a diversity of perspectives. I don't speak from these fields of expertise, but have learned from reading them, and believe that Rhetoric has something to gain from engaging in this work and something to offer in return.

The case studies in this volume include "sacrifice" in the "war" against COVID-19, where I read the emergent cultures of pandemic "resistance" alongside suicide terrorism and military suicides (chapter 1); the California mass hunger strikes of 2013, read as performative speech that "begins after death" and proleptically claims the human right to die (chapter 2); two legal cases of "preventable" and "untimely" childhood deaths, which figure the irreconcilable sovereign claims of anti-vaxxers and Indigenous peoples, respectively (chapter 3); and finally, the video-recording of the death of a disabled Black man read in the context of racist speech/acts digitally remediated across our social media platforms (chapter 4). The concluding Refrain invokes the trope of apostrophe and self-reflexively returns, in refrain, to the painful question of writing and how "I" might address, and hearken, the dead. While each chapter might be interpreted as a discussion on "suicide," this term only makes sense in the old grammar of sovereignty, where suicide is a (criminal) usurpation of the sovereign's prerogative to take life.[46] I seek instead to problematize the liberal agency and possessive individualism, as well as the psychopathology, presumed in discourses on suicidality and suicidal ideation. This is not to exalt suicide or other forms of dying, but it is an occasion to reflect on the ways that many are "suicided by society" in our postsovereign age, here, on the knife's edge of epochal disaster.

In the end, my choice of case studies was deeply personal: they moved me, and I hope I have honored the voices that spoke to me from their particular places of abandonment. But more than this, they enjoined me to critically reflect on and expose something of my own relation to them and to my writing and speaking on them, ever mindful of the inherent risks of appropriating them, exploiting them, or colonizing them. Parataxis has been my writerly trope, bringing into proximity distinct and incommensurable case studies that do not permit the syntactic construction, sequential coordination, or subordination of the stories they tell. The cases are not representative examples of neoliberal biopolitics so much as they are occasions to hear and to analyze situated disaffirmations. Textually grounded in this way, I hope to surface some of the wider ethical tensions and collisions at play in the political project of making live and letting die. I think of myself as critically curating these cases, in Cara Finnegan's sense of this term: I don't claim mastery over these scenes, but rather, would contest the assumption that critical research "discovers" the meaning or truth behind a representation.[47] Indeed, since the cases constellate around death, what mastery or truthful representation could anyone sovereignly claim? A critical rhetorical reading should instead shine light on the subject of speech and writing. And finally, the particular resonances between the four sites—and the deaths they ask us to hearken and to hold—make of the whole an artificial construction: given their incommensurability, their relation remains open and is curated here with the hope of generating unforeseen interpretations, connections, critiques.

Cantley, Québec
October 2, 2020

# 1

## The Cost of Living | On Pandemic Politics and Protests

In this world, there are two things without voice: the rich man's sins and the beggar's death.
—Persian proverb

Just before our first lockdown, in the early days of the COVID-19 pandemic, the mayor of Canada's capital city tweeted a screenshot of an internal email to City Council written by Dr. Vera Etches, the chief medical officer at Ottawa Public Health.[1] In her memo to elected representatives, she emphasized the need for the public to stay at home and to practice social distancing: "We each need to do our part to ensure that our healthcare providers do not have to choose between who lives and who dies." No doubt Dr. Etches was mindful of the harrowing life-and-death choices that some Italian doctors had faced during the worst of Italy's first pandemic wave. Later that day, however, when her text was published as an official statement on the Public Health website, Dr. Etches's rather blunt sentence was amended to the following: "We each need to do our part to ensure that our healthcare providers have the capacity to provide life saving measures for all, and to care for the most vulnerable people."[2] It would seem that, in official terms at least, some things are unspeakable because they touch on something the public cannot or should not hear: death. And, in the place of death, we must hear instead words chosen from a biopolitical lexicon: "capacity," "life saving," "measures," and "vulnerable people."

In her internal memo, Dr. Etches had named death and ascribed to her reader (and herself, "we") a kind of linguistic agency, or perhaps even a sovereignty, over the transitivity of death, and indeed, the transitive vectors of the virus itself. But in the amended public statement, if the virus remains communicable death does not. Biopolitical discourses privilege the life that is made—preserved and pro-longed—while silently repudiating any agency over the deaths of those it lets die. Death becomes almost intransitive, unvoiced and unspeakable, presumably non-agentic. It is no longer a question of responsibility for death or for the choice "between who lives and who dies"; now the agency is focused on "making live" in biopolitical terms. If "we each need to do our part," the referentiality of the "we" may well have shifted from the internal memo to the public statement. And while the implicit "they"—"our healthcare providers"—are named once again, they now appear in the context of a systemic "capacity" for "life saving measures," referring to wider biopolitical and biomedical systems, and only indirectly to anyone's personal responsibility. Indeed, it is difficult to imagine how "we," as individuals, could assume responsibility for such complex systems. This "we" is unreconstructed and presumably names a liberal subject, self-possessed and in the first-person, whether singular or plural.

Biopolitically, the life-and-death relation is impersonal, mediated by a vast regulatory apparatus comprising laws and policing, public policies, public health mechanisms, biomedical technologies, economies, and bureaucracies. "Life" arises in this nexus as part of a political economy focused on data-driven forecasts, statistical estimates, measures, capacities, and profiling: socio-biometrics that inform security mechanisms intended to optimize, to protect, and to prolong biological life. The apparatus targets—in order to manage, to regulate, and to administrate—particular "populations" or "masses" with an efficient generality, rather than individuals in their unique and sometimes shambolic singularity. These "populations" are typically defined in biological terms, and in the third-person plural, "they"—artifacts constituted by confirmed diagnoses and risk-factors, such as potential exposure due to recent travel, the presentation of symptoms, as well as through quantified hierarchies of biological susceptibility, from preexisting medical conditions and comorbidities to someone's age.

This chapter homes in on the "we" and its shifting referent and agency (mine, yours, ours, theirs) to problematize our claim on those biopolitical paradigms in which we have been claimed in advance. Globally, in the response to COVID-19 there have been sweeping biopolitical measures to "flatten the curve," such as face-covering bylaws and shelter-in-place orders intended to contain those who might be silent (asymptomatic) vectors. In the early days, this terminology quickly became widespread and embraced as the truth of transmission and risk, our new reality and social lexicon, our new immunological identity. But not quite. To be sure, a sizable and vocal minority rejects public health messaging as overblown or views the pandemic itself as a political hoax and fake news, even a "liberal" or Communist or "deep state" conspiracy. What is the relation of the "we" to those among us who protest public health protocols—lockdowns, facemasks, physical distancing, and eventually, vaccines—and who ostensibly resist biopolitics but who end up reduplicating its lethal effects, exposing to death those among us who are disproportionately susceptible or at-risk? To what extent is this resistance a form of violence, or terror?

In this context, biopolitics is both the medicalization of politics and the politicization of medicine. This is not to suggest that biopolitical and biomedical discourses are prima facie untrue or that ongoing public health measures have been unwarranted. A criticism is not a critique. And while it is important that we continue to criticize the many egregious state responses to COVID-19 (including falsehoods and flagrant lies), a *critique* of biopolitics would shine light on the underlying powers, pretexts, and preconceptions that drive these responses and inform their popular uptake—or resistance—alike. A critique would seek to understand their moral and rhetorical conditions of possibility, the powers by which they propagate, and the ways these are mobilized to silence and suppress the deaths of those we (will) have let die. The compass of this "we" is central to any critique—"who speaks?"—and to any assignation of agency, real or imagined. This chapter thus makes no definitive claims about pandemics or political protests. After all, these are nothing without human transmissions. And so, this chapter turns back on us—those agents who transmit and who resist, whether willfully or haplessly—to call into question our self-givenness and the persuasive force of our speech/acts.

Setting aside our concrete criticisms, one way into a rhetorical art of critique is to ask, What can be said, in this moment, and perhaps more importantly, what can't be said? And relatedly, what can we hear and what can't quite be heard? These correlated questions are themselves critical because a biopolitical "commonsense" organizes the scene of political speech and belonging, almost imperceptibly circumscribing in advance our communicative repertoire—the words, ideas, decrees, and attendant responsibilities that will be transmissible, persuasive, and that will order human will and behavior. Written in the context of the COVID-19 pandemic, in the pre-vaccine late summer of 2020, this chapter addresses the (bio)political problem of this moment. It demonstrates how the biopolitical apparatus operates almost anonymously in its vast and pandemological powers.

Unlike sovereign or repressive powers, biopolitics is not centralized or top-down; it is widespread, diffuse, and incorporated as part of our ethos, where "life itself" is the sacred (but no less biophysiological) object and objective, the means and the ends, of state power. And as I discuss below, it is all too easy in this moment to hear neoliberal voices hailing a liberal political subject who is the vital link (we are told) in the value chains of global capital. These strident voices—which also invoke a "we"—call for us to reopen the economy, COVID-19 infections notwithstanding. In this din, it is hardly considered ironic that the global transactional flows of contagion are coextensive with economic capital. Both, together, are increasingly virtual and invisible to the naked eye, even as they seize on bodies and cause visible devastation, sometimes unto death. If we act with enlightened self-interest (we are told) and if only we have faith in the invisible hand of the "free" market economy, we will ensure the greatest good for the greatest number, an equitable distribution of health and wealth. This is nonsense, of course, and as this book's case studies demonstrate, the state-sanctioned power to make live is never far from its unspeakable counterpart, the power to let die. Biopolitics is nothing if not a sacrificial economy. Some will—and some must—die in order that others may live: a condition of relational vulnerability or precarity that is structurally produced and inequitably distributed. Here, it does not make sense to speak of responsibility as individual choice, of the rights or obligations of a liberal political subject. Perhaps this was always so, but the reality is now pressing in from all sides.

And yet, biopolitics is a deceptively salutary narrative. Hailing us, it promises life tomorrow through the technologies of today, projecting into counterfactual futures whose spectral deaths, if hearkened, return to haunt the present moment. The life that is promised never ceases to announce itself in a discursive frenzy at once socializing, moralizing, materializing, and militarizing—albeit unevenly and unpredictably across the differentiated populations that are seized, identified, mobilized. To be sure, for many the available means of "making live" selfishly appeal to individual self-interest and, understandably, one's desire for self-preservation. And as I argue throughout, the ruse of biopolitics, its unwitting agent, is the liberal individual—the "I"—fed by a delusional sense of rationality, autonomy, and entitled agency, which together belie the fact that we are nonautonomous beings, tethered inexorably to others, human and nonhuman, and to a planet in geopolitical and ecological crisis. At the same time, the voices of those we let die are seldom heard. If they speak, it is to be spoken (of) in the third person, as "they," and not in and from the first-person address of an "I" or a "we." Ghostly, they reside and resound on the other side of the pious project that makes live: those who belong to the masses or (sub)populations exposed to increased situational vulnerabilities that are more likely to be pathogenic.

In the COVID-19 pandemic, workers who face the greatest risk of exposure include cashiers and grocery store employees, warehouse workers and meat packers, janitors, nurses, personal care workers, maids, and teachers, among others—many now suddenly deemed "essential" workers and "heroes," even as a considerable number of them continue to subsist below the poverty line.[3] Indeed, a heightened risk of exposure is too often destined for those who already carry in their bodies an increased risk of premature death, as if History and Nature had conspired in the design of a foolproof eugenics program. As we know, poverty and socioeconomic status are powerful social determinants of health comparable to traditional clinical risk-factors. And the pandemic has certainly exacerbated widespread poverty and devastation, especially for those whose lives and livelihoods were already precarious. In the United States circa 2020, for example, 60 percent of earners are financially worse off than they were before the recession of 2008–9 and have no "wealth buffer" to weather another financial crisis. And ironically, the very institutions—governmental and corporate—responsible for this inequity and recently so very vocal in "our" need to protect human life are the same institutions that have failed to provide adequate personal protective equipment to workers, exposing them to disease and untimely death. It's an old story. Vulnerable yet "essential" populations are often stratified by class, ethno-racial identity, gender, and sometimes citizenship status and ability to access health care services. Life's order is subtended by a normative structural, impersonal, and ritual violence. For death and dispossession are no less "essential" to the livingness of biopolitical life, where death is euphemized as collateral damages, negative externalities, or sometimes as opportunity costs. We—or "they"—must be kept alive in order to die a *slow* death, as Lauren Berlant has called it. "They" are afforded only "lateral agencies" that kill in the exercise of minor, negligible freedoms "in a zone of ordinariness."[4] Human resources. Human capital. But is a prolonged life by slow death a better "choice" because it permits prolonged consumption?

In this dark light, the COVID-19 pandemic offers a rare occasion for a critique of biopolitics, and the chance to expose life-and-death powers that are normally clandestine in their operation. "We each need to do our part to ensure that our healthcare providers do not have to choose between who lives and who dies." In its barely perceptible gesture, soon expunged, Dr. Etches's unedited statement had the courage to name death and, briefly, to problematize human agency and identity in a way that epidemiological statistics on COVID-19 deaths fail to do (they read like a ticker tape—factual but unreal). If we were able to hear in this moment, it was as if death spoke, rather than life itself. The statement conscripts the reader rhetorically: I am asked to imagine myself as responsible for the harrowing life-and-death choices that health care providers will be forced to make in the event that coronavirus transmissions remain unchecked and our health care system is stretched beyond capacity. But sovereign agency and responsibility are something of a ruse here. After all, these difficult decisions are made every day, and not just in times of pandemic crisis or states of emergency. More critically, then, Dr. Etches's memo invites us to think beyond individual responsibility, and to reflect on what responsibility and agency could mean in the context of a *public* good. What is our personal relation to an impersonal system with inbuilt constraints, limited structural capacities, and even ritual violence? This system operates, in our names, as a regulatory apparatus that makes live anonymously, with structural decisions executed largely in our absence. But by *naming* death, we are perhaps fleetingly made aware that letting die has been part of our unspoken moral and medical (and economic) calculus all along.

If this word is avowed only to be disavowed in revision, if death is unnamed and unnamable in the official public statement, its transitivity is nevertheless secreted in the long shadows of our biopolitical lexicon, threatening to irrupt on the scene, much as we saw in media images of Lombardy, Italy, when caravans of military trucks were deployed to remove the coffins of COVID-19 victims, whose sheer numbers had overwhelmed the hospital morgues and cemeteries. In the end, the biopolitical "life" that is promised is at best affirmed without assurance, for life ultimately holds no final or definitive meaning in the absence of death. Death, even unspoken, is always the impossible possibility to which all are destined. And this is perhaps a lesson in what we prefer neither to say nor to hear. Apart from our rituals—many of which have been suspended in the pandemic— we remain unprepared to attend to the dead, to hear a cry, or to interpret that cry as a meaningful address communicating pain and loss, for this would make of us its aversive addressees.

## On What We Can(not) Hear

Language cannot get any purchase until it carves up the unity of experience: *my* pain, spoken by a sovereign "I" imagined to name it, to possess it. Ludwig Wittgenstein has remarked that "the verbal expression of pain replaces [*ersetzt*] crying, it does not describe it."[5] In other words, the cry of pain is neither a description, an observation, nor a report that takes place *in* language.[6] Rather, the cry is "forced from us."[7] And its signification should be immediately recognizable. Maurice Blanchot phrases it somewhat differently: "The cry tends to exceed all language, even if it lends itself to recuperation as language effect."[8] In our pandemic moment, it seems there are some constellations of voices and cries that we remain unable to hear. Any effectual recuperation, any verbal expression, remains still largely uncomposed in the writing of our unfolding disaster. Blanchot: "If I say: the disaster keeps watch [*veille*], it is not in order to give a subject to the vigil [*à la veille*]; it is to say: the wake [*la veille*] does not occur under the sidereal sky."[9] Less as disaster's vigil than as a cry, then, I write these pages in solidarity with the dead: with those who (will) have been destined to die, and whose deaths (will) have been language-effects too: with those who—to borrow a turn of phrase from Antonin Artaud—(will) have been "suicided by society."[10] From disaster's structural, impersonal, and ritual violence an absence would cry forth, would speak. Blanchot once again: "When the subject becomes absence, the absence of the subject, or dying as subject, subverts the whole sequence of existence, causes time to take leave of its order, opens life to its passivity, exposing it to the unknown, to the stranger—to the friendship that never is declared."[11] Under our own skies, with disaster keeping watch, I wonder, and hope. What unstructured solidarities and undeclared friendships will gather to write or to speak, in care of deaths unnamed, in and from a fragile "we"?

Drowning out death's hues and cries, other voices have risen up instead. Occupying once-credible positions of power, they refuse to be silenced. Reflecting on death as ritual language-effect, I offer a few uncomposed excerpts—roiling sound bites—from the violent timeline that marked the early days of American pandemic disaster. In a March 23, 2020, segment of Fox News, lieutenant governor of Texas Dan Patrick was among the first to advocate a speedy return to work for Americans, many of whom found themselves under recent state or local government orders to shelter-in-place. Patrick asked his older viewers, "As a senior citizen, are you willing to take a chance on your survival in exchange for keeping the America that all America loves for your children and grandchildren?" To this he answered, "I'm all-in"—a wager wherein the economy of sacrificial exchange is preferable to presumably short-term losses in the American market economy. Evidently, some lives are expendable, of lesser value than others, and this valuation itself is a patriotic duty. Patrick's sentiments were echoed by Glenn Beck, the popular conservative commentator, who on March 24 declared, "I would rather have my children stay home and all of us who are over fifty go in and keep this economy going and working, even if we all get sick, I would rather die than kill the country. 'Cause it's not the economy that's dying, it's the country." With these hymns, we are meant to accept a kind of economic nationalism, a nation that is no more and none other than its "free" economy. Somewhat later, on May 4, New Jersey governor Chris Christie stated on CNN that we must reopen the economy despite what would certainly result in a higher rate of mortality from COVID-19. "The American people have gone through significant death before," he said, citing World Wars I and II as examples. "We've gone through it and we've survived it. We sacrificed those lives." One wonders if Christie imagined the possibility that he, too, could become a sick or sacrificial lamb?

In a Collège de France lecture on biopolitics, Michel Foucault raises the singular specter of "an absolutely racist State, an absolutely murderous State, and an absolutely suicidal State."[12] These converge, he suggests, when "the field of the life [that the State] manages, protects, guarantees, and cultivates in bio-logical terms [is] absolutely coextensive with the sovereign right to kill anyone, meaning not only other people, but also its own people." It's a peculiar moment in Foucault's oeuvre because elsewhere he repeatedly argues that, since at least the early nineteenth century, sovereign power has gradually been supplanted by biopolitical power, and we have shifted both ideologically and technologically from a disciplinary anatomo-politics that individualizes toward a biopolitics that massifies and seizes on the "life" of particular human populations. In his brief discussion here, however, these two forms of power—the sovereign right to "take life or let live" and the biopolitical power to "make live and let die"—are superimposed: "That is where this mechanism inscribed in the workings of the modern State leads."[13] Foucault will ask, "How, under these conditions, is it possible for a political power to kill, to call for deaths, to demand deaths, to give the order to kill, and to expose not only its enemies but its own citizens to the risk of death?"[14]

To answer this question on the "suicidal state," in a rarer moment still Foucault turns to the concept of racism, characterizing it as the "basic mechanism" of modern state power. Racism, he writes, is "a way of establishing a biological-type caesura within a population that appears to be a biological domain." This estab-lishes a transactional economy wherein race and racism inform "biological" deci-sions over who will be made to live and who will be allowed to die—a racial hygiene that eliminates the enemy race within and thus regenerates one's own, that cleanses and purifies. The logic is simple: "As more and more of our number die, the race to which we belong will become all the purer." The state thus becomes suicidal by deploying a racism that is "not a truly ethnic racism, but racism of the evolutionist kind, biological racism." In other words, this is not an "ordinary racism" that is "bound up with mentalities, ideologies, or the lies of power"; rather, it is "bound up with the technique of power, with the technology of power." In this, Foucault is describing the Third Reich, and he claims, "Of course, Nazism alone took the play between the sovereign right to kill and the mechanisms of biopower to this paroxysmal point."[15] Foucault offers striking instances of Nazi scorched earth dogma turned back on the German *Volk* themselves.

Despite the judicious scholarly criticism of Foucault's problematic treatment of race,[16] in our context we might venture that Foucault was in part correct in his brief treatment of "biological racism" (I offer an extended critique of this concept in chapter 4). And yet, we must hasten to offer a qualification: while COVID-19 indeed occasions a biological racism, this is perhaps *only* by virtue of the long history of "ethnic" or "ordinary" racism that is coextensive with the techniques and technologies of power that are in this moment being extended, retooled, and operationalized for application in what appears to be a biological domain organized by "endemic" inequities and vulnerabilities. Race, after all, is a sociohistorical and biopolitical *process*, a performative effect—something that is done, rather than something that is. In the words of Kendall Thomas, "We are 'raced' through a constellation of practices that construct and control racial subjectivities."[17] One part of this constellation is the biologization of race, something that is done but that is taken, by sleight of hand, as something that is.

Contingently, and with care, we must insist that the histories and experiences of Black, Indigenous, and other People of Color are diversiform and incommensurable with the instantiations of "biological racism." The state has proven perennially indifferent to the sociocultural and racialized realities of these lived lives. Their differences are effaced in the name of life itself ("All Lives Matter!"), while some lives nevertheless remain exchangeable according to the differential embodiments and economies (something that "is") that the state exposes and exploits (something that is done). From the earliest hours of our pandemic present the state was already poised to mobilize—passively, to be sure, and in the name of a virus—the terrorizing principles, the vicious animus, of historical racist oppression for use elsewhere, a sham biologism rewritten into the "real," effectively redrawing the battle lines in the march toward a new civil war. The state's enduring strategies of systemic ethno-racial oppression together with a resurgent alt-white/right nationalism are all too easily mapped onto biosocial vulnerabilities, this time in the name of a natural or providential biological order.

The infrastructures of systemic violence are architectonic. Who will get a ventilator or hospital bed when demand outstrips supply? Some version of utilitarianism will prevail in triage protocols, the same old "utility"—ostensibly biologized—of lives informed by neo-Malthusian economies and histories of net "value," "worth," and "acceptable" (or even "necessary") losses. The protocol is familiar and demonstrates the extent to which we are willing to cede to and apply an economic framework to calculate the worth of a human life. It is dressed in clinical garb to lend an air of impartial, presumably colorblind authority. And of course, hospitals are not the only sites of triage; segregation and the hierarchization of "value" are quotidian occurrences. Here, Hurricanes Katrina or Maria might offer object lessons in the differential calculus of (racialized) lives that (don't) matter. Ruth Wilson Gilmore's definition of racism remains resonant: "the state-sanctioned and/or extra-legal production and exploitation of group-differentiated vulnerabilities to premature death."[18]

In the suicidal state epitomized by a Trump rally, some may find a caustic irony—and take cynical flight—in the specter of a "biological" racism coming home, in some instances, to infect proud racists themselves. We have arrived at a new paroxysmal point of state biopower, an ostensibly world-historical animus that Trump's presidency has courted, and his court has presided over. For a long time, of course, plagues and pogroms have gone hand in hand. This time, however, it would seem that the pogrom is providential: it is the plague and acts in the name of a tiny virus. Our daily delivery unto slow death has been accelerated—no longer a slow surrender to poverty, microplastics, toxic pesticides, greenhouse gas emissions, and climate crisis. COVID-19 is the perfect pretext for a pogrom that needs little oversight once in motion. It is autogenous, and it will suffice merely to do too little for too long—a fact amply evidenced by infection rates and body counts circa 2020. The toll will be greatest among those who are elderly, poor, unemployed, incarcerated, homeless, disabled, marginalized, racialized, without health insurance, or with preexisting medical conditions. Many will be permitted to perish as a tribute—nay, as paean—to the national economy.

The rhetoric of sacrifice verges on the militaristic. It is murderous, but indirectly and biopolitically, in the passive voice of letting die. "Language-effect" is not a recognized cause of death. And not least, of course, COVID-19 exacerbates existing biosocial inequities and vulnerabilities—so much so that one is tempted to personify the virus and assign to it a certain malicious agency and intent: it exploits precisely *these* inequities and vulnerabilities, further replicating the very conditions of American poverty and plutocracy. In Jacques Derrida's terms, "There are historical and political 'situations' whose terror operates, so to speak, as if by itself, as the simple result of some apparatus, because of the relations of force in place, without anyone, any conscious subject, any person, any 'I,' being really conscious of it or feeling itself responsible for it."[19] How should "we" (presumably good liberals) situate ourselves in relation to this apparatus, and wage a critique on its conditions of possibility, when we, too, form part of these conditions and seem ill equipped to do little more than self-righteously criticize?

In his early writings on the pandemic, Giorgio Agamben quickly averred that the Italian response to the crisis was "disproportionate" and represented yet another instance of the "state of exception" as an increasingly normal paradigm of government: "It is almost as if with terrorism exhausted as a cause for excep-tional measures, the invention of an epidemic offered the ideal pretext for scaling them up beyond any limitation."[20] In a text published some days later, he would clarify: "Our society no longer believes in anything but bare life. It is obvious that Italians are disposed to sacrifice practically everything—the normal conditions of life, social relationships, work, even friendships, affections, and religious and political convictions—to the danger of getting sick."[21] Agamben's statements have been met with spirited criticism, but in the American context it is perhaps more fitting to ask, Isn't the American state already founded, historically and economi-cally, on the mobilization of bare life? How else might we reckon the enormous wealth and plutocratic power generated by the Atlantic Slave Trade, premised on the dispossession and differential fungibility—the exchangeability—of human lives for personal profit and "national" economy? "Getting sick" or dying is a foregone conclusion, and secondary to economic interests (that have never been equally shared anyway).

If in this context we search for the "pretext" of the state of exception or bare life, we need look no further than the socioeconomic and political legacy of slavery and the terror that has followed, undead, in its wake. State biopower is not quite (as Agamben argues) the exercise of a sovereign exception so much as a vast and diffuse apparatus that presides over a sacrificial economy that is not—and has never been—for or by "the People." In recent decades, these conditions have been intensi-fied under neoliberalism (or some will say "optimized"), where government's role has been radically reduced to the administration of the economy (corporate tax cuts, bailouts, market interests). Today, individuals are left on their own, many isolated, some still sheltering-in-place, and forced to imagine mortal illness, life and death—and not just for this moment, but across the future waves of epidemic, and the murderous memes and militias that will surely attend them. Revising

Agamben's statement, we might say that some of us are disposed to sacrifice practically everything—not for the danger of getting sick but for the risk of losing a long-standing social order purchased on privilege, plutocracy, and (social) death.

A depraved president, incapable of expressing either comfort or mercy, announced without irony on March 18, 2020, that he had deployed the US Naval hospital ships *Comfort* and *Mercy* to house American patients "offshore." By April 2, in New York, the one-thousand-bed *Comfort* was comforting just twenty patients.[22] Three years ago, the same *Comfort* was deployed to Puerto Rico to offer medical assistance to victims of Hurricane Maria. In that natural disaster the ship admitted, on average, a mere six patients per day.[23] And some ten years ago, the *Comfort* had been deployed to Haiti following a catastrophic earthquake near Port-au-Prince. Christina Sharpe's critical reading of the American response in Haiti gains added poignancy as we shuttle between epicenters, from earthquake to hurricane to pandemic. Homing in on the *Comfort*'s administrative and ethnographic gaze, Sharpe presents as evidence a ghostly photograph of a gravely injured young Haitian girl: "Affixed to her forehead is a piece of transparent tape with the word *Ship* written on it."[24] In Sharpe's reading, "Ship" is both material and metaphor in the afterlives of slavery and in the conveyances of disaster: "Is *Ship* a proper name? A destination? An imperative? . . . Is *Ship* a reminder and/ or remainder of the Middle Passage, of the difference between life and death?"[25] Cold comfort for Black "cargo," containerized, in the "wake" of slave ships, migrant ships, military ships. Turning to the *Comfort*, she writes:

> We should pause . . . on the name and provenance of the ship. . . . "US," "military," "comfort," and "allopathic medicine"—each and together being terms whose connection in the lives and on the bodies of Black people everywhere and anywhere on the globe—warrant at least a deep suspicion if not outright alarm: from those experiments on board the floating laboratory of the slave (and migrant) ship, to J. Marion Sims's surgical experiments conducted without anesthesia on enslaved women; to the outbreaks of cholera in Haiti introduced by UN troops; to experiments with mustard gas on US Black soldiers in World War II to produce an "ideal chemical soldier"; to the Tuskegee and Guatemala syphilis experiments and their ripple effects; to the dubious origins and responses to the crisis of Ebola; to the ongoing practice of forced sterilization; to recent studies that show again and again that Black people in the United States receive inferior health care because they are believed to feel less pain.[26]

The inaudible cries and afterlives of these evils have now begun to find themselves transcribed on the mortal bodies of those who, now fungible for reasons other than just the color of their skin (though surely that, too, still), will be exchanged "for keeping the America that all America loves." Is this a lesson we are capable of hearing?

In his testimony to the US Senate on May 12, 2020, the nation's top infectious disease expert, a beleaguered Dr. Anthony S. Fauci, issued the stark warning that reopening America's economy too soon would result in "needless suffering and death."[27] Dr. Fauci was already being sidelined by the Trump administration and many in power simply refused to listen: rates of infection and death climbed exponentially in some parts of the country. But after all, the definition of "needless"—and its opposite, "necessary"—will differ depending on who you ask, and much the same holds true for measures of "suffering." These are slippery and age-old terms, sometimes even personified. Necessity was known to the ancient Greeks as the goddess Ananke, who dictated the fates of gods and human beings alike. She sometimes appears alongside the goddess Bia, a word that means force, power, or violence. And at first glance, those among us who blithely ignore public health orders or more defiantly protest government lockdown and facemask orders seem to inhabit such a mythological world, animated by fate and the specter of violence. For them, reopening the economy is demanded as a necessity, or is claimed as a Constitutional right, along with the freedom of movement, assembly, and religious worship, as Trump's Supreme Court would soon affirm (pandemic deaths be damned!). For them, the state's management of the crisis is seen as little more than a crisis of state management, where state intervention is deemed unnecessary and unwelcome, highly suspect or even "socialist."

Throughout the spring and summer months of 2020 we were bombarded with media images from many major US cities depicting militia-style vigilantes, some with assault weapons, occupying state buildings and claiming to defend their "rights" and "liberties," spurred by Trump tweets goading them to "LIBERATE MICHIGAN" and "LIBERATE MINNESOTA."[28] We have witnessed anti-lockdown and anti-facemask protests in the United States and, indeed, worldwide. From my perspective in the North American context, it's difficult to determine the extent to which local protests are driven by politics, ideology, or necessity. Organized on social media platforms and some funded by conservative groups (at least one, in Michigan, with apparent ties to a devout member of Trump's soulless administration), the protesters present as a ragtag collection of radicalized libertarians, Trump supporters, Second Amendment "defenders," anti-vaxxers, conspiracy theorists, and anti-globalists. Despite their differences, protesters do seem united in their singular will to tempt fate, to assume risk—or more accurately, to force others more vulnerable than them to assume it, as if by necessity.[29]

These spectacles have made it difficult to conduct reasoned debate over how we should navigate between the demands—and collateral damages—of the competing claims for public health and economic health, for lives and livelihoods. In other words, when communities begin to see sustained downward trends on their epidemiological curves, how will they know the right moment to reopen, and at what cost? And conversely, when there is a resurgent wave of infections, what will suffice to close things back down again? The metrics have been as inconsistent as their application, and we have had to factor in mental health and the human need for sociality. Nevertheless, even the most progressive democratic governments must admit a tolerable threshold of death—an acceptable loss of human life—as a result of reopening their economies. A few deaths might be called "unfortunate," perhaps "inevitable," but at what threshold do otherwise preventable deaths become too many to accept? If we knew these numbers, I suspect we'd find them shockingly high (as a society, we seem to tolerate repeated school shootings, "thoughts and prayers" notwithstanding). But there is little doubt that someone, somewhere, is crunching these numbers and quietly considering the voting public's levels of tolerance to death. It is a balancing act. But for all the talk of life's "pricelessness," every life does have a price, and some are valued more than others. This is the morbid calculus of an actuarial "science" as much as a political wager. The threshold will depend in part on who dies and who counts. If this is macabre it is also quotidian. It's just that these sacrificial economies are typically more discreet than they are in the time of COVID-19. It's just that the locus of power, its structural, impersonal, and ritual violence, has become unstructured, and for many, deeply personal, and worth the increased risk of protesting or simply ignoring public health orders.

In an interview published on April 8, 2020, Pope Francis remarked, "We're realizing that all our thinking, like it or not, has been shaped around the economy. In the world of finance it has seemed normal to sacrifice [people], to practice a politics of the throwaway culture, from the beginning to the end of life."[30] The moral bankruptcy, it would seem, is not simply our shortage of PPE and medical personnel, or even our godlessness. Rather, our vocabulary is morally bankrupt, and as a consequence, our imagination and capacity to think and to act otherwise. What would it mean if our thinking and, indeed, the very terms by which *to* think have been colonized by economic vocabularies, metaphors, and idioms? In the fierce competition of crises—between public health and economic health—it would mean that we could not objectively navigate between them. The very terms by which to navigate would impose their bias. To speak of economic "health" is itself a misuse of words and a mixed metaphor. But we barely bat an eye, even though we know that the economy is not a biological entity, and a "healthy" economy is always achieved by the suffering, ill health, or death of human beings. Such is the law of capital accumulation, the poisonous "freedom" of free markets. Again, these calculations are not new, it's just that they become less covert in the time of COVID-19. Our "throwaway culture," as Pope Francis called it, is usually discreet and anonymous, part of a global financial system and worldview. For example, we seldom consider the value of our own lives in relation to those rendered precarious or who are maimed and killed as a result of our nation's lucrative foreign arms deals, pharmaceutical testing, or child sweatshop labor. Closer to home, we might consider the implicit "value" ascribed to the poor, the homeless, Indigenous communities or People of Color, prisoners, and those in long-term care facilities. The precarity of other human lives is the hidden "utility" that props up the apparent value of our own.

But then what, after all, is the "utility" of a human life? And what, the "utility" of a virus? To test the survival of the fittest among us, to test our collective will, or our compassion and care for others? On these terms the virus, too, might resemble a god. It is perhaps fitting that Ananke and Bia, necessity and violence, go hand in hand.

The protesters, much like the virus, have something of value to teach us—not so much for what they say as for the animus they do not quite articulate in words. Yes, the protestors are a ragtag lot; they have no manifesto and do not speak in one voice. Some are surely misinformed, believe in conspiracy theories, or mistrust the science. Others may gesture to a fundamentalist religious faith, claim Constitutional "rights," or despise state power, while still others are perhaps simply reckless or selfish for any number of reasons—deniers who may not even deny the science but narcissistically deny that they themselves have a moral responsibility for others. And a radical fringe undoubtedly militates for the overthrow of the state and would hasten the "boogaloo"[31]—a slang term twisted and appropriated by the alt-white/right signaling the coming civil war, a race war to be waged, this time, with the providential help of a virus that exploits biological and socioeconomic vulnerabilities. The protests, then, expose the fault lines where the collision of biologic and economic crises erupt as a social crisis that has been simmering for generations. The mythological "fates" and "necessities" of protesters, their saber-rattling and neo-tribalism, share much with the worldview of religious fundamentalists, anti-vaxxers, and a swath of libertarians and far-right extremists who locate their faith elsewhere. They seem committed to other gods or demons, are distrustful of evidence-based science and medicine, and are fearful of state power. And arguably, they have wielded considerable influence over the hastened reopening of the economy in many jurisdictions. This has resulted in otherwise preventable (yet presumably "patriotic") suffering and death.

To be sure, the protestors do not offer a critique of biopolitical onto-logics or neoliberal economies—but they ought to occasion one. Instead, however, the liberal establishment is quick to scorn and to criticize, sometimes with fear, loathing, or self-righteous censoriousness. But a *critique* ought instead to turn our gaze inward and might discomfit us rather than reproduce and rhetorically validate what we already think we know. In some respects, the protestors' mytho-logical worldview courting fate and violence almost parodies the cool efficiencies of our biopolitical state, which for so long has in its own right enshrined the ageist, ableist, racist, and economic rhetorics of "tolerable" suffering and death as a matter of (neo)liberal public policy. We, good liberals, are complicit in such structural, impersonal, and ritual violence, as much as we might disavow it in the name of life itself. How different are we really? The protestors parody our hidden economies of "utility" and sacrifice, putting them on obscene display. If we manage not to stop up our ears, we might for a moment hear our own hypocrisies echoed in these scenes. And we might find the courage to submit our own preconceptions and vocabularies to critique—to question what seems "natural" and "just," and to ask why these are neither fated nor necessary.

## Thanatopolitics

What can we say of (or to) those who protest public health orders, refuse to wear facemasks, attend large gatherings (beaches, bars, parties, synagogues,[32] mega-churches,[33] etc.), and generally behave as if everything is "normal"? COVID-19 is both a virological and socio-behavioral malady. The examples of these "types" and their discourses—in some cases parroting rogue state "authorities"—are legion across the mainstream media. I need not reproduce it here.[34] We know it, and we know, too, the standard lines of reproach and public shaming, along with the moral outrage and righteous indignation directed at these "covidiots" whose self-proclaimed "liberties" do, in fact, encroach on others' right to life. Their diversity notwithstanding, they nevertheless demonstrate at least three common—and interrelated—features. First, their struggle is foremost a matter of *resistance*, typically directed against powers perceived to be false or odious. Second, this resistance is expressed as—and iteratively shores up—their individual identity and will, or even their "sovereignty," as they arrogate to themselves (liberal) "rights" and "freedoms." In this, they seek to reclaim a sense of agency fashioned as a perverse "right to life." And third, if death should come for them, that death (imagined to be unlikely) will be perceived as divinely willed or fated. In these ways, we might say that they are the embodiment and logical fulfilment of a liberal order the apotheosis of which is neoliberal biopolitics.

They are extremists or radicalized, we might say, although many conceive of themselves as the true patriots—and in a sense this is correct: they enshrine in their identity the values of self-possessed (indeed, mercenary) individualism, life, personal liberty, and the pursuit of happiness. And yet paradoxically, as I suggested above, they end up reproducing and enacting the very logics of neoliberal biopolitics—its sacrificial economies, its ruse of individual sovereignty and free choice, its routine disavowal of death, and its impassioned valorization of "life itself." They are, ironically, agents of an order they imagine themselves as resisting. Most of these people, I suspect, are not "suicidal" and don't *intend* to cause harm to others, to infect or to kill, to weaponize their bodies: if these are the consequences of their actions, they amount to accidental or aleatory effects. We might even call them *accidental terrorists*.[35] And to be clear, I'm not particularly sympathetic toward them, but nor am I sympathetic toward the moralizing and self-righteous good liberals (myself among them) who rush to condemn but who also end up unwitting agents of neoliberal biopolitics, whether in our demands for more laws and enhanced law enforcement, or more passively, by acting as the cultural conduits of normative state discourse and its language-effects. In this respect, good liberals are the new conservatives, while good conservatives increasingly cleave to a phantasmatic nostalgia for pre-liberal and pre-modern forms of governance enacted as illiberalism, neo-feudalism, or even political theology. How, then, might we on the Left suspend our impulse to scorn and to criticize—perhaps even despite our own pain, identity, politics—in order to rethink resistance outside of biopolitical logics, and without further implicating ourselves in them or reaffirming them unwittingly? In other words, how might we critically *disaffirm* biopolitics, *disclaim* its claim over us, without quite capitulating to and recirculating its tropes?

Some fifteen years ago, in an essay on what I called "thanatopolitics," I made an early and clumsy attempt to navigate this paradox.[36] I used "thanatopolitics" mindful that I was using an existing term in a new way. When Giorgio Agamben uses the term (albeit rarely), he intends only to signal the deathly, reverse face of biopolitics: "biopolitics can turn into thanatopolitics,"[37] he writes, as if to suggest that biopolitics is not always constitutively tied to death. Roberto Esposito follows suit: "The Nazi experience represents the culmination of biopolitics . . . absolutely indistinct from its reversal into thanatopolitics."[38] And Foucault, too, uses the term in a similar vein (but more rarely still): "The reverse of biopolitics is thanatopolitics."[39] In hindsight, I might have done well to choose a less freighted word! In my formulation, thanatopolitics was intended to offer a critical response to biopolitical life, where the deaths of those we let die would at times become a *productive* (rather than privative) power and would "speak" in order to expose and disrupt biopolitical logics from within. As Foucault teaches us, discourse is productive, and I had hoped to contest the biopolitical production of "life" by imagining those it lets die and silences in death as staging their own productive counter-discourse that would expose the biopolitical ruse.

Too hastily, I characterized thanatopolitics as a "resistance" to biopolitics. This was mistaken. As I argue above, resistance is not quite thanatopolitical because it often succeeds only in shoring up and reproducing the biopower it ostensibly resists. In this book, I argue instead for an understanding of thanatopolitics in and as disaffirmation—a response brought home in the productive rhetorics of dead speech, sometimes lyrical and apostrophic, spoken neither in sovereign grammars nor in the normative and teleological embrace of "logical" content or epistemic closure. To disaffirm, in response, is to have hearkened those we (will) have let die a biopolitical death carried out precisely *in* the execution of teleology and logic. If the dead make a claim on us, our response shouldn't simply usurp that claim, domesticate it, possess and reclaim it, in the language of logic and life itself.

For me, then, thanatopolitics is not the reversal or inversion of inherently "affirmative" rhetorics, for the affirmation of *making* live is unreconstructed and always linked, however clandestinely, to *letting* die. The active-passive binary calls for deconstruction. Moreover, in emphasizing the productive, critical valences of thanatopolitics, I also wished to distinguish my use from Achille Mbembe's signal use of "necropolitics" in a postcolonial African context.[40] I nevertheless take a great deal of inspiration from Mbembe, who issues the following challenge for postcolonial studies: "We need to go beyond the binary categories used in standard interpretations of domination, such as resistance vs. passivity, autonomy vs. subjection, state vs. civil society, hegemony vs. counter-hegemony, totalization vs. detotalization."[41] Mbembe exhorts us "to discuss the status of *death-as-such* or, more precisely, of death's life or *the life of death*."[42] Through thanatopolitics, I had hoped, we might find that the repudiated *life of death* opens a critical space between conventional (logical) antinomies. Finally, in my own formulation of thanatopolitics I preferred the invocation of Thanatos, whose cultural (and psychoanalytic) counterpart is typically Eros. These terms suggest a *topos* distinct from the more "clinical" and corporeal connotations of *necro-* and *bio-*, which infect and inflect biopolitics. Again, a disaffirmation of biopolitics should not reduplicate its normative tropes and tendencies but should arrive, instead, from another order of discourse, beyond mere corporeal life and death, and beyond the epistemic remit of our words' work.

In this early "thanatopolitics" essay I staged a discussion on deaths classified as either suicides or sacrifices—a distinction that ultimately says more about one's (living) positionality and perspective than about these particular deaths themselves. I invoked what is perhaps the most reviled and extreme figure of resistance: the suicide terrorist. And I insisted, as I do throughout this book, on the interconnectedness, often elided, between making live *and* letting die, and on the gradual "disqualification" of death in our culture. In Foucault's terms, "it is now not so much sex as death that is the object of a taboo."[43] This taboo was clear to me in 2004–5, as I was writing my earlier essay. The Second Palestinian Intifada (2000–2005) had received a great deal of media attention in the United States, particularly its suicide bombing missions. The United States itself had recently been the target of Islamist suicide terror attacks, and while the deaths of September 11, 2001, were meticulously counted and variously (repeatedly) invoked, there was still "no time for mourning," as Barbara Biesecker rightly argued.[44] Offered a Manichean choice at the time, we were either with President George W. Bush or with "the terrorists." And so we went to war. In official terms, Americans were said to "value life," whereas the terrorists did not. "Life" in America was being rhetorically rewritten by the "culture of life,"[45] as Bush repeatedly called it. This rhetoric was highly militarized, and its ethos extended into other nominally civilian domains—medical, juridical, political, technological, economic. In truth, however, under the guise of "freedom" we were subject to the progressive surveillance and militarization of public culture as the new norm—a permanent state of emergency and a disaster capitalism compelling (and outsourcing) mass death.

My interest here remains focused on the relative unspeakability of death, and the rhetorical intransitivity of letting die, which is eclipsed by the biopolitical transitivity of making live. If the death of the suicide terrorist hardly counts as a death (for "us"), this figure is nonetheless widely invoked in the training and desensitization (also a recruitment and radicalization) of Western military personnel. Specifically, on the intransitivity of death, I invoke my early essay on thanatopolitics in the context of the current pandemic, for the global War on Terror is the enduring legacy under which the pandemic plays out, rhetorically, on the home front. The pandemic, too, is a "war" against an "invisible enemy" (in Trump's terms). The trope of invisibility also recalls Cold War rhetorics retooled and redeployed in the global War on Terror, and now once again against a new Chinese communist enemy—a "Chinese virus," the "kung flu"—that (we are told) threatens to destroy the American way of life. And the invisible threat extends, in Republican Party propaganda, to "fake news" outlets as well as to "radical" or "socialist" liberals who have apparently infiltrated the Democratic Party. When a threat is invisible, it is easily displaced, much in the way that the Pentagon diverted $1 billion in bailout funds—intended to "prevent, prepare for, and respond to coronavirus"—toward military materiel instead.[46]

The long-standing economies of sacrifice that are conjured—now in the many forms of resistance to public health orders, scientific elites, globalists, the fakestream media, bluepilled libtards and normies, facemasks and social distancing—have weaponized lives and resulted in widespread illness and death, particularly across vulnerable and marginalized populations whose lives were discounted to begin with. To resist an invisible enemy can easily turn you into one, whether as suicide or as heroic freedom fighter (again, terms relative to one's point of view, self-identity, and source of information). Resistance can terrorize, even if it doesn't warrant the official label of "terrorism." As Derrida has asked, in a distinctly Foucauldian vein, "Does terrorism have to work only through death? Can't one terrorize without killing? And does killing necessarily mean putting to death? Isn't it also 'letting die'? Can't 'letting die,' 'not wanting to know that one is letting others die'—hundreds of millions of human beings, from hunger, AIDS, lack of medical treatment, and so on—also be part of a 'more or less' conscious and deliberate terrorist strategy?"[47] Of course, "not wanting to know" and knowing are two different, yet related, epistemic commitments. Thanatopolitics, as I imagined it, would surface this knowing as an ontological commitment, where it might find a political voice to declare—in words and deeds—that we are unable to continue to *live* in the shadows of silence, unable to condone a violence committed in the name of our own lives.


## Suicide by Society

Suicide terrorism has been widely decried as an act of "asymmetrical warfare." In one telling instance, the "asymmetry" of the suicidal *acte de guerre* was invoked following mass hunger strikes (met with force-feeding) and three detainee suicides at Guantánamo Bay in 2006. The military commander of the camp, Rear Admiral Harry B. Harris Jr., said of the suicides, "They are smart, they are creative, they are committed. They have no regard for life, neither ours nor their own. I believe this was not an act of desperation, but an act of asymmetrical warfare waged against us."[48] His message was clear: "we" are the true victims of these suicides and "we"—whose regard for life is apparently beyond reproach—are justified if we have no regard for *these* lives, either because they do not count as life or because their purported disregard for life disqualifies them in this, "our," regard.[49] There is no hint of irony in his words, and no acknowledgment that asymmetry could be measured otherwise, whether racially, socioeconomically, technologically, geopolitically, in military prowess and resources, or even in a nation's willful hostility or rapacity.[50] But these systemic asymmetries apparently pale in comparison to the "asymmetrical" act of taking one's own life.

The ostensible transitivity and sovereignty of the suicidal act is not only a sin against God across the Abrahamic religious traditions, it also profoundly disrupts the secular-sacred of biopolitical life and making live. As Jacqueline Rose has remarked, "Dropping cluster bombs from the air is somehow deemed, by Western leaders at least, to be morally superior. . . . Why dying with your victim should be seen as a greater sin than saving yourself is unclear."[51] We are meant to believe that those who drop bombs do so because of their morally superior regard for life. "Suicide bombing kills far fewer people than conventional warfare," Rose reasons. "The reactions it provokes must, therefore, reside somewhere other than in the number of the dead."[52] And indeed, terror is less about the number than the means—a sudden and visceral irruption of death into our everyday places of life-making. Cluster bombs often strike similar places, of course, but *our* death-making is at-a-distance, meant to be shrouded in the intransitivity of letting die, mediated by Hollywood heroism, and coded in the fictive "proportionality" and "necessity" of war. To say that suicide terrorists target civilians, and then to reason that this "justifies" our horror, is disingenuous. All war does just this: it kills civilians, physically and psychically, socially and economically. In World War II, Allied forces dropped two nuclear bombs on Japan and countless firebombs on Germany and Japan, massacring hundreds of thousands of civilians. These particular acts of war often occasion a discourse of "necessity" and some utilitarian calculus by which such preemptive killing would ultimately save more lives than those incinerated. More recently, in the global War on Terror, we might consider American military adventures post-9/11 in Iraq and Afghanistan (and beyond), each with its own terrorist insurgents, and each calling for progressively preemptive counterinsurgency tactics, US state-sanctioned murder (and in some cases bodily desecration), extraordinary rendition, and torture (euphemistically, "prisoner abuse"), at least some of which escaped military censorship to expose quotidian abominations at Abu Ghraib, Guantánamo Bay, and countless American "black sites" around the world. This haunted me and still does.

The rich man's sins and the beggar's death are related by more than their coincident voicelessness; they are interdependent in the silent bargain known as the cost of living. The shameless human carnage caused by the 2003 US invasion and occupation of Iraq (self-righteous, and with no more than a phantasmatic casus belli),[53] the enormous civilian death toll, and the suffering of those left alive, is widely documented but never officially acknowledged in America as a crime against humanity. In 2006, *The Lancet*[54] reported the Iraqi body count ("excess deaths") at 654,965; more recently, in 2015, the international organization Physicians for Social Responsibility[55] placed the number "conservatively" at one million and did not hesitate to qualify the US military adventure as genocidal. And so, long after the celebrated disposal of Osama bin Laden's (invisible) remains, Americans remain under the bloody legacy of ongoing Overseas Contingency Operations (OCO budget in 2020 = $71.5 billion), including Enduring Activities, that the global War on Terror is said to necessitate, its violence meted out in the logics of "preemption" and "self-defense." In the war of these asymmetries figured as sites of "vital," "humanitarian," and purportedly "surgical" interventions, we have developed highly lethal autonomous weapons systems—drones, smart bombs, et cetera—that are remotely and algorithmically driven and powered by complex networks supported by satellites and publicly traded commercial industries.[56] This delivery unto death is highly mediated, sanitized, and gamified. What imaginable resistance could emerge from within such a vast neoliberal-biopolitical apparatus that operates as if by its own (highly profitable) inertia? What, if not something horrific and unimaginable?

Reading media reports of suicide terrorism, over the years I became increasingly preoccupied with the steadily growing number of suicides among Western military personnel, who, it seemed to me, are themselves ultimately also the victims of missions that killed other human beings in the service of a delusional world-historical cause. I followed these stories and began to gather an archive of soldiers' suicide notes, typically published in fragmentary form, in news stories, on blogs, or tucked away in Reddit feeds. I have many in my archive, but they are each exceptional because publishing them contravenes a Department of Defense Directive stating that all members of the military, including "retired and separated Service members, former DoD employees and contractors, and non-active duty members of the Reserve Components[,] will use the DoD prepublication review process to ensure that information they intend to release to the public does not compromise national security as required by their nondisclosure agreements."[57] The dead, of course, cannot submit their words for prepublication review, and the nondisclosure agreement (Standard Form 312) is binding "during the time I am granted access to classified information, and *at all times thereafter*" (my emphasis). The interests of "national security" hide a multitude of sins in patriotic perpetuity—sins often unjustly ascribed to persons who take their own lives, but whose last words and final acts frequently betray the structural, impersonal, and ritual violence of a system that kills by letting die, and then (as their loved ones frequently attest) lets die once again when life becomes unlivable for those soldiers who come home bearing war's "invisible" scars.

Selecting from some suicide notes that have been verified and are in the public domain, I offer just a few words from these dying dead voices, seldom heard:

"I had once thought that I could leave with my thirteen dead: the thirteen who kept me from sleeping, who assaulted my psyche in my modes of consciousness. They became legion. I thought back to all the missions I had witnessed. I couldn't believe the numbers. I felt like my soul had fled and I knew my judgment would be damnation. But I was still there. . . . In the hospital, my dead stood in judgment of me in my nightmares." (A letter from a remote sensor operator)[58]

"Time's finally up. . . . I am not a good person, I have done bad things. I have taken lives, now it's time to take mine." (A veteran of Operation Iraqi Freedom)[59]

"The simple truth is this: During my first deployment, I was made to participate in things, the enormity of which is hard to describe. War crimes,

crimes against humanity. Though I did not participate willingly, and made what I thought was my best effort to stop these events, there are some things that a person simply can not [sic] come back from. . . . To force me to do these things and then participate in the ensuing coverup is more than any government has the right to demand. Then, the same government has turned around and abandoned me." (A veteran of Operation Iraqi Freedom who describes his suicide as a "mercy killing")[60]

These voices tell a story of overwhelming moral injury,[61] and a truth that is otherwise silenced by military propaganda and "patriotism." I hate my archive, it sickens me, but I feel that it dishonors these voices to stop up my ears. In their agonies, in their fraught resistance, they invite us to think beyond individual responsibility, to reflect on the "we" and what responsibility and agency could mean as a *public* good. I have no grounds to dispute these soldiers' documented behavioral health diagnoses, including PTSD (in 2017 this officially included just 50.8 percent of all US military suicides).[62] I would note, however, that the posthumous psychiatrization of such acts tends to reinscribe these individuals into a biopolitical order, effectively robbing them of the very resistance to which their last words—and their deaths—often attest. Compare the words of Saeed, a twenty-one-year-old Palestinian: "In honesty, if life is like this, and work is like this, death is more honourable."[63] Suffering and death are visceral, notwithstanding a politics of "necessity." And what of honor?

Suicide terrorists and Western military suicides: I paratactically place these figures of repudiated death and resistance alongside those who, in the warring asymmetries of COVID-19, also variously resist an invisible enemy. This includes those who have been infected by the virus and whose resistance might be fought as a personal medical crisis, as well as those who resist state and public health protocols, who protest, who refuse to wear facemasks, and are thus potential agents of contagion and, in some cases, themselves become infected and will demand health care. I do not equate these figures of resistance nor do I suggest their contexts are commensurable. They are not. And yet, it will not do to categorize these casualties as either "ours" or "theirs," according to the patriotic economies of war. They speak to and of a death that we'd prefer remain unspeakable—a death (to recall Blanchot) that "subverts the whole sequence of existence, causes time to take leave of its order, opens life to its passivity, exposing it to the unknown, to the stranger." If we bracket, for a moment, questions of individual intent (for as I've argued, such liberal agency is unreconstructed and uncertain), at a community level it becomes difficult to distinguish the enemy terrorist from the Western soldier from COVID-19's accidental terrorists: strangers to us, their lives are weaponized and convey an unknown threat, exposing life—ours and theirs, too—to its passivity. How much does it matter if needless suffering and death are immediate or highly mediated through techno-military or capitalist or bio-social networks? Death need not be highly wrought.

In our unending wars of purported "symmetry," "proportionality," and "necessity"—now indispensable to the national economy—it is vexing to distinguish the terrorist from the freedom fighter. In an effort to exalt the latter, we struggle in vain to locate a liberal-humanist agency—a purity of intent, an identity, a desire to make live—that in spite of it all is nevertheless implicated in the covert agencies of intransitive death-warranting. As Talal Asad has noted, "However much we try to distinguish between morally good and morally evil ways of killing, our attempts are beset with contradictions, and these contradictions remain a fragile part of our modern subjectivity."[64] These extreme examples shed light on the institutionalized and normalized failure of otherwise "progressive," "enlightened," or "tolerant" good liberals to associate our livingness with the dispossession and death of others who (will) have been suicided by our society. Might these deaths not attest to a strange "life of death,"[65] as Mbembe puts it—lives already negated, whether as unlivable or unsurvivable? What is the agency of letting die here, this quiet power to disavow certain lives, to count them as already dead, as destined for death, and to disavow (yet again, and still) their deaths as deaths?

"Terrorism," Asad writes, "is an epistemological object in modern society."[66] And while the terrorist is "dismissed as being essentially part of a nonmodern, nonliberal culture,"[67] Asad points out that terror—however (re)mediated or (re)framed—is integral to liberal subjectivities as well. We tend to treat both as epistemological objects, including the soldier suicide and those who variously defy and protest COVID-19 protocols. We attempt to understand them, too, by advancing knowledge claims, and yet our epistemological objectivity—transitive in its grasp on those subjects of violence—fails to comprehend the ontological claim, the "life of death," that consumes them. Indeed, those who resist often reclaim a lost sense of agency through the intransitivity of their pain and suffering that is then transitively redirected through acts of violence and self-harm. In an earlier exploration of pain and agency, Asad offered a critique of "romanticized" notions of resistance and moral agency, which, he argued, carry the false assumption "that power is external to and repressive of the agent, that it 'subjects' him, and that nevertheless the agent as 'active subject' has both the desire to oppose power and the responsibility to become more powerful."[68] Romanticized notions of agency—"self-empowerment,""individualism"—are invoked, he argued, in order to advance a "triumphalist" vision of history, much as we saw above across our various figures of resistance. This promised life to-come, this triumphant futurity, is the salutary ruse of biopolitics, but there is something harrowing in the ways that the intransitivity of letting die is not only secreted in the biopolitical apparatus, but is at times willfully mobilized as a transitive death-making, however mediated or indirect.

## Postscript

At the time of writing, American deaths due to COVID-19 already far surpass the combined deaths of every war since World War II (including the Korean War, the Vietnam War, the Gulf War, the War in Afghanistan, and the Iraq War).[69] Given the state's pandemic rhetorics of war, its calls for "patriotism" and "sacrifice," we might feel galled that, over the course of Trump's presidency, there was little to no state reverence for the dead and dying, no celebration of the heroic dead (as in times of war), no official moments of silence, no public rituals of recognition or mourning. On the contrary, Trump's White House succeeded in fueling the pandemic with its botched response, disinformation, and a maskless super-spreader president who touted a drug proven not to work, suggested injecting household disinfectants, and promoted a witch doctor who believes in the pathogenic effects of demon sperm. It was all singularly surreal, seemingly unstoppable, a satyricon come to life. And as for death? Trump summed it up coolly: "It is what it is."[70] "Live and Let Die"—the Guns N' Roses song blasted during the president's summer 2020 campaign stops in Arizona and again in Ohio. At least this merciless spectacle had the virtue of a certain honesty, however grim.

   And yet, it is far easier for me to criticize the state's hypocrisies and biopolitical crimes than to reckon, in my grief, with my sentimentalizing desire for the state's sovereignty in these moments, my yearning for leaders who might mirror my own commitments and affects. I feel powerless to interrogate my own compulsions. My narcissistic desire is tempting, but the romanticized promise of resistance and moral rectitude risks turning my disaffirmation into the triumphalist terror of sovereign grammars and "master" tropes. Is this who "we" are? Instead, I turn away from the spectacle. I come closer to home: that is where disaster strikes. Life opens to its passivity. Time takes leave of its order. A cry, but not just: a call. Attending to the dead, alongside those left behind, we may stumble into spaces where the state is ultimately senseless and irrelevant. For, in anguished moments, together, we have held discreet vigils for those we have lost, sought solace in makeshift rituals of mourning, in summoned strangers, perhaps, or in undeclared friendships, and, for now, community among our dead.

# 2

## Speech Begins After Death | On Claiming the Human Right to Die

In what extreme delicacy, at what slight and singular point, could a language come together in an attempt to recapture itself in the stripped-down form, "I speak"?
—Michel Foucault

In a 1968 interview published posthumously as *Speech Begins After Death*, Foucault reflects on the relationship between death and writing—a term he uses interchangeably with speech. "Speech," he says, "isn't only a kind of transparent film [*pellicule transparente*] through which we see things, not simply the mirror of what is and what we think. Speech has its own consistency, its own thickness and density, its way of functioning. . . . It's this density characteristic of speech that I'm trying to interrogate."[1] Interrogating the density of speech, its materiality and texture, Foucault opens here with visual metaphors for speech as "a kind of transparent film," and then as a mirror that reflects "what is and what we think," the relation between reality and representation. But he qualifies these metaphors: speech is not only, not simply, these rather two-dimensional things, whether transparent or reflexive. It is also, paradoxically, a thickness, a density. Drawing on Christian Lundberg, I would call this latter its "rhetoricity," which Lundberg characterizes as "the functions of discourse that operate without, and in advance of, any given context." "Rhetoricity," Lundberg continues, "serves as a kind of negative constraint, hindering the presumption that any definition of rhetoric can capture the functions of discourse without remainder."[2] I bear this preliminary definition in mind as Foucault, several pages later, offers us an interpretive clue to his paradoxical definition of speech when the metaphor of the film appears once again.

Asked by his interviewer why most of his texts concern distinctly *historical* systems of knowledge and modes of speech, Foucault replies that he finds it difficult to speak or write about the present: "Naturally, it seems to me that I could talk about the things that are quite close to us, but on condition that there exists [*qu'il y ait*, 'that there would be'], between those very close things and the moment in which I'm writing, an infinitesimal shift, a thin film [*cette mince pellicule*] through which death has entered."[3] Here, the space and time in between what is and what we think, speak, or write is mediated by the "thin film" of death; death, the rhetorical condition of speech. And it is this death that lends speech its density, its thickness, its gravitas. "For me," Foucault says, "writing ... basically means having to deal with others to the extent that they're already dead."[4] Recalling Lundberg's definition of rhetoricity, we might say that death is the remainder, the density or thickness, that thwarts the mistaken presumption that discourse can function without remainders or remains—from without, and in advance of. This is Lundberg's Aristotelian exhortation for rhetoric to "let it be," echoed here in Foucault's subjunctive, *qu'il y ait*, that there would be—or should be—death. But rather than a "negative constraint" on speech—the mirror image of a negative right that we couldn't be free *from*—I would like to read Foucault's subjunctive as a positive or productive exhortation for the irruption of death in and as the moment of speech and writing.

Speech is not always in the service of a biopolitical *telos*. The positive or productive constraint, if we can call it that, would be thanatopolitical. It would be spoken from death, rather than in and of life itself. Life would no longer be the condition, neither the objective nor the means, of such speech. Nor would such a speech *make* live: it would neither preserve nor prolong life. And it would not resurrect the dead. Rather, speech and death are reclaimed here, together, as mutual events—a transparent film, infinitesimally thin—a threshold that distinguishes the living from the dead at "the moment in which I'm writing." And, if we wish to distinguish the living from the dead, we must not presume that the living speak and the dead do not. "For me," Foucault says, "speech begins after death and once that break has been established. For me, writing is a wandering after death and not a path to the source of life."[5] Foucault's anxious and repeated qualification here—"for me"—indicates that he is constrained by his own "use" of death, in writing and in speech. Wandering after death, speech comes posthumously, seeking errantly in the shadows of death and hearkening a death that remains forever without, in advance of, any context. Hence, the "inexhaustibility of language, which always holds speech in suspense in terms of a future that will never be completed, is another way of experiencing the obligation to write."[6] We are not, then, directed toward "the source of life" or the origin of speech. And we are not in pursuit of the autonomy or agency of living speakers who would speak in order to express their unique identity or "interiority." Rather, to speak or to write in care of death is to attend (to), to hearken, the voices of the dead, exteriorly, and to place ourselves in a rhetorical relation of obligation as much political as ethical.

I do not speak *of* death so much as I *speak death* so as to speak. I do not anticipate or go to meet my death. Rather, death fractures all anticipation from a future that will never be accomplished or lived-out, and from which death comes in time to make its claim, lending density and force to speech as my obligation. I can have no proper relation to death if death is understood merely as the cessation of biological life, which occurs at a particular place and time. To speak *of* death in clinical or strictly biological terms is reductive and dehumanizes the dead, rendering the person and the life lived as no more than and forever a thing, an epistemic object. Things as such don't die; they can be dispatched or disappeared with little consequence, administratively or through a police function, as much through violence as by "benign" neglect. This is the voice of biopolitics, if we were to conjure *its* voice: it tells me to "stand my ground," to value (my) life at all costs, and it makes live and compels me to live that life, such that "for me" to die is almost a social and moral failure on biopolitical terms. Of course, biopolitics itself doesn't exactly speak: as we know from Althusser, ideology never speaks in its own name, and doesn't show itself for what it is. There is no annunciation. For those we silently let die, their death is the condition of this, our, biopolitical life—a death that does not fully count as death because it befalls a life that did not fully count as living.

These expedient lives and losses may be enumerated, as they are so frequently, so fleetingly, in statistics that tender them flatly as line items, as bodies that lack density, thickness, gravitas. Biopolitics is tropological, even seductive, but evacuated of all self-conscious "rhetoricity," to recall Lundberg's term. It's a joke without laughter or any sense of its own irony. It advances a claim on what is to-come by anxiously filling "the functions of discourse," foreclosing on what is "outside," disavowing its inassimilable remains, or gobbling them up. If biopolitical discourse is hegemonic, if it constitutes subjects, regulating the terms in and through which we are tropologically constituted *as* subjects, I'm asking how a shift in perspective from biopolitical life to death might help us to imagine a conception of political agency that doesn't return us wholesale to the phantasmatic sovereignty, the moral agency, of a liberal subject. That is, if biopolitics promises life by consuming the lives of some, then how might a thanatopolitical discourse on these deaths critically disaffirm biopolitics and give voice to its silent and unspeakable remains?

It's not quite that the unspeakability of death would at last be spoken or positively known as a thetic "content," but, rather, that the event of death and the act of speech would lift the veil on the unspeakable, gesture toward another order of discourse, and reveal what is unspeakable *as* unspoken. And so, if we are tacitly party to a biopolitical nondisclosure agreement, a social compact, here we might *say*, however paradoxically, that we *cannot* say, and we might understand by this that we are destined for speech as for death, given over to death as we are to language, and obligated to speak and to write at the limits of this foreclosure, where speech folds back on itself in the struggle to say what cannot be said.

Turning to the case of California's mass prison hunger strike in 2013, this chapter explores the power of a speech that begins after death. In what follows, I argue that the hunger strike claims the human right to die, and I theorize the rhetoricity of this claim by bringing Foucault into conversation with J. L. Austin's understanding of performative speech acts. The hunger strike makes a claim on death, from without, and in advance of, its particular context. It traverses the thin film to bring us face-to-face with those who speak death and who are themselves the conditions and casualties of biopolitical life, condemned in the quotidian to endure slow death, civil death, and social death. "I'd like to reveal something that's too close to us for us to see," Foucault says, "something right here, alongside us, but which we look through to see something else. To give density to this atmosphere that surrounds us and allows us to see things that are far away, to give density and thickness to what we don't experience as transparency."[7] We tend to look through the biopolitical veil of death and see only the splendor of life; we look through human suffering and see security and civil peace. Death is our atmosphere, too close for us to see, and too much a part of us for us to comfortably reckon its work in our vital economies.

## Claiming Death

On August 19, 2013, the California Department of Corrections and Rehabilitation (CDCR) won a court order from a federal judge authorizing the force-feeding (euphemistically, "refeeding") of hunger-striking prisoners scattered across six prisons in the state's carceral archipelago.[8] In the early days of the protest some thirty thousand prisoners were fasting and refusing to work.[9] But these were not bodies locking arms to occupy streets or public squares: many staged their protest from the extreme isolation of solitary confinement,[10] their voices echoing from a legal black hole with highly tenuous and unverifiable support networks. Hunger strikers were protesting their living conditions, the most notable being the state's use of long-term and indeterminate solitary confinement.[11] Prisoners of moral conscience as well, we might say, they continued to uphold the five core demands for reform set out during two previous hunger strikes in 2011.[12] The 2013 mass hunger strike was (and remains) unprecedented in size, a remarkable display of solidarity by inmates across the California prison system, peacefully uniting prisoners despite geographic, social, and ethno-racial differences. These men were supported by breakout hunger strikes across the United States and in many other countries as well. Yet the CDCR told a different story.

The court order allowing the force-feeding of these captive bodies was motivated in part by CDCR claims that violent prison gangs were orchestrating the protest and "coercing" inmates to take part. Less than two weeks before the court order was issued, CDCR rehabilitation secretary Jeffrey Beard had published a scathing op-ed in the *Los Angeles Times*, presumably part of a public relations campaign to delegitimize prisoners and their demands: "Don't be fooled," he wrote. "Many of those participating in the hunger strike are under extreme pressure to do so from violent prison gangs, which called the strike in an attempt to restore their ability to terrorize fellow prisoners, prison staff and communities throughout California."[13] As with so much that goes on behind prison walls, Beard's claim is extremely difficult to corroborate, but as I discuss below, his claim is suspect because many prisoners from rival gangs took part in the strikes and joined in solidarity with sworn enemies from other prisons as well.

Unsurprisingly, the court proved obedient to the familiar tropes of terror, security, and innocent (presumably white) communities under threat, authorizing force-feeding and declaring invalid any Do Not Resuscitate directives the prisoners had signed.[14] The CDCR court request itself was framed as a medical humanitarian response, and the court order as a state-sanctioned intervention purporting to honor prisoners and to value their lives. The CDCR cited concerns over "inmate-patient autonomy" and specifically invoked Policy 4.22.2 of California Correctional Health Care Services,[15] which pertains to the provision of "medical services" during a "mass organized hunger strike," and which, the CDCR somewhat vaguely alleged, "may be insufficiently flexible or detailed to address a number of issues posed by the hunger strike."[16] As the state's hyphenated appellation "inmate-patient" suggests, prisoners' bodies are doubled in this legal rhetoric: objects of competing forces, these bodies are caught between the conflicting paradigms of punitive *control* and medical *care*, between powers that would let die and make live.

But any real concern for inmate-patient "autonomy" is risible in this context. It is the last thing that prisons want from docile bodies within their walls. If inmates are routinely allowed to languish in solitary confinement, to experience slow death, civil death, and social death, their decision to protest this treatment and to engage in the accelerated death of a hunger strike suddenly seemed to qualify them as "patients" in need of "sufficiently flexible" health care. Normative conceptions of autonomy, it would seem, cannot or should not extend to one's capacity to refuse food or treatment, in solidarity, or to die in or on one's own time. If patient-inmate "autonomy" was really so compromised, it is ironic that the hunger strike wielded such power: the state was compelled to watch the strike unfold in real time and to respond. And as I argue below, while individual prisoners would surely find some agency in the hunger strike, it was not first by virtue of their individual "autonomy." Speech across difference, and the forging of collective bonds in solidarity, requires us to abandon the principles of autonomy and possessive individualism, those sovereign tenets of political liberalism and law. As Giorgio Agamben writes, "What the State cannot tolerate in any way . . . is that the singularities form a community without affirming an identity, that humans co-belong without any representable condition of belonging."[17] In sum, the *nomos* of the hunger strike—refusal, protest en masse, and ultimately death— is ungovernable. Across the threshold that separates life from death, might we accept the living and the dead as co-belonging in such a way that disrupts the impositions of political identity and representability? By turning to death, we threaten to expose the biopolitical body that is caught in between, neither living nor dead—a body that can make no normative claim to the right to die, that cannot die, and that can only be misrepresented in biopolitical terms.

The *topos* of liberal political autonomy becomes profoundly troubled in this moment. No longer anchored in the individual's living body, free will, or personal agency, prisoners drew inspiration from and allied themselves in collective action. From the state's perspective, of course, normative autonomy has always been little more than a fungible fiction and a biopolitical technology of control. By forcibly restoring "autonomy" (itself a performative contradiction—a joke that isn't funny) the state would regain the capacity to govern the lives of those in custody, effectively quashing collective action, annexing prisoner autonomy, and co-opting it by administrative procedures and policies, ultimately undermining any political agency by preemptively adjudicating and appropriating all normative claims to it. In a rhetorical register, this marks the struggle over who holds the right to speak and to claim a right, and who controls the terms in and through which such speech might be heard across its communities of reception—themselves often constituted in and by the claim. And it is the struggle as well over whose actions will be able to enter into discourse and appear as legible and just. If nominally autonomous speech/acts are conceived as a positive right—a freedom *to*—this freedom is refashioned here, whether cynically or ironically, as a negative right policed by state authorities—as a freedom *from*.

The apparent right to be "free from" even *potential* coercion by prison gangs, whether voiced or not, is considered sufficient grounds to disregard an inmate's will and suspend his purported rights for the ostensible purpose of safeguarding them. And it is ironic, too, that *actual* coercion is not mentioned, as when, for example, segregated prisoners are routinely pressured by prison staff to "inform" on each other during post-segregation debriefings. This information alone can be used to justify someone else's solitary confinement, the absence of corroborating evidence notwithstanding. The choice, as prisoners themselves describe it, is stark: "parole, snitch, or die."[18] Yet, despite these ironies, legally sanctioned force-feeding was the ploy by which CDCR officials sought to dodge what they no doubt perceived as a public relations problem. On the one hand, the state would either cede to prisoners' demands and structurally undermine its own disciplinary authority, or, on the other, it would allow them to die, which would undermine the state's moral authority and fuel a crisis of public trust. The CDCR wagered that force-feeding administered under the aegis of a court order would symbolically permit the state to preserve its authority: to refuse prisoners' demands, and yet to demonstrate that it cherishes life and respects the legally sanctioned human rights of those locked inside.

This is an instance of what Colin Dayan refers to as the "sorcery" of law,[19] here taken up as a rhetorical force, the power of language and of speech to conjure a particular understanding of law and life, and conversely, to obscure or conjure away state-sanctioned dispossession, degradation, and death—all the while surreptitiously producing it. My own writing here, my speech, is incited by these dissident protesters who are condemned to a living death, but whose proper death they are not permitted to claim. The prison as a limit case offers a glimpse into the ways that biopolitical power functions across social structures more broadly to control and confine our administrated lives in the quotidian. As Dayan suggests, "We should ask not how we allow the existence of 'black sites' (our overseas prisons), 'frozen zones' (in the borough of Brooklyn), 'security housing units,' 'special management units,' or 'supermaxes' (throughout the United States), but rather how we live and breathe with a status that exempts us for the moment from being labeled as threats. For, even if we are safe today, we live on a slippery slope."[20] We are sliding down that slope, and it is increasingly unclear which forms of life will soon become a public security interest, subject to violent police functions, biomedical orthopedics, public health surveillance, law, policy, popular media campaigns, and intersecting paragovernmental administrative bodies. In the name of these "agencies," a normative conception of "life" is securitized, preserved, and prolonged—at least "for the moment," while nonnormative lives are subjugated according to shifting fortunes, fates, and economies.

Biopolitics operates ideologically through the cruel fiction of an absolute and inalienable right to life typical of liberal political conventions.[21] And yet life itself becomes a moral responsibility, and sometimes a burden rather than a right, if we do not also consider the human right to die. For death is that without which life becomes a hollow and senseless notion, little more than the prolongation of unqualified (bare) biological life. Liberal right-to-life discourse does not map onto the right to die, and yet the right to die, I'm suggesting, is primordial and implicit—if obscured—in any claim that invokes a right to life. In this respect, I do not follow scholars who theorize the hunger strike as the strategic wielding of one's *life* against a sovereign power whose prerogative is "to take life or let live"[22] (for these lives have already been as it were administratively and "autonomously" revoked). And although the state deploys its pseudo rhetorics of sovereignty, in and as the rule of law, we nevertheless find ourselves subjects not of a sovereign power but to a biopolitics that differentially "makes live and lets die." After all, force-feeding is an obvious effort to make live, and the state doesn't wish to be perceived as a power that arbitrarily and intentionally kills.[23]

Another approach is called for because within the biopolitical paradigm life's givenness is not presumed, life is not quite what the subject always-already "has" to willfully wield or surrender to a Hobbesian sovereign in return for protection, as the tradition of liberal political philosophy would have it. Rather, biopolitically, life and its expression are not presumed so much as produced and sustained by anonymous powers that make live. From this it follows that one has the moral duty to go on living, and that the state has the duty to intervene to safeguard and prolong that life. Thus, I address the hunger strike neither as a strategic or symbolic expression of "life itself" nor as "free speech" that ought to be entitled to First Amendment protection.[24] Nor am I in a position to argue for the justness of the prisoners' demands. Liberal approaches such as these tend to presuppose life and exalt individual autonomy and agency, which become entangled in instrumentalist disputes over whether fasting to death constitutes suicide, rightful nonviolent protest, a political tactic, or a decisive escape from living conditions experienced as unlivable.[25] I suspect it is all of these, and more besides. But these formulations become dubious if we take seriously the ways that conceptions of vital agency and autonomy are normatively produced and historically constrained by juridical, penal, and medical biopower fixed on an unreconstructed—and thin—conception of "life itself." And besides, in their claim, hunger strikers *have* no life to wield: they are already unalive because their living conditions are unlivable, and so it becomes a real question here whether any resulting death should be attributed to the actions of an "autonomous" individual, or whether it's a "suicide by society."

To claim the human right to die is, paradoxically, to claim a right *to live*. This is not quite the same as a right to life. Recalling Foucault, we might say that the right *to live* is claimed in speech that begins after death—a proleptic claim *on* death as that which will qualify the life that one lives, ensuring that that life is not unqualifiedly bare life. Claiming the right to die, then, would wrest death from neoliberal biopolitics and disclaim the passivity of letting die. And indeed, the protestors' demands focused on their living conditions—the right *to live* without the abuses of prison officials in their arbitrary application of "policy" and punishment. They do not wield or wager life so much as they "risk" a living death. Rather than a clear exercise of liberal agency or autonomy, then, and rather than a straightforward act of resistance, the specters of this speech/act—through bodily mortification and death—suggest the abandonment of normative autonomy, not to the state, but in the name of the dead and by the power of death itself. In claiming the human right to die, one's speech/acts frustrate the ways that "autonomy" is biopolitically produced and regulated by the state. Here, the human, no longer quite a political category or substance of rights or dignities, becomes an unruly instance that unworks the state's power over human life-making and death-warranting. The state may of course intervene to prevent one's biological death, to forestall it for a time, and yet to die is to be claimed by a power that the state cannot quite assimilate. Indeed, death remains ultimately indifferent both to the state's interventions and to one's autonomy, for, by death, one doesn't of course win back autonomy for oneself. In its own time, death will mock any powers that purport to possess, sustain, or guarantee life.

As I argue below, the state can neither see nor hear that the death that is claimed in claiming the human right to die is not mere biological death. Rather, a murmuring voice remains, in death, to haunt the biopolitical insistence on life itself, and to expose the sleight of hand by which biological life is "doctored" and duplicitously affirmed as the highest ethical good. And so, we must conclude that hunger-striking prisoners are force-fed and obliged to persist—both unalive and undead—not out of humanitarian kindness, but because the state dreads most that they should become persons in some sense only *in* death, and through death gain a ghostly agency and voice—an unregulable irruption into the administrative efficiencies and grammars of our biopolitical order. Officially, force-feeding prisoners engaged in a hunger strike ostensibly saves their lives: a "humanitarian" intervention apparently intended to preserve or restore the conditions of their humanity—but with precious little care that the very conditions of their continued existence effectively foreclose on it. Foremost, it is order that is preserved or restored. The "humanitarian" act may well be experienced as vengeful rather than just, and ultimately, as a murderous gesture—to bring about the death of death, to foreclose on the possibility of death, and to rob from life that which makes it meaningful. The intimate and proximate *speaking* of death lends contour to and humanizes the living of a life. But if we repudiate the intimacy and proximity of death, and smother life's mortifying speech/acts, then to forcibly impose this repudiation—to deny any possible claim to it—redoubles the violence by sentencing one to the unending silence of a living death.

## Speech/Acts

Claiming the human right to die opens us toward a reconception of voice, toward a dead speech or writing that would act despite—and even critically disaffirm—the living death of biopolitics. To recall Foucault, "Writing . . . basically means having to deal with others to the extent that they're already dead.'""But this doesn't mean," Foucault explains, "that writing would be like killing others and carrying out against them, against their existence, a definitively lethal gesture that would hunt them from presence, that would open a sovereign and free space before me."[26] The force of such speech is not biopolitical: it does not let die in order to make live, silence in order to make speak. I'm not free to say whatever I wish, and there is no question here of a sovereign "I" freely at play. To claim a speech that begins after death is to problematize the subject who speaks and that subject's relation to death. "Who" becomes a troubled placeholder. "Who," we must ask, has the right to speak and to *claim* this right, for the claim is not the same as the right, and each stand in some respect as the necessary condition of the other. To speak, even as an impostor, the claim must have been granted, and to have that claim granted, one must have been entitled to speak. From the above, we might say that death adds a "cryptic" dimension to speech: to claim the human right to die is in some sense to be claimed *by* death, to speak in its name and to invoke the dead. If speech begins after death, speech claims will travel under the sign of death, and, under certain conditions, will hold the power to re-politicize the operant terms of biopolitics, to bring death to discourse, and to expose the powers— however clandestine or silent—that kill in the name of life.

Claiming that speech begins after death, Foucault has in mind the philosophy of Maurice Blanchot. Not only does he mention Blanchot by name during his interview,[27] but just two years had elapsed since his 1966 essay on Blanchot, "The Thought of the Outside."[28] In this earlier text, Foucault reflects on the troubled position of the subject who speaks, and he begins in part one of that essay with the titular utterance "I LIE, I SPEAK." This is an odd speech act. If we ignore for a moment the claim that the speaker is lying, and focus instead on the claim "I speak," it would appear to say no more and no less than that I'm speaking at the moment I utter these words. "I speak" seems to be hermetic in its logic and self-evidently true, demonstrating how it is that speech is said to act efficaciously, even transparently. Indeed, it is what J. L. Austin might call a performative utterance: doing or performing the very thing that it names or says. And yet Foucault destabilizes any such certainty. "I speak" is preceded by "I lie," united by a simple comma—a breath or a pause in speech, a parataxis—which leaves it to the reader (or listener) to join them significatively.

Am I lying about the apparent obviousness of the claim that "I speak" or in that speech/act itself? Do lying and speaking stand in a causal relation? Is one the necessary condition of the other? Do I speak in order to lie, or is my speech in some sense always a lie, one that redounds on the purported veracity of the speaker, the substance and trustworthiness of the "I"? "I lie, I speak" invokes the ancient liar's paradox, and we may recall the fable of Stesichorus, who was struck blind by Helen of Troy when he called her a whore. Blinded, Stesichorus immediately writes his palinode or "counter-song" to appease Helen, declaring that, in truth, he was a liar when he spoke.[29] How do we know that this latter "truth," this palinode, is not a lie? This is not simply the riddle of how to distinguish the truth of a declared lie from a lie declared as truth (and besides, isn't a lie by definition the false declaration of truth?). Where logicians will rush to draw up their "truth tables," finding in them some solace perhaps, rhetoricians and literary scholars may just shrug and say that some truths are best told as lies because rhetorical matters come into play, and truths and lies are sometimes staged and performed independent of exactly *what* is said—in the form of songs, stories, metaphors, or allegories. This is what we called "rhetoricity," above. As for old Stesichorus, Helen seems to have been satisfied: his sight was immediately restored. Perhaps she was simply moved by the sweetness of his song?

Foucault mobilizes and himself performs the performative contradiction of the truthful liar. What, he asks, are the conditions under which I myself or others might hear and comprehend my utterance "I speak" and recognize it as coming from me, truthfully, as an avowal of the "I"? And if "I lie" and truthfully avow my lie as I speak, I may, after all, be lying about lying, avowing a disavowal or disavowing the "I." Who or what is the referent, the transitive object, of the expressions "I lie" and "I speak"? What do "I" lie or speak *about*? Speech is something the subject does, but equally in some sense something the subject *is*, self-referentially and self-reflexively: "The speaking subject is also the subject about which it speaks."[30] Along the thin film that would distinguish doing and self-reflexive being, I occupy an ambivalent existential place, and "I" am held as a placeholder between the ontology of the subject and the work of words themselves. The referent is, then, implicitly self-reflexive, even centrifugal: speech about speech, but speech also about the subject herself, and the subject reflected in and by her language. Holding open the parataxis, we must somehow imagine that one does not necessarily precede the other. "Speech about speech leads us," Foucault writes, "by way of literature as well as perhaps by other paths, to the outside in which the speaking subject disappears."[31] Disappearance is a death of sorts, a forceful surrender of self-sovereignty, but equally the place of an ambivalent (and at times, insurrectionary) appearance. In an effort to distinguish "I lie" from "I speak," the subject must, Foucault writes, "slyly fold" discourse back on itself. "I lie, I speak" is to begin, so to speak, as an impostor. So to speak, and so as to speak.

We might say, then, that the baldness of the utterance "I speak" relies on a subtending discursive field that momentarily, fictively, props up the substantive agency of the speaker, and secures her place in a socio-symbolic order, which would grant meaning to that speech and to that "I." A Cartesian conceit operates here, an hypostatization akin to the "I think" of the *cogito*, where a silent discourse must steal in to encumber one's agency and autonomy, an advance claim that operates furtively. When I say that I speak, that supporting discourse, Foucault argues, is missing: "The sovereignty of 'I speak' can only reside in the absence of any other language; the discourse about which I speak does not preexist the nakedness articulated the moment I say 'I speak'; it disappears the instant I fall silent." Foucault then asks, "In what extreme delicacy, at what slight and singular point, could a language come together in an attempt to recapture itself in the stripped-down form, 'I speak'? Unless, of course, the void in which the contentless slimness [la minceur sans contenu] of 'I speak' is manifested were an absolute opening through which language endlessly spreads forth, while the subject—the 'I' who speaks—fragments, disperses, scatters, disappearing in that naked space."[32] The contentless slimness in this beautiful passage is reminiscent of that thin film (cette mince pellicule) through which death enters and makes speech possible, immediately evacuating the speaking subject into the naked space through which language itself appears, speaks, and "endlessly spreads forth." The subject is held together, then, conjured, through the "absolute opening" of language and by an unabsolvable obligation to write, to speak. Here we might imagine that the death of the fragmented, dispersed, scattered, and disappeared subject heralds a different kind of speech and writing, a "cryptic" thanatography.

The kind of cryptic speech I'm suggesting has no obvious propositional content, is not intentional, and radically calls into question—rather than presumes or props up—the subject of speech and that subject's "use" of language (I return to a discussion on "use" in the Refrain). In an earlier essay dating from 1963, Foucault had deployed the metaphor of the mirror to draw an "essential affinity" between death and speech: "Headed toward death, language turns back upon itself; it encounters something like a mirror; and to stop this death which would stop it, it possesses but a single power—that of giving birth to its own image in a play of mirrors that has no limits."[33] The "mirror to infinity" reflects on death, opening a void, a "density," and a "virtual space" through which language endlessly spreads forth and "speech discovers the endless resourcefulness of its own image."[34] If we speak so as not to die, our speech nevertheless begins after death and performatively enacts its claim on us, from the crypt. No doubt, Foucault inducts us into a cryptic speech act theory. And yet the performativity that is suggested here helps to shed light on those who claim the human right to die, which, if it were to speak in a Foucauldian vein, might say, "I die, I speak."

For a somewhat more conventional account of speech act theory, I turn to the work of J. L. Austin, which, it will turn out, is cryptically productive in its own right. Together with Foucault, I hope to demonstrate how Austin might nuance our understanding of the prison hunger strike as a performative speech act. Of course, in Austin's understanding of performativity, "I speak" is not so terribly fraught. Drawing on his analysis from How to Do Things with Words, "I speak" might be treated rather straightforwardly as a successful or "felicitous" performative, saying what it does and doing what it says. To say "I speak" would seem to perform my speech and to evidence the fact that I'm speaking, there and then. "I lie" is no doubt much murkier. And yet, neither "I speak" nor "I lie" appear as examples in Austin's text. Instead, his examples favor performatives that include "marrying," "betting," "bequeathing," "christening," and so forth, typically spoken in the first-person singular and in the present indicative active tense. They revolve around social bonds. "I speak" and "I lie" may have been too self-referential for Austin. If they are performatives, in his sense, they are less obviously transitive. I can never quite vouchsafe the subjective conditions that would secure my own speech/acts. Such speech/acts may say what they do, performatively; as transitive verbs, however, it is difficult to say how they do what they say they are doing *to* the addressee when that addressee is always in some sense me myself. There is, then, what we might call an intransitive dimension to "I speak," "I lie," and also "I die." And as I suggested in chapter 1 apropos biopolitics, *to let die* verges on the intransitive, and yet its intransitivity does not sentence us to passivity: a thanatopolitics would work to disaffirm this passivity, and speech would begin after death. Nevertheless, this is not Austin's worry, not at all. For him, it would seem that the "I" is given from start to finish, independent of its speech, and, by virtue of this, "I" am free to speak. The marriage ceremony is often taken as Austin's paradigm example: "*I do* take you to be my lawfully wedded . . . ," where to utter these words is to commit the speaker and to *do* the very words that the "I" has uttered (provided I know and mean what I say). In these moments we can say that our speech *acts*, transitively, and that saying makes it so, "felicitously" consummating our speech.

Austin takes pains to elaborate the conditions under which such speech acts are successful or felicitous: "*There must exist an accepted conventional procedure having a certain conventional effect, the procedure to include the uttering of certain words by certain persons in certain circumstances.*"[35] For him, spoken words are not enough. The personal identity of the speaker also matters, including the speaker's intentions, as well as the unbroken social scene of address in which these words are spoken. For example, a stage or film actor who utters the marriage vow will not be considered married to the actor who receives this vow. Austin enumerates six types of conventions or procedures that must be satisfied if the performative is to be successful or felicitous. When these rules are not met, the utterances are performative failures or infelicitous, and infelicities are of two types: "misfires" and "abuses." The latter, abuses, devolve on the psychology of the speaker, where my utterance rings hollow because it was insincere. I may have lied or I may have had no intention to fulfill my promise, and so forth ("I lie" is unspoken, conceived as interior and intentional, context rather than address). The misfires, however, are sociological in nature. They result from "misinvocations" or "misexecutions" of speech, where social conventions are not obeyed. I may, for example, offer marriage vows to my favorite sheep, goat, or chicken, but this is a misexecution of convention, and I will not be considered married simply on account of uttering these words, no matter how sincerely or ardently.[36] As Austin himself admits, his schematics are boring, dry, and unpalatable. My students skim these passages, but they do matter if we hope to understand the kind of social ontology that Austin presumes. In schematizing, I don't want to lose sight of my question: Is the hunger strike a speech act, and if so, of what sort? Bearing this question in mind, I return to Austin to see if we might fathom an answer on his terms.

Austin initially introduced performative speech acts (or "illocutions") because he was dissatisfied with the way that Anglo-American philosophers of language had until then understood speech. Austin argues that these philosophers mistakenly take illocutions for "locutionary usage," thereby falling prey to the "descriptive fallacy"—namely, analyzing speech according to the truth or falsity of its so-called propositional content, and ignoring its normative force. In other words, they fail to see how we actually *do* things with words because they treat performatives as mere "constatives." Constatives are rather straightforward locutions: statements that impart information, describe, or report—much like a bad undergraduate essay that discusses a Jane Austen novel by offering little more than a plot summary. The summary may be true enough, but it *does* nothing, or, as an instructor might say in frustrated tones, the essay makes no claim, has no voice. As a corrective, Austin identified performative or illocutionary uses of language, and roughly the first half of How to Do Things with Words clarifies this distinction of utility between straightforward locutions and performative illocutions. Austin describes performative illocution as the "performance of an act *in* saying something" and refers "to the doctrine . . . of 'illocutionary forces.'"[37] Illocutionary speech acts draw on the symbolic positioning of the speaker and the "total speech situation," from which they draw their illocutionary force or conventional (citational) agency.

Recall for a moment the claim above that biological life is not quite living and that death is not quite the mere cessation of biological life. If clinical definitions of life and death were the end of the story, then life and death could be fully contained in constative utterances, without remainder, and communicated as neutral and impartial information. Life and death would *do* nothing and have no claim on us. In this manner, we can of course account for the abstract facts of someone's life or death: date, time, location, death by what means, et cetera, and all the while fail to convey the "density" or the "thickness" of a life lived. And this, I have suggested, is one inflectional modality of biopolitics, its means of reducing the deaths of those allowed to die to insignificance, to the banality of reportage. Meanwhile, for those it makes live, neoliberal biopolitics renders us as living human capital, and biologizes life so as to prolong and extend it. Biopolitics exalts life while simultaneously flattening it—and yet, strangely, this leveling is its exaltation, a negation that takes on a positive value in the numb continuation of life. In stark contrast to the constative world of bare life, performative speech might be conceived as a political and rhetorical form-of-life, a way of life that is political because it speaks, and in speaking, constitutes the *polis* as a reflexive condition for speech. And here Austin would be correct: the agentic force of the illocutionary speech act does not reside solely in the speaker. Nor does it reside in language as such, but as the prefix *il-* of his "illocution" attests, it acts *in* language—language is its vehicle, its subtle body. Again, the illocutionary force—the *doing*—that emerges *in* speech relies on received social conventions, rituals, and ceremonials. Amidst various caveats, Austin offers the tidy formula: "*in* saying *x* I do *y*."

And yet for Austin it is nevertheless the task of the speaker and sometimes the auditor(s) too—all presumably good liberal subjects—to ensure that these rituals and conventions are met, and to obey and to marshal them as a part of the force of truthful, efficacious speech: "It has to operate through the conventions of language and is a matter of influence exerted by one person on another: this is probably the original sense of 'cause.'"[38] Cynically, we might say with Foucault, "I lie, I speak," and see performative speech of this sort as the posturing of the impostor, a lie taken for truth (or vice versa). For Foucault, the agency of speech is not vouchsafed by the speaker's obedient marshaling of social conventions, as it is for Austin. Foucault will not seek recourse in the subjectivity or identity of the speaker. Across much of his work, it is the "agency" of discourse that animates speech, while the subject of that speech fragments, disperses, scatters, and disappears: "The subject that speaks is less the responsible agent of a discourse (what holds it, what uses it to assert and judge, what sometimes represents itself in it by means of a grammatical form designed to have that effect) than a non-existence in whose emptiness the unending outpouring of language uninterruptedly continues."[39] In this moment, the very moment in which the "I" seeks the linguistic means to affirm itself, to traverse the "transparent film" or mirror that mediates reality and representation, it falters, unsovereign, unable to close the chasm between the "I" who speaks and the "I" who is spoken, what "I say" and what "I do."

Foucault's terms are certainly foreign to Austin and the two are not easily reconciled. And yet, Austin, over the course of his lectures, begins to call into doubt his own schematic division between constatives (locutions) and performatives (illocutions)—the domains of meaning and force, respectively—to suggest instead that all constatives might properly be considered performative speech acts. At one point, he declares that constatives are little more than oversimplified abstractions from performative speech: "The traditional [constative] 'statement' is an abstraction, an ideal, and so is its traditional truth and falsity."[40] This represents a full-frontal attack on the linguistic philosophy of his day and an assault on a certain understanding of scientific positivism. I would add that it should also destabilize a worldview whose legacy has been resurrected more recently in the reductive calculus of neoliberal biopolitics, new "materialisms," and object-oriented ontologies that wish to claim that matter "speaks." They have no sense of rhetoricity, no ear for poetry or song, and even less for an ironic or self-deprecatory quip (and Austin's text is positively jocular if you warm to his dry wit). An impartial voice is always potentially partial, constatives are always potentially performative, and descriptive claims may well be normative in their remit. Who can deny that even the most seemingly clinical speech that reports or describes—in the most neutral of terms—calls on a set of preexisting conventions, institutions, and practices that authorize this speech and lend it significance? Even the benign clinical description carries normative force and is often more malignant for its apparently neutrality, as with, say, statistical prognoses and rates of survivorship relating to one's possible cancer treatment. And it is here, with an eye to power, that Foucault and Austin begin to speak to one another.

Midway through his text, Austin turns his attention away from the now questionable binary between constative (locutionary) and performative (illocutionary) speech acts to introduce a third term: *perlocutionary* speech acts. At least two of his later lectures tackle what now suddenly seems to have been his principal intention all along: the distinction between illocutions and *perlocutions*. And things start to become somewhat more cryptic. Like illocutions, perlocutions are performative, but not in the same way. Where illocutionary speech is summed up by the formula "*in* saying *x* I do *y*," perlocutionary speech, true to its prefix *per-*, is summed up as "*by* saying *x* I do *y*." Sadly, perlocutions occupy scant space in Austin's text, and in his final lectures he returns to a dry schematization of illocutions. Still, he offers us some worthwhile insights to develop: "Saying something will often, or even normally, produce certain consequential effects upon the feelings, thoughts, or actions of the audience, or of the speaker, or of other persons: and it *may* be done with the design, intention, or purpose of producing them."[41] Austin elaborates by way of example, in which he distinguishes between locution, illocution, and perlocution. I cite his first example:

Locution:
He said to me "Shoot her!" meaning by "shoot" shoot and referring by "her" to *her*.

Illocution:
He urged (or advised, ordered, &c.) me to shoot her.

Perlocution:
He persuaded [or convinced] me to shoot her, [or] He got me to (or made me, &c.) shoot her.[42]

In addition to the perlocutionary verb "persuade," Austin includes "rouse," "alarm," "convince," "deter," "surprise," "mislead," and "intimidate" (distinct from "threaten,"[43] which he classifies as illocutionary). While the agentic force of illocutionary speech is conventional, the force of perlocutionary speech is nonconventional, which is to say, it might even defy or flaunt conventions, or mobilize a convention catachrestically (by misusing or abusing it) in order to achieve its effects. As such, its effects are unpredictable and precarious, guaranteed neither by the speaker's intentions nor her obedient marshaling of conventions. In other words, while illocutionary speech embodies the transitive force of a convention, by contrast perlocutionary speech is intransitive and disembodied from the start; its force may well come from elsewhere, without seeking recourse or affirmation in the intentional agency of a liberal subject who speaks (*he* persuaded, convinced, got me to, or made me . . .).[44] Illocutions draw on and often cite (as in law) conventions as the force of their agency (they are citational practices), whereas perlocutions produce effects that are properly events: they might draw on convention but do not directly take their force from conventionality or citationality, even as they may generate effects and "sequels" in these realms. They may, for instance, stage the ethical collision of competing discourses. We saw this in chapter 1 with the suicide bomber and the soldier suicide—those "suicided by society," and whose "message" or "speech," *by* saying, challenges a normative conception of "life itself" and appears for us as unassimilable, untranslatable, in biopolitical terms. And yet, these speech acts produce unanticipated and uncontrollable perlocutionary effects, which range from autoimmunitary political responses to retributive justice to vengeance. "Terrorize" is perlocutionary. (In chapter 4, I offer a critique of the perlocution in the context of digital hate speech, which further troubles our understanding of "consequences" and "sequels" in the temporality of instantaneous digital transmission.)

Austin only takes us so far. And in the end perlocutionary effects threaten to pop up everywhere: "For clearly *any*, or almost any, perlocutionary act is liable to be brought off, in sufficiently special circumstances, by the issuing, with or without calculation, of any utterance whatsoever, and in particular by a straightforward constative utterance (if there is such an animal)." In *sufficiently special circumstances*, and *by* the uttering: even so-called constatives can carry perlocutionary effects, very real consequences—"brought off" with or without human calculation. This situation threatens to be ungovernable. And worse, Austin's schema (he calls it a "programme") does not easily accommodate what he refers to as physical actions—hunger strikes, for example—which *say* something by *doing* something (an inversion of his illocutionary speech act). "If the action is not one of saying something but a non-conventional 'physical' action, this is an intricate matter."[45] His rather comical example, buried in a footnote, is "hurl[ing] a tomato at a political meeting." This is as political as Austin gets, but even here, while the action is conceived as a form of speech, and while it will undoubtedly enjoy perlocutionary effects or consequences (even if no more than someone's dodging the tomato), for Austin these redound on the liberal speaker as an expression of her presumed interiority and intentionality: "The consequence will probably be to make others aware that you object, and to make them think that you hold certain political beliefs."[46] Probably?! Austin is surely being droll, but this leaves too much unsaid, and too much hinges on his wit. This is why it is crucial to read Austin alongside Foucault, who helps us to think the perlocution beyond speech, discursively, and outside the domain of a liberal, autonomous speaker—where a self-possessed "I" is not presumed from the start. And it is here, I submit, that we might begin to fathom what kind of speech begins after death, and what sort of speech/act characterizes the hunger strike.

## Truth or Consequences

Allow me tentatively to posit the hunger strike in terms of perlocutionary speech in intimate discursive proximity with bodily mortification and death. In Austin's language, then, I'm attempting to surface some of the consequences or effects of such speech/acts. And yet, I'm not altogether happy with Austin's language. By "consequences" and "effects," he seems to commit us to the sovereign grammars and temporal conventions of cause and effect. But "consequences" are irreducible to temporal sequences. Rather, as Foucault suggests, relations of cause and effect sometimes slyly fold discourse back on itself. They can be paratactical. Effects can and sometimes do assume a causal force in relation to their own purported "causes"; consequences can be and sometimes are taken not as contingent but as necessary grounds, origins, or a priori truths. Those we let die, for instance, are usually not seen as the systemic and systematic consequences of neoliberal bio-politics, but instead as *causae sui*, as if they died of their own necessity, by their own hands. And this ruse, in its turn, stands in a causal relation to our own liberal postures of moral innocence, which we are invited to experience as an origin and identity. We must understand how particular consequences and effects are, in themselves, the conditions of possibility for biopolitical power. A conventional rendering of consequences and effects will rob speech of its perlocutionary potential, its nonconventionality and contingency, however dangerous or droll. Speech is not language, as much as it draws its force *from* language. As Foucault says, "Speech, on the contrary, no matter how long or how diffuse, how supple, how atmospheric, how protoplasmic, how tethered to its future, is always finite, always limited."[47] The finitude of speech marks its essential affinity with death. It is not a neutral instrument of communication on the tongue of a liberal subject who has always-already won the claim to speak. If it were, communication would be no more than the constative utterance of "facts," the mobilization of preestablished conventions, or the utopian free exchange of ideas among equals in the public sphere. This is the constitutive violence of philosophy's *ceteris paribus*—"all things being equal"—for, as we know, in the public sphere all things are never equal.

Sometimes, we *do* manage to subvert conventions, not so much *in* what we say but *by* saying it. To understand perlocutionary speech of this kind, we might speak not of consequences or effects, but of moments, events, ruptures in the fabric of existence and signification. Here, it is better to speak of voice. I have struggled writing this chapter, deferring my return to California's carceral archipelago, where I might at last have offered up the voices of hunger-striking prisoners in lieu of my own. But how, in the end, would the voices of a few "speak," from these pages, as the speech of the hunger strike itself? How would they speak the shadow of the death they have claimed because, in some sense unbidden, death has already made its claim on them? I could not ensure that reproducing their speech would succeed as a perlocutionary speech act in the context of this book; I believe I share their disaffirmation, but what is theirs cannot here and now be wielded as my own.

I could report, constatively, and momentarily overwhelm, perhaps, with a litany of harms inflicted by extreme isolation and unlivable living conditions. The evidence is legion, and barely contested, across myriad professional discourses: psychiatry, medicine, nursing, social work, criminology, sociology, philosophy, and even from correctional officers themselves, when they, by some miraculous sense of self, have not been fully interpellated by the prison-industrial complex. (In my own prison research,[48] allied health professionals reported despair at feeling co-opted and censored by corrections, and this had profoundly deleterious repercussions on caregiving and their own mental health.) Or I could reference Supreme Court decisions condemning solitary confinement, United Nations reports, the American Civil Liberties Union, Amnesty International, Human Rights Watch, and many others. But what would this speech *do*? As important as this speech is, another form of speech is called for, a stylistic break with the performative conventions of liberal rights discourse—all self-evidently "true," by convention. Turning instead to the force of perlocutionary speech acts, however, we recall that its agency is not *in* language, as it is with illocutionary speech: perlocutionary agency is occasioned (not caused) *by* speaking, *by* language. Perlocutionary speech is not, then, what we would call linguistic agency in any straightforward sense. Rather, the protoplasmic force of the perlocution is occasioned despite its rupture with performative conventions and conventional constraints. It would attend (to) the forms that rise in the face of a total speech situation, intervening into those conventions that preauthorize a speaker's claim to speech.[49] It would enjoy, in other words, a certain uncertain rhetoricity.

It is not, of course, that the speech emerging from and responding to the hunger strike is entirely nonconventional. Indeed, so much of it relies on the conventions of litigation through the courts. There are, as well, published demands, threats, protest fliers, websites, Twitter and Facebook feeds, rallies, public lectures by critical intellectuals such as Angela Davis, and some mainstream media attention. Speech proliferates, both beautiful and banal. Sometimes it invokes the powerful conventions of kinship relations. A prisoner involved in the hunger strike wrote, "I look at the photo of my daughter Jawanda. I've never seen her face in real life or heard her laughter. . . . I'm convinced my daughter Jawanda hates me for not being there for her and her brother as they grew up."[50] A twenty-one-year-old Texas woman in solitary confinement wrote, "I am somebody's daughter. I have a great family. I should be home."[51] These are humanizing voices, when they can be heard. And with this in mind, the stated mandate of the Prison Hunger Strike Solidarity website is to amplify "the voices of those in solitary confinement."[52] Speech proliferates, and yet much of it becomes domesticated, diluted, or dismissed as unsanctioned, radical, or even coerced.

Meanwhile, other language invokes somewhat less conventional expressions of solidarity. Joining the hunger strike of 2011, solitary prisoners from California State Prison–Corcoran wrote the following in solidarity to prisoners at Pelican Bay: "Pelican Bay Collective is not alone in this struggle and the broader the participation and support for this hunger strike and other such efforts, the greater the potential that our sacrifice now will mean a more humane world for us in the future."[53] Our sacrifice now, they write, will ensure a more humane world for us in the future. There is a radical expression of solidarity in these words, across geography and across time. The "we" who writes, the "we" who sacrifices, speaks indistinguishably from an indeterminate "we" who will enjoy a more humane world in the future. However, in the context of a hunger strike, there is no guarantee that those future selves will belong to the ones who speak here and now. Our sacrifice now: the thin film by which death enters in the moment of speech or writing. The sacrifice for a future, and for those to whom "we" bequeath this future, is all the more palpable under the claim of death. We begin to break the bonds of convention, exceeding them, disembodying them, in and by those voices that speak. It will not do to classify such speech as simply propositional in its "content," as truth or lie. And it is impossible to account in linear or logical terms for the temporality of its sacrifice: imagining a contingent future perfect in which the grammatical subject will no longer exist or speak, but also, in the moment of utterance, a subject who speaks and acts as the voices of others unseen and unheard—a subject fragmented, dispersed and scattered, but not altogether lost in between the one who speaks and the one who is spoken. We find, then, occasional moments, events, ruptures when we return to the scene of California's hunger strikes. Those who committed to fast to death, together, alongside those they did not and likely would never know or even see, did so in extreme isolation from one another, and far from the public eye.

It is not, then, the living speech of hunger strikers that so threatens the state, for the state regulates the terms of this barren livingness, and its expression, co-opting such speech as one modality of biopolitical control, refiguring it as coerced by violent prison gangs, as a security or terror threat, a threat to fellow prisoners, prison staff, and law-abiding communities alike. Rather, it is dead speech that is intolerable to the state because it unites these voices from an elsewhere to haunt state discourse from outside or beyond its administrative purview. It haunts my words as well: What sort of solidarity, in or by my own writing, can be achieved? How might I escape the language of bland affirmation as I join in to disaffirm? As an extreme case, solitary confinement is disembodying, and the solidarity invoked by the hunger strike happened virtually—through writing and some form of speech, yes, policed and curtailed and subjected to brutal retaliation by prison officials, but these words nevertheless carried with them a perlocutionary force, beliefs and effects, wrought on bodies here and now and for tomorrow. "We would rather starve ourselves, to risk inevitable death, than to be indefinitely subjected to the deprivations of the torture unit."[54]

To be sure, these "inevitable" deaths are not mine, not ours. How, then, to speak and to write, to call and be called, across the chasm that opens up between what I say and what such saying could do, across what Dayan calls the "background of reasonable assault, where sanitized language leads us to accept unlimited restraint and its attendant terrors, less spectacular because legally inflicted"?[55] We might, rather, marvel at how isolated, mortified bodies managed to speak at all across social, racial, geographic, and ideological differences, let alone to establish an incipient, unconventional sense of community, tentative trust, and belonging. If death is here the condition of speech, it also conditions the moments—in the days and months—preceding this speech, when prisoners in extreme isolation, and in defiance of the usual conventions, were able, through unsanctioned speech and writing, to cooperate and join in solidarity across our administrated spaces of cruel abandonment. What kind of "uncertain reservoir," as Dayan writes, might be summoned "to cast doubt on the robustness and transportability of the onto-logical partitions that we so easily presuppose: body and mind, animality and humanity, matter and not matter, feminine and masculine"?[56] What sort of force, by speech, if not by death?

Since their first hunger strike in 2011, Pelican Bay protesters remained largely silent concerning the legitimacy of the criminal justice system as a whole, referring instead to the violation of individual bodily and psychological rights. They did not claim that their individual sentences were illegitimate, but only that within the prison system they must suffer and bear witness to particular, concrete, and illegitimate abuses. Framed in conventional legal terms, they communicated a formal complaint to the CDCR and the governor outlining reasons for their planned hunger strike, citing US Constitutional violations, UN human rights violations, and contraventions to the 1984 Convention Against Torture and Other

Cruel, Inhuman or Degrading Treatment or Punishment.[57] They published modest and measured requests that might be perceived by the wider public as reasonable, humane, easily met. This performatively positioned them as rational and realistic, not as irrational security threats or "the worst of the worst." In the context of this "legitimacy paradox,"[58] the decision to fast to death takes on a particular moral force. These actions operate within—and yet on—the norms of the prison and legal systems themselves. The leaders of the Pelican Bay hunger strike came from various racial backgrounds, "validated" by the CDCR itself as belonging to rival prison gangs: the Black Guerrilla Family, the Aryan Brotherhood, and the Mexican Mafia. "In other words," as legal scholar Keramet Reiter notes, "the hunger strike leaders lacked the kind of shared political ideology of participants in other, international hunger strikes, like the Irish Republicans, the Palestinian nationalists, or even the Guantanamo enemy combatants."[59] Reiter offers a detailed summary, reporting that hunger strikers were able to overcome rivalries and join in solidarity in part by invoking resistance efforts across international communities, and allying themselves with them.

In an unpublished transcript of the face-to-face meeting of July 20, 2011, between Scott Kernan, CDCR undersecretary, and four hunger strike leaders at Pelican Bay, one of the strike leaders, Todd Ashker, is reported to have said, "We all know we're dead already. We're dead here. None of us are going nowhere. So what do we have to lose? . . . We have no other way . . . to expose what's really been going on to the public, the main street public."[60] The "conversation" (the CDCR insisted it was not a "negotiation"—it would remain constative rather than irrupt as performative) focused on the daily lives of prisoners in solitary, a life framed by prisoners as a living death.[61] Already dead, the specter of death here marks the beginning of speech, with its own thickness and density, its own way of functioning. It is the condition of this "conversation," but it also haunts the total speech situation, which includes and gives voice to the hunger strike itself. In response, then, to the agency—of law, "humanitarian" medicine, the CDCR, the state—that force-feeds and conjures a perverse, biopolitical lifeform, we glimpse here the force of voices that cannot be conventionally contained. Who speaks here and what is this speech/act? Is this speech self-referential? Does Ashker lie? Does he tell the truth? Posing questions of this nature is to presume that the speaker is free to marshal the operant conventions of meaningful speech and truth-telling, and in so doing to lend his speech the illocutionary force of a recognizable claim. But the speaker has been granted no such authority over his own words or those of the many others, unknown and unseen, who he represents.

If, together, they make a claim, at least part of its force is non-propositional. This speech is less a question of its truths or lies, intervening instead into the conventional truths and consequences of the prison system itself. Perlocutionary speech *acts* on these conventions and challenges the illocutionary forces that regulate in advance "who" may speak and be spoken.

Together, they speak *from* death through the trope of prolepsis—where the specter of a future death is set free to travel across other kingdoms, other socio-symbolic fields, here and now. *Death speaks* and performs the manner in which the protestors are (literally) fragmented, dispersed, scattered, and disappeared. The "naked space" of disappearance, to invoke Foucault once again, is also that time and place in which these bodies are warehoused, times and places of inhumane confinement, where words no longer promise to outrun death. We might say that by speaking, they yield to the power of language and death, straddling the "contentless slimness," the "thin film," or the "mirror," so that we might see through a glass, darkly, a shimmering death. Is this critical work not equally a conjuration, one that nourishes the *illusion* of the conjuring constitution that biopolitics hopes to disappear? In hearkening this language, and in care of death, we are forced to admit a poetic conceit, which would open up rather than foreclose on this scene of address.

In his poem "The Hollow Men," T. S. Eliot writes, "Shape without form, shade without colour, / Paralysed force, gesture without motion."[62] For what, in the end, is a gesture without motion, a voice with no vocation, a trope without a turn, if not the terror of hearkening "Those who have crossed / With direct eyes, to death's other Kingdom." Voices "quiet and meaningless," the "dried voices" of the dying, the dead, hail us, and remind us that we too inhabit the kingdom of the dead, that ours is the other of death's other kingdom, another death, and that we too are hollowed out by these words' work. This kingdom was once held fast by Christianity in the West but has for at least two centuries belonged to an increasingly biopolitical state, now managed according to neoliberal efficiencies (our pieties are simply displaced). What then is the force of critique if not by contingency and revolt in the face of necessity and the "necessaries" of biopolitical life? There is something about this death that cuts across the "thin film" that separates reality and representation, in imprisoned and solitary performatives that are in no wise "free" speech. Death speaks: it names us, it calls us, it commands us to remember. It is perhaps more primordial a relation than the invocation of life, the word made flesh. Here and now, rather, flesh becomes word, death desires, and ultimately possesses us. And it is death's desire—rather than a desire *for* death—that surfaces in the hunger strike, speaking through the mortification of the flesh, arising in the name of the dead: "Remember us—if at all," Eliot writes, "—not as lost / Violent souls, but only / As the hollow men / The stuffed men." The poetic gesture that closes this chapter would ask us to suspend, for a moment, our cherished conventions, our sovereign grammars, that police the limits of speech and recognition, to imagine them coming undone. "Between the idea / And the reality," Eliot writes, "Between the motion / And the act." In-between, the hollow men in this mirror: straddling a thin film stuffed full to brimming with the mediating turns and tropes of biopolitics, a noisy business that would conjure away the paralyzing silences of death and anxiously fill these times and spaces of human abandonment. This is the taking place of language, its occasion and occasioning, which attends (to) a living death somewhere along the hyphen— the *trait d'union*—of the in-between, and a speech about speech that we are dying to speak.

# 3

## Necessaries of Life | On Law, Medicine, and the Time of a Life

What, then, calls me into question most radically? Not my relation to myself as finite or as the consciousness of being before death or for death, but my presence for another who absents himself by dying.
—Maurice Blanchot

On April 26, 2016, David and Collet Stephan were found guilty in the death of their eighteen-month-old son, Ezekiel, who, according to the autopsy report, died from bacterial meningitis in March 2012.[1] Invoking Section 215 of the Criminal Code of Canada, a jury in the Lethbridge, Alberta, courtroom found the Stephans guilty of "failing to provide necessaries of life." Duties "tending to the preservation of life" are written into the Criminal Code, and include the legal responsibility "as a parent, foster parent, guardian or head of a family, to provide necessaries of life for a child under the age of sixteen years."[2] This archaic phrase—"necessaries of life"—hinges on the genitive "of," which suggests possession or origin: that which is *of* life, emerging as it were *from* it, and belonging properly *to* it. In contrast with the more prosaic "*for* life," "the necessaries *of* life" is a formulation in which it is difficult to conceive of one term without the other, even as each term is uniquely contingent on particular contexts, whether socioeconomic, historical, racializing, et cetera. Specifically, in this case the necessary and sufficient provisioning of *biomedical* care was understood implicitly as the parents' legal duty, advancing the terms in and by which life and its "necessaries" might be invoked through the frame of criminalization, and where medicine and law act in concert to regulate what life and its possible preservation might mean morally and materially. And, as the trial revealed, while the Stephans had been treating their son with various naturopathic medicines and home remedies, the jury found this care to be insufficient in tending to the preservation of life. In the jury's verdict, then, mainstream biomedical and pharmacological treatments are enshrined as de jure necessaries of life: life biomedicalized and subject to medico-legal jurisdiction and veridiction. Crown prosecutor Lisa Weich summed it up bluntly in front of television cameras: "Sometimes love just isn't enough," adding "One of the goals of the case was to provide Ezekiel with a voice."[3] Through the trope of prosopopoeia, it was as if life itself had spoken, in that dead mouth, to pass judgment.

Given testimony that Ezekiel's bacterial infection had been treated naturo-pathically with "hot peppers, garlic, onions and horseradish,"[4] the guilty verdict may strike us as unremarkable or even banal. And yet, the banality of the verdict is itself remarkable for indexing the long reach of biomedical and pharmacological power, which configure popular conceptions of life and of care—as it were by necessity. A fiduciary as well as a medical and (bio)ethical duty, the parental duty to provide the necessary and sufficient conditions of life must be balanced against a parent or guardian's legal right to choose what they believe to be best for the life of the child under their care, including what kind of life that child will live. But what kind of lived life will be deemed legitimate and what will be judged necessary and sufficient to it, particularly with the rise of vocal anti-vaxxer cam-paigns and similar cultural and religious contestations of law and medicine? For example, should courts and public health officials order parents to vaccinate their children against their parents' will? The "choice" is not simply personal, as COVID-19 and the resurgence of diseases like mumps and measles impact population immunity, placing the lives of others at risk. As Ezekiel's case demonstrates, our ostensibly free choices are circumscribed by a regime of medico-legal best prac-tices, evidence-based protocols, and drug and health technologies, together informing the prevailing cultural imaginary in which "life" and life's "timeliness" have already made an ineluctable—and normative—claim on us.

In the case of Ezekiel Stephan, the verdict at first appears to be relatively straightforward: it is probable that Ezekiel would not have died from bacterial meningitis, which is considered a curable infection, had he been treated with antibiotics under the care of a physician. The presumption is and perhaps must be in favor of life and, moreover, in favor of a certain futurity that presumes as much as fulfills it. However, as this chapter argues, what life means in this moment—and indeed, across time—is not altogether self-evident. Biopolitically, its meaning is tangled up in a temporality that is oriented toward a future life that, in the face of death, haunts us as a medico-legal counterfactual, but no less as that ethical moment in or from which we shall judge, retrospectively, that the "necessaries of life" were not provided, whether willfully or through (criminal) negligence. In its judgment of prior life-events, law operates forensically and factically, on the one hand, while on the other it would speak for the dead from a biomedically mandated future that ought to have been—that is, from a prognostically probable and ghostly temporization by which legal speech derives a good deal of its moral authority, and life its meaningful articulations in time. This is not merely the moral authority of the courts, but also law's prior (ontological, rather than simply temporal) ascription of morality in those cases that come "before" the law.

Let it not be said, however, that I'm advancing a crypto-skeptical argument in favor of the wholesale rejection of law or medicine. Rather, this chapter asks a rhetorical question instead, a question about the normative *time* of a life, and how biopolitical life and life-time figure for us as a normative "timeliness" promulgated across medical, legal, and (bio)ethical discourses—full-throated avowals whose temporality and "timeliness" secrete their own deficiencies, monstrosities, mistakes, and morbidities. The figures of biopolitical life and life-time normalize and neutralize the thresholds of tolerable death. Through the rhetorics of medicine, law, and (bio)ethics, the moral obligation to a discursive "timeliness" informs our existence, our livingness, temporally circumscribing—however fictively—our exercise of autonomy and moral agency as living beings born to die. By "rhetoric" here I do not have in mind an idle or abstract theoretical reflection on life and life-time, but, rather, an inquiry into the generation, the everyday uptake, and material effects of medico-legal and (bio)ethical idioms, and the attendant norms that inform the "timeliness" of life and death, which seems to decree that none shall die "before their time." My suggestion here is that medico-legal "life" and its "timeliness" operate as discursive figures—biopolitical tropes—that stand in as self-evident norms that *appear* to arise from the facticity of biological life as much as from life's sacred value. And as with the trial of Ezekiel Stephan's parents, there is a palpable tension between these dimensions of livingness. If one purpose of the trial was to provide Ezekiel with a voice, that voice has been sovereignly claimed by law and it is not quite a toddler's voice that we are able to hear. The normative force of "timeliness" seizes on and fixes that "voice," but cannot quite shake off its counterfactual futures or that dead time in which certain deaths do not speak in our time, or appear as it were as uncaused (virtually atemporal), or as "aleatory" events, errors, errancy.

I would like to pause here to note that biomedical futures are always only statistical probabilities and prognostications—the domain of an uncertain knowledge, a certain nonknowledge, of Nietzsche's *Unwissenheit um die Zukunft*. Medical arts are not scientific certitudes. Indeed, as Ivan Illich argued many years ago,[5] medical diagnoses and treatments carry iatrogenic risks that occur in the execution of the duty to preserve life, sometimes directly resulting in the loss of life, and the loss of a loved one. These risks are not trivial. A 2016 meta-analysis published in the highly respected medical journal *BMJ* calculates medical error as the third-leading cause of death in the United States, following heart disease and cancer.[6] And yet, as salient a risk as medical error may be, it remains shrouded in silence: in the United States, Canada, and the United Kingdom (among many other countries) medical errors are not reported on death certificates, in coroners' reports, or in rankings of cause of death because there is no International Classification of Disease (ICD)[7] code in which to capture them.[8] We can infer that other causes of death are thereby inflated. In Michel Foucault's terminology, we would call death by medical error an "aleatory" event[9]—contingent, accidental, random, unpredictable—and the regulatory domain par excellence of biopolitics and its psychic and political economies.

If, then, an estimated 251,454 people die each year in the United States as a direct result of medical error,[10] then these lives—those we let die an unclassifiable death—must amount to a tolerable loss of life in the name of those whose future lives might probabilistically be sustained by virtue of *non*-fatal or otherwise *non*-erroneous medical treatments: those we ostensibly make live, those who otherwise might have died, or might have died sooner, or might have lived with illness or in pain. This cannot quite be described as medical sovereignty over life. It's not exactly the sovereign right or decision to take life or let live. Rather, it is biopolitical—a diffuse power that intervenes to make live and let die, where the lives that are preserved and prolonged cannot so decisively be decoupled from the deaths that are produced and permitted. Tolerable deaths by medical error must then also count, in some macabre moral calculus, as "necessaries of life." (These deaths we seem to accept as quotidian and banal, and we need not, for example, raise the extreme biopolitical specters of human experimentation or "Right to Try"[11] legislation to make the case.) In other words, these risks and these deaths are necessary and intrinsic to our biomedical futures, as counterfactual as these futures always are. But they rarely haunt either medicine or law.

In this light, futurity takes on a dubious moral status, narrowly construed as the possible persistence of your life or mine, a hopeful postponement of death implicit in disputes over necessary and sufficient health care, whether for specific treatments today or prophylactic interventions for tomorrow, such as childhood vaccinations or preventative bilateral mastectomies and oophorectomies for carriers of the BRCA1 or BRCA2 gene mutations associated with some breast cancers. Here we face an ethical collision between individual experience and the anonymizing statistics of biomedicine, between the person and the population, and between forensic facticity and prognostic probability. And there is something self-sealing about probabilistic claims, which cannot so easily be disconfirmed by appeal to discrete examples quickly swallowed up in the arithmetic. How might we weigh an individual's right to choose against the medico-legal and (bio)ethical duties to preserve (future) life and well-being, particularly when these duties induct that individual into the responsible and quasi-actuarial self-management of statistical risks, including human error and iatrogenic effects? The terrain is murky and difficult to navigate, foremost for the patient whose life hangs in the balance. We cannot answer these questions decisively, but not for lack of available information (try to google your symptoms!). Our choices are always in part tendered by a leap of faith or—in the absence of faith—hope or charity. If we coolly concede that some people must die through fatal errors, and that this is the normal order of things, then how many and in what ways? Are we prepared to say *too* many and in *this* way only when a national ribbon campaign gains public traction? Or when a loved one is the fatal victim of illness, violence, negligence?

Perhaps it is true, as Foucault remarked in his introduction to Georges Canguilhem's masterwork, that no "science of the living" should fail to take into account what is "essential to its object," namely, "the possibility of disease, death, monstrosity, anomaly, and error."[12] "For," Foucault continues, "at the most basic level of life, the processes of coding and decoding give way to a chance occurrence that, before becoming a disease, a deficiency, or a monstrosity, is something like a disturbance in the informative system, something like a 'mistake.' In this sense, life—and this is its radical feature—is that which is capable of error."[13] Darwin himself had made a similar observation. But our biopolitical understanding of life is emphatically more capacious than this, comprising physiochemical mechanisms and genetic codes, yes, but also something sacred, transcendent, angelic, which resounds in and across medico-legal discourses on life—part of a biopolitics that would devotedly and with good intentions (profits notwithstanding)[14] *eradicate* disease, death, monstrosity, anomaly, and error. Is it any surprise that, in its project of fixing (in both senses of this word) life's errors and errancy, biopolitics ends up reduplicating life's "mistakes," this time in another domain, but which it then quietly disavows? Error and errancy imply their own temporality, at odds with the biopolitical time and timeliness of medico-legal life. Caught between two incommensurate temporizations, I myself am not in a sovereign position to propound a tolerable threshold of collateral damage or acceptable loss, silent or spoken, in the providential practice of medicine, nor am I authorized to adjudicate between individual rights and medico-legal responsibilities, private and public health.

Instead, we must ask ourselves about the ethical "legitimacy" of those medico-legal powers that inform our lived understanding of life and life's timeliness—an understanding and a way of life that rhetorically structures the sanctioned articulation of bodies and persons as moral agents in time. In other words, we must question the normative embrace of biopolitics, an ostensibly affirmative ethic of making live that is at once complicit in the tolerated voicelessness of those it lets die. Is my death always untimely if, according to the speculative futures of biomedicine, it might have been forestalled, for days, weeks, years? Health economists will predictively calculate my future "quality-adjusted life years," or QALYs. But what sort of power would subtend such econometric claims? And what kind of life is being calculated, "qualified," and "adjusted" (for) here? What kind of normative livingness is affirmed and preserved? Foucault argues that "a certain type of power—distinct from both medical and judicial power—has in fact colonized and forced back both medical knowledge and judicial power throughout modern society."[15] For Foucault, it is the power of normalization that "colonizes" and "forces back" both medicine and law. And I would like to read "normalization" here as the progressive and processual hold, the cultivation, of a particular normativity—or *normativization*, if this word is not too ugly. It is not simply that norms regulate *what I am*, epistemologically or ontologically; more critically, and in advance, norms also inform *who I ought to be*, ethically, including what I ought to *desire* and to *do* in order to secure this ethical future, today and for a promised tomorrow. I argue that there is a normative, indeed, normativizing force transmitted by the "timely" rhetorics of life and life-time—the biopolitical sleight of hand by which the technologies of law and medicine themselves become "necessaries of life," deeply desired, and life becomes hardly conceivable in their absence. Moreover, these rhetorics seem to be immunized from critique because they authorize in advance the permissible terms of legitimate public discourse, of publics, and of public time. Such livingness, it would seem, is that which we cannot not desire.

I opened this chapter with the case of Ezekiel Stephan in part because it is so deceptively straightforward: a tragic death that likely strikes us in retrospect as preventable if only some antibiotics had been administered, if only his parents had respected the obvious "norms" of care. Legal scholars have weighed in, suggesting that belief in naturopathic medicine is "like a religion"; the bioethicist Juliet Guichon declared, "There's an element of irrationality in the rejection of physician advice," further opining "I wonder if it's a distrust of people in authority in general."[16] The sentence handed down to the Stephans ensured that Ezekiel's case is as much about public moralization as it is about legal culpability and the policing of what is deemed "rational" by commonsense "people in authority." As a group of protestors from across North America stood outside the courthouse, Collet Stephan was sentenced to three months of house arrest—except to attend church and medical appointments, presumably unironic exceptions that accord religious faith and medical science the same legal favor.[17] The judge ordered her three remaining children to be treated by a medical doctor at least once annually and to visit a public health nurse every three months. And if there was any doubt that this case should serve as a late-modern morality tale, Collet Stephan was also ordered to post a full and unedited transcript of the sentencing decision on her various social media sites. For his part, David Stephan was sentenced to four months in jail—a harsher sentence because he "demonstrated a complete lack of remorse for his actions," according to Justice Rodney Jerke.[18]

Mr. Stephan continues to make broad appeals to anti-vaxxers and libertarians in the United States and Canada, and prior to sentencing he had posted a "Dear Jury" letter on his Facebook page, claiming "The flood gates have now been opened and if we do not fall in line with parenting as seen fit by the government, we all stand in risk of criminal prosecution. . . . How many parents have lost children for various reasons, all of which could be concluded [sic] that the child's life was endangered and that the parents should have been able to foresee it?"[19] Beyond his defense of "parents' rights," David Stephan poses difficult and salient questions: To what extent should biomedical consumerism be inscribed in and as law, in and as a parent's fiduciary duty? And what, moreover, is the tense and timeliness of biomedical life, law's life, in the retrospective judgment that one should have been able to foresee—and forestall—risk and death? In the months that followed the trial, the courts heard two distinct appeals: the Stephans appealed both the guilty verdict and their sentences, while the Crown appealed their sentences as too lenient and "insufficient."[20] I return below to summarize the many turns of this case, through appeals that ultimately made their way to the Supreme Court of Canada, resulting in a retrial and yet another appeal, which (at the time of writing) is still pending.

In what follows, I take up these questions and complicate them further by juxtaposing the case of Ezekiel Stephan with that of Makayla Sault.[21] Makayla was also a minor treated by nonbiomedical therapies under parental care, and many commentators have similarly characterized her death as both preventable and untimely. Moreover, both cases advance a claim on the basis of what is both ostensibly "natural" and ordained by a Christian God, and each is an inflection of law and life that righteously spurns the prescriptive futures of state law and biomedicine. In some respects, they represent analogous contestations of neo-liberal biopolitics. Nevertheless, I will suggest that Makayla's case haunts Canadian medicine and law in ways that Ezekiel's does not. In her case many believe that her Indigeneity was the most salient factor in her death, that there was no legal closure, and that justice was not served. Her parents were never charged under the Criminal Code. Makayla's story calls to be read alongside Ezekiel's because, as I argue below, "Indigenous exceptionalism" and sovereign rights claims based on ethno-cultural difference are increasingly co-opted and deployed by anti-vaxxers, libertarians, and religious fundamentalists alike who also take "exception" to state law and medicine, and who seek recognition of their own "way of life," traditions, and faith. In a nutshell, if an Indigenous community can claim medico-legal "sovereignty" on the grounds of race, ethnicity, culture, and tradition, it should be no surprise to find these claims echoed in the rhetorical posturing of fundamentalists and anti-vaxxers who, like David Stephan, also invoke ancient healing arts, natural law, and the sovereign right of the pater familias. If we believe that Indigenous rights ought to be recognized as distinct from those claimed by anti-vaxxers, fundamentalists, or libertarians, how will we adjudicate between these groups' claims, and by what or whose authority? In any such adjudication, both groups will righteously spurn the further incursions of state law and medicine—and with them a host of regulative mechanisms, such as DNA tests, the logics of Indigenous blood quantum, and so forth. And both groups know that the sovereignty of their sovereign claim will be undone if it can be recognized only by first capitulating to the sovereign state authority it repudiates.

Bringing these two cases into conversation, I argue that while each seeks to disaffirm the futures of neoliberal biopolitics, neither does so through a straight-forward invocation of sovereign right. Indeed, I'll argue that traditional concep-tions of sovereignty as the power to "take life or let live" rely on historical convention and are typically applied to the jurisdiction of bodies, lands, and territories—a strategic spatializing power. And yet today, land and territory, much like the human body itself, are as much temporal displacements as they are spatial colonizations, subject to risk management, investment, amortization; they are mapped projectively and regulated as resources for extraction and capitalization in future markets. Makayla and Ezekiel therefore raise contemporary challenges for justice and community that cannot easily be addressed by a "return" to sovereign jurisdiction or to legal precedent. Nor can their cases be dismissed outright as matters of archaic, primitive, or pre-modern thinking, which is what biopolitical technoscience does from its linear-progressive futures. Between these two orientations of power—sovereign and biopolitical, the past and the future—I offer a temporal argument situated at this moment, now, in the present. This moment, I argue, constellates around the temporization of death rather than life. Here I'll turn to the work of Georges Bataille, along with its reception by Maurice Blanchot and Jean-Luc Nancy. Bataille proposes an original conception of sovereignty linked to death in the temporality of the present moment or instant (l'instant). My reading will suggest that the biopolitical tropes of life and life-time might be disaffirmed through Bataille's temporization of death, holding open a momentary but momentous encounter with other lives and life-times that are lived and lived-out in tenses and intensities that may not conform with our own. But first: Makayla's story.

## Indigenous Life and Indigent Sovereignty

Diagnosed with acute lymphoblastic leukemia (ALL), the most common childhood cancer, eleven-year-old Makayla Sault had been undergoing a series of potentially life-saving chemotherapy treatments at McMaster Children's Hospital in Hamilton, Ontario. Under Canada's system of socialized medicine, most treatments are paid by the state, including most chemotherapies. In late April 2014, Makayla voluntarily withdrew from treatment, and on May 13, near Brantford, Ontario, on the Mississauga-Ojibwe reserve of New Credit First Nation, Makayla explained this decision in a video-recorded letter read in the presence of her band council and posted online. The following is an excerpt: "I know that what I have can kill me, but I don't want to die in a hospital on chemo. . . . When Jesus came into my room, [He] told me not to be afraid. So if I live, or if I die, I am not afraid. . . . Jesus told me that I am healed, so it doesn't matter what anybody says. God, the Creator, has the final say over my life. . . . I wish that the doctors would listen to me, because I live in this body and they don't."[22] Withdrawing from chemotherapy, which oncologists estimated to have a 70–90 percent statistical likelihood of cure,[23] Makayla reportedly pursued Ongwehowe Onongwatri:yo, Indigenous medical therapies administered by a traditional healer on the Six Nations.

Unsurprisingly, for its part the Canadian Cancer Society is clear that while Indigenous therapies may offer cultural benefits, "there is no evidence at this time that Aboriginal traditional healing can treat cancer itself."[24] And while we don't know what Makayla's therapies involved, we learned from investigative journalists that Makayla also traveled to Florida to receive "alternative" New Age spa therapies—perhaps in combination with Indigenous medicines—at the controversial Hippocrates Health Institute, which was known to promise snake oil cures for cancer. As a consequence of Makayla's case, one month after her death on January 19, 2015, the state of Florida ordered Brian Clement, the owner of the spa, to cease practicing medicine.[25] Failing to treat ALL with chemotherapy is almost certainly fatal, which prompted several media commentators to invoke the term "suicide" in this case (I return to this freighted word below). We might cautiously say that it is statistically probable that Makayla Sault's death from cancer would have been forestalled or prevented had she followed the recommended course of chemotherapy treatments. And finally, in stark contrast to the case of Ezekiel Stephan, Makayla's parents were not charged with failing to provide the "necessaries of life." At the time of her death, her parents issued a statement that her fatal stroke had been caused by the twelve weeks of chemotherapy she had received one year earlier—a claim that oncologists dispute.[26]

Makayla's withdrawal from treatment prompted a series of institutional medico-legal actions to determine if the state ought to intervene, and to force her to resume chemotherapy treatments. Makayla's physicians reported her case to Brant Family and Children's Services (the regional Children's Aid Society, or CAS), which organized an undisclosed number of *in camera* interviews with Makayla, her family, and band representatives to determine, in the context of the Child and Family Services Act, whether Makayla was a "child in need of protection." According to the wording of the Act, this is when "the child requires medical treatment to cure, prevent or alleviate physical harm or suffering and the child's parent or the person having charge of the child does not provide, or refuses or is unavailable or unable to consent to, the treatment."[27] However, while this Act remains in force for child and youth social welfare, broadly construed, since 1996 medical decision-making is typically governed by the Health Care Consent Act, which hinges on whether the person in question is "capable" to refuse a prescribed course of treatment. (In Ontario, laws on child protection are often seen as conflicting with laws on medical consent where a minor is concerned.)[28]

According to the Health Care Consent Act, in the first instance "capability" is decided by the attending physician, and an individual is deemed capable "if the person is able to understand the information that is relevant to making a decision about the treatment . . . and able to appreciate the reasonably foreseeable consequences of a decision or lack of decision."[29] However, the physician's decision is open to appeal by the province's Consent and Capacity Board, which is an independent tribunal made up of experts and lay members (e.g., physicians, psychiatrists, nurses, and members of the general public). Although the CAS interviews with Makayla and her family were not made public, after a short time, on May 20, 2014, the CAS deemed Makayla to be "capable" and no further legal action (or appeal) was pursued. It is possible that the CAS decision was informed by its policy on Diversity and Anti-Oppressive Practice, which is meant to ensure "that every person's values, beliefs and practices are being honored and respected accordingly."[30] If so, we might easily see how Ezekiel Stephan's parents, antivaxxers, and religious fundamentalists who diversely refuse a prescribed course of medical treatment could invoke such vague wording in a demand for similar "honor" and "respect."

The province of Ontario is unusual in that the Health Care Consent Act does not specify a minimum age for consent, nor does it stipulate what it might mean in practice, or in speech, to "appreciate" the "reasonably foreseeable consequences" of a health decision. In the case of an appeal, this kind of futurity, both prognostic and personal, ultimately rests on the judgment of Consent and Capacity Board members. However, where religious belief is a factor, there is nevertheless ample legal precedence for deeming a minor incapable of such a momentous decision and forcing, by court order, a minor into treatment against the wishes of that individual and typically those of the individual's parent(s) or guardian(s).[31] It is significant then that, in her public video-recorded statement, Makayla reported witnessing the figure of Jesus Christ, who told her that she had been healed of her illness, though she logically contradicts this conviction—with a nod to the "reasonably foreseeable consequences" of her decision—when she states, "I know that what I have can kill me."

News media reported that Makayla's parents are both pastors in an evangelical Christian church, a fact that might have raised concerns over the extent to which she had been influenced by her parents' religious faith, and how this might have played into her "capacity" to withdraw from treatment. In early May 2014 she had traveled to the border town of Sarnia, Ontario (about one hour's drive from Detroit, Michigan), to share her religious vision with a congregation presided over by the US televangelist Ted Shuttlesworth.[32] Given legal precedence concerning Jehovah's Witness minors, religious grounds alone might have been cause to legally deny Makayla's "capacity": in this case, the state would have been obligated to intervene, to forcibly provide the "necessaries of life" by removing her from her family and community, hospitalizing her, and submitting her to biomedical treatments as prescribed. Rightly or wrongly, this course of action was not followed. If Ezekiel was posthumously reclaimed by law and given a ghostly voice, we might say that Makayla was abandoned by law while still alive, and unto death—and it is this economy of abandonment, to employ Elizabeth Povinelli's phrase,[33] that haunts Canadian law and medicine in ways that Ezekiel's death does not. Makayla was of course correct when she addressed her doctors: "I live in this body and they don't." This was never contested. But does it follow that she had the right to die in her own body as well?

It must be said that, in Canada, decisions concerning Indigenous child welfare are entangled with Indigenous rights and ongoing claims to Indigenous sovereignty and self-governance. It was perhaps politically more expedient for the CAS to bestow autonomy and "capacity" on an eleven-year-old than to, as one "expert" opined, incite the "wrath" of Indigenous "warrior societies" across the country who had threatened collectively to defend their territory and prevent state authorities from removing Makayla into treatment.[34] In this reading, Makayla's Indigeneity was the operative locus of the "capacity" ascribed to her. And her body became the site of competing claims, here played out over life-and-death decisions affecting a little girl with cancer. These competing claims to and on behalf of Makayla raise ethical challenges for politico-legal and philosophical conceptualizations of autonomy and informed consent: Who or what authority presides over—and by what prior entitlement or right—an individual's "capacity" to refuse treatment, and the right to live, and to die, in one's own time and place?

If First Nations were truly sovereign and self-governing, they would not be subject to Canadian law. But the CAS remained silent on all matters of Indigenous sovereignty and did not *decline* to rule in this case; rather, the CAS deemed Makayla "capable" on *its* terms and in *its* socio-symbolic order. The CAS thus effectively safeguarded its own nominal sovereignty—and that of the Canadian state—through the ruse of "capacity." It is as if the CAS declared: *You* have the right to make a claim on *our* terms, the right to speak and be heard, as long as *we* bestow on you this right and accord you this standing "before" the law. In other words, *your* claim is a claim always and only by virtue of *our* prior act of recognition, *our* claim on *you*, which remains ours to bestow or withhold. *You* are beholden to *us*. Makayla was freed, on the one hand, even as she was held firmly within the remit of Canadian law, on the other. Of course, it is this presumptive authority that those who advance Indigenous sovereign claims find so odious and reject. Whether such a compromise was the CAS's legal prerogative, or was conceived as its moral duty, we must nevertheless wonder when state administrative-legal bodies hold the power to declare someone "capable" and to decide the future of one's bodily life and death. Indeed, capacity itself is an artifact of state power, part of the architecture of law, and presumes a possessive individualism that clashes both with Indigenous worldviews and, as I will conclude below, with the disorienting temporality of anyone—Indigenous or not—living in the shadows of a cancer prognosis.

On the one hand, then, we must reckon with structural elements, the transitive agency and authority of medico-legal institutions, while on the other we are faced with a subjective dimension, which includes the normative process of subjectivation and the exercise of an individual's artifactual "capacity." Structural and subjective factors are not altogether distinct; the *time* of one's life—or life-time—is bound up with normative medico-legal state power as just one facet of settler-colonialism and of biopolitical state power more generally. Foucault has usefully problematized the two faces of such power through the concept of governmentality. In a famous passage on governmentality, Foucault defines modern Western power as follows: "The exercise of power is a 'conduct of conducts' and management of possibilities."[35] In other words, the exercise of state power is indirect, mediated, and not strictly a matter of individuals' capacity to consent, but is regulated through a field of possibilities and incentivizations: "Instead, it acts upon their actions: an action upon an action, on possible or actual future or present actions."[36] The structural and infrastructural dimensions of governmentality are therefore interlinked, in a "complicated interplay," as Foucault writes, with subjectivity and subjective comportment.

We glimpse here the manner in which subjects are massified biopolitically and normalized in part through social and institutional (infra)structures or "technologies" that privilege a hyperindividualism driven by competitive self-interest and personal rights. And yet here, paradoxically, presumably enlightened self-interest and responsibility bind that individual every more intimately to a host of state services and expert service-providers in and by which that entrepreneurial individual will be "freely" and efficiently (self-)managed. The modern state, according to Foucault, is thus both totalizing and individualizing—a power "in which individuals can be integrated, under one condition: that this individuality would be shaped in a new form, and submitted to a set of very specific patterns."[37] I'm interested in the "complicated interplay" of (infra)structures and subjectivities, particularly as these normative "patterns" are instantiated in the temporizing tropes of life and life-time. The temporal and temporizing dimensions of state power are absent from many scholarly discussions, particularly in the context of settler-colonial racism.

State power is not easily disambiguated from the agencies of medico-legal authority. It is perhaps easier to grasp the ways that life and life-time function, tropologically, through the widespread and generalized uptake of these "very specific patterns" across popular media. To offer one example, in an open letter to Makayla published in the *Globe and Mail*, Toronto-based writer Heather Cleland offered Makayla the insights of her own experience. As a young woman, Cleland also had cancer, and she speaks of the drugs that helped manage the side effects of chemotherapy treatments. Without chemotherapy, Cleland avers, "I wouldn't have finished school. I wouldn't have spent nine whole months travelling around the world. I wouldn't have gotten my master's degree. . . . Chemotherapy was the only reason I was able to do all those things."[38] In a direct and public address to Makayla, Cleland suggests that without chemotherapy she will not live to go to university, to travel, to pursue relationships, and to live a full life, as Cleland imagines it. In other words, without chemotherapy Makayla's death will be untimely, it will come too soon. Makayla's "childish" fears of bodily discomfort, however understandable, and her decision to pursue Indigenous therapies, will keep her from that future from which Cleland writes, a promised and prognostic future, a redemptive time to-come. The biomedical determination of life's futures, the will to "make live," here become conditions for the untimeliness of death's proximity in the present, figured in how long one is expected to live, statistically, and how medicine and sometimes law ought to intervene into that proximity.

But how can we know for certain the contours of the untimely in its proximity to Makayla Sault, or how the temporization of biopolitical "life" manifests for her on the frontiers of an ontological struggle for meaning, a life lived under the specters of colonial history, part of which is her Christian faith itself? What sort of imaginable future announces itself from these ruins?

This ongoing legacy of ruin has not been forgotten by Indigenous peoples. And this is surely one sense in which death speaks in Makayla. In the Canadian context, Indigenous youth statistically are more likely to be incarcerated than they are to finish high school. They are more likely to live in poverty and more likely to be diagnosed with HIV, hepatitis C, and tuberculosis. The correctional system, too, has become a site of further racialization. According to the Canadian corrections investigator, the hyperincarceration of Indigenous persons is staggering: nearly 50 percent of all incarcerated women, and 32 percent of the federal prison population in general, while Indigenous peoples represent less than 5 percent of the Canadian population—a shameful overrepresentation that far exceeds the per capita overrepresentation of African Americans in the US slavocratic prison system.[39] These statistics must be understood together with the historical crimes committed in and by the residential school system in place until the early 1980s, when children were for decades routinely stolen from their families in order to be "civilized." These were also the crimes of the Church, and a colonial history of institutional barriers to resources, of systemic racism, and a medical system that condoned human experimentation on Indigenous persons. Canada's system of socialized medicine is still segregated and unequal in its provisioning of health care for Indigenous populations.[40]

In 2010, the Office of the Chief Coroner conducted a "Death Review" of youth suicides in the remote Pikangikum First Nation,[41] another Ojibwe community some distance from Makayla's, home to approximately 2,400 people. The Coroner's Office was tasked with understanding the deaths by suicide of sixteen children and youth, aged ten to nineteen, which occurred between 2006 and 2008. The Pikangikum First Nation has been called the suicide capital of the world, with the highest recorded per capita rate of suicide.[42] Among First Nations across Canada, suicide is a public health crisis, often reported as an "epidemic" or "state of emergency." The coroner's review paints a bleak picture of poverty, neglect, substance abuse, sexual abuse, domestic violence, teen pregnancy, unemployment, and widespread depression, and considers in detail myriad governmental issues relating to "infrastructure, policing, health, education, the delivery of child welfare as well as the social determinants of First Nations' health." From 1951 through 1980, large numbers of children were taken from the Pikangikum First Nation into the care of a CAS; decades later, in 2010, the report notes that the number of Indigenous children in care is still disproportionately high—province-wide, 17 percent of all children in care are of Indigenous descent. The report ends with a list of twelve key recommendations, few if any of which have been implemented. There is a perennial lack of resources, a lack of public will, and perhaps uncertainty over how to act justly. The suicide crisis is ongoing across Canada's First Nations communities.

This context was largely ignored in mainstream public debate over Makayla's future. In the months following her withdrawal from chemotherapy, many media outlets were happy to offer a platform for those decrying "Indigenous exceptionalism," expressing incomprehension, frustration, and even outrage directed toward Makayla, her family, her community, and the administrative-legal authorities who had refused to force Makayla into treatment, and to make her live. The bioethicist Juliet Guichon (once again) weighed in, together with three pediatricians from the University of Calgary, stating that a "young Canadian girl is being denied a good chance for a cancer cure because she is aboriginal."[43] They argued that the courts should decide Makayla's treatment, consistent with legal precedence, and their text sovereignly claimed Makayla as a "Canadian girl" whose rights were being denied on the basis of her Indigeneity. In their eyes, Makayla is the responsibility of the Canadian state, and they expressed their frustration that "our" legal authorities, acting in "our" name, have somehow betrayed "us" in failing to force Makayla to resume chemotherapy, which they see as "our" legal and moral obligation to her. Failing to do so represents for these scholars—and many other non-Indigenous commentators—a grave injustice, a moral wrong, and discrimination, and these considerations must, they argued, supervene on an Indigenous right. After her death, one white journalist opined, "if she'd been a white girl, she'd still be alive."[44]

Significantly, however, not one of them asked, What is the "capacity" of the law and its institutions in this case? Whence *their* capacity to judge and to bind Makayla to that judgment? And is this capacity not founded in the historical legal violence that sanctioned—when it did not altogether orchestrate—the abduction of Indigenous children, and sometimes their rape, their destitution, before the law, in the holy name of Jesus and in the name of the Crown? Unsurprisingly, then, across mainstream media accounts of the case there was no mention of the Pikangikum First Nation or a host of innumerable deaths by suicide, all ostensibly preventable, untimely. In the utter absence of these reflective questions, and in the myopic scope of biomedical treatments and obsessive legalisms, these commentators—and many others in Canadian society—seem to apprehend life in the abstract, proclaimed without argument as the highest good and without any connection to Canada's violent colonial legacy. Sentiments such as these— ostensibly rational, scientific, and just—suggest the challenges ahead as Canada seeks truth and reconciliation with Indigenous peoples who live and die within its "sovereign" borders.

I return in the final section to the difficult questions of community and identity, but I would first like to focus on the word "exception" and the kind of "sovereign" rhetorical work that it is summoned to do in the context of "Indigenous exceptionalism." "Excepted" from what, exactly? As if from a truth that is manifestly originary, and yet that flows from a dominant culture that steadfastly refuses to question itself and its questionable authority to *decide* on the exception? And this, I must add, from a culture predicated on its very own privileged exceptionalisms: whiteness, ableism, first-worldism, manifest destiny, and so forth? This unreflective prerogative is the hallmark of conventional sovereignty, which thinly veils its foundational—and abiding—politico-theological violence. In Carl Schmitt's formulation, "Sovereign is he who decides on the exception."[45] And Bataille would write, "Traditional sovereignty is conspicuous. It is a sovereignty of exception (a single subject among others has the prerogatives of all subjects as a whole)."[46] This is what Ezekiel's and Makayla's deaths reveal to us and of us: the base and utter baselessness of our "sovereign" decision to except or accept, even as we find ourselves taking a side, impulsively lining up, compelled or simply seduced, whether by sovereign claims, on the one hand, or neoliberal biopolitics, on the other.

We might, then, read a disaffirmation in Makayla's refusal to continue treatment—a complicated interplay of forces distinct from the normative exercise of an individual's "capacity" or power to "consent," whether real or an artifact of governmentality. Instead, we might read a repudiation of a particular temporization in the time and timeliness of one's life and death. And we might hear contempt for the set of binaries that unreflectively informed much of what was written by "us" in the mainstream press, obedient as "we" are to the world-historical temporization that sharply distinguishes a dark past from the enlightened future: primitive/modern, savage/civilized, faith/knowledge, religion/science. In the popular imaginary, Indigenous peoples are often relegated to the past and seen as failing to cede to the beneficent biopolitical futures that characterize settler-colonial time in the non-Indigenous present. But there is much to learn from such untimely "failures," errors and errancy. The binaries above impose a progressive history toward a life lived within certain normative coordinates, fixed within certain temporal regimes and managed conditions of possibility—obedient to the "necessaries of life," apparently as self-evident as they are sanctifying. Notwithstanding the wider sociohistorical and economic contexts that, in the treatment of Indigenous lives, utterly belie the necessary and sufficient provisioning of care, we are meant to apprehend life-time here as triumphantly encoded in the auspicious story of technoscientific progress, the battle against disease and death, written into the linear narratives of biomedical futures. Makayla *can* be biomedicalized, while Indigenous suicides cannot; she *should* therefore be made to live, even as Indigenous suicides are abandoned to the silent ignominy of their "endemic" death.

## Beyond Sovereign Time and Biopolitical Time

In this book's focus on biopolitics, I have stressed the Foucauldian view that sovereignty has been obsolesced by biopolitics (sovereignty is neither "deconstructed" nor "critiqued" by biopolitics).[47] And yet sovereignty continues to function as a biopolitical ruse—the parasymbolic warrant for a biologized "life itself" stripped of its symbolicity (or rather, when we make a conspicuous show of this very lack, which is made manifest and majestic). For many, the obsolescence of sovereignty is a contentious claim, but I believe it is justified when we examine the divergent temporalities that distinguish sovereign from biopolitical power. Sovereignty stands on precedent and draws on the past, much as we see in legal judgments. The sovereign enjoys an inherited power, established historically by convention; indeed, sovereign speech/acts rely on convention, which is to say that in Austin's sense they are illocutionary (see chapter 2). The sovereign's dominion is also said to be God-given. If the sovereign holds the originary divine right "to take life or let live," the life that is killed or spared is a life whose very livingness was never in doubt—a life that was already living and was (or continues to be) subject to sovereign jurisdiction. In practical terms, then, sovereign speech/acts are typically jurisdictional (*juris*-dictions), legal claims over bodies, lands, and territories. This is not quite the case with disciplinary and biopolitical forms of power, which are temporally oriented toward the future. Indeed, our spaces and bodies have been neoliberalized and biopoliticized as a function of future-time: as things to be surveyed and mapped according to the market futures of resource extraction, commodification and transportation (e.g., pipelines), future profits, livelihoods, and the "necessaries of life."[48]

Arguably, today most sovereign invocations are little more than a ruse for that which is demanded—as necessary, as normative—by neoliberalism and biopolitics, obedient to their futures. Foucault parses these divergent temporalities in the following way: unlike with sovereign power, he writes, "there is no reference to an act, an event, or an original right in the relationship of disciplinary power. Disciplinary power refers instead to a final or optimum state. It looks forward to the future, towards the moment when it will keep going by itself and only a virtual supervision will be required, when discipline, consequently, will have become habit."[49] And what discipline does to the individual, anatomo-politically, biopolitics does to the population or mass. Disciplinary power individualizes, whereas biopolitical power massifies by seizing on "life itself"—and life's futures— as its means and its end. Both discipline and biopolitics are therefore *futural* temporizations, truth claims (*veri*-dictions) that normalize with a kind of anticipatory resoluteness. The future becomes a normativizing and transitive force to be embodied and lived-out as "timely" moral obligations in the lifeworld, here and now.

"Sovereignty" is, then, a fraudulent and freighted trope whose turns and returns demand what Frantz Fanon has characterized as a psycho-affective attachment to colonialism and colonial history.[50] In his use of Fanon in the context of Indigenous lives, Glen Coulthard states, "The liberal recognition-based approach to Indigenous self-determination in Canada . . . has not only failed, but now serves to reproduce the very forms of colonial power which our original demands for recognition sought to transcend."[51] In following Fanon, Coulthard argues that Indigenous peoples are unwittingly interpellated by, and reduplicate, forms of structural hegemony, both economic and political. I'd add here that the widespread use of the term "sovereignty"—often by Indigenous activists—is also hegemonic *rhetorically*, structuring in advance the terms of recognition and the manner in which such claims can be advanced, and by whom. Coulthard writes, "In settler-colonial contexts such as Canada—where there is no formal period marking an explicit transition from an authoritarian past to a democratic present—state-sanctioned approaches to reconciliation tend to ideologically fabricate such a transition by narrowly situating the abuses of settler colonization firmly *in the past*. In these situations, reconciliation itself becomes temporally framed as the process of individually and collectively *overcoming* the harmful 'legacy' left in the wake of this past abuse, while leaving the *present* structure of colonial rule largely unscathed."[52] The ideological fabrication of the past *as past*, indeed, a claim to and in the name of history, proclaimed as fact, is a sovereign ruse. It is one we are called to witness time and again.

But it was with no irony when, in May 2016, the Canadian government sovereignly renounced its objector status to the UN Declaration on the Rights of

Indigenous Peoples. Met with a standing ovation at the United Nations in New York, the minister for Northern and Indigenous Affairs declared that Canada would implement the Declaration "without qualification . . . [as] an important step in the vital work of reconciliation."[53] Despite the "vital" work ahead—and repeated calls to account for the living *and* the dead—the Declaration is not legally binding, and it remains to be seen how its tenets might be squared with Canadian law, state "sovereignty," and a dark colonial legacy. The Declaration itself problematically adopts the architecture and language of political liberalism, in which the tradition of human rights and capacities is based on the purported sovereignty of the self-possessed individual—a politico-theological avatar, we might say. And yet a framework founded on possessive individualism and personhood does not quite fit a collective frame, or peoples. This ontological incommensurability poses an insurmountable problem of recognition—a word anxiously asserted in so many state documents and again in the preamble to the Declaration: "*Recognizing in particular* the right of indigenous families and communities to retain shared responsibility for the upbringing, training, education and well-being of their children."[54] In the Declaration, Indigenous peoples "in particular"—not persons—are said to "share" the particular right to "self-determination," which includes the right to "autonomy."[55] And yet we must stumble here when "selfhood" and "autonomy" become the fungible postulates of a collective, shared existence. What could they mean in this context? We would need to ask, rhetorically, who speaks and in whose name? Or, what is the locus, the time and place, the when and where, of such an address? The Declaration itself does not dare to use the word "sovereignty" in relation to Indigenous peoples. The word "sovereign" appears just once, in the Declaration's final, unequivocal article: "Nothing in this Declaration may be interpreted as implying for any State, people, group or person any right to engage in any activity or to perform any act contrary to the Charter of the United Nations or construed as authorizing or encouraging any action which would dismember or impair, totally or in part, the territorial integrity or political unity of *sovereign* and independent States."[56] Nothing . . . any . . . any . . . any . . . any . . . any. . . . Vehemently, categorically, this closing gesture undermines the entire Declaration by reaffirming the sovereignty of existing states and territories. Only the sovereign can confer recognition, and there can be but one.

In upholding Makayla's *individual* right to refuse treatment, the CAS of course remained silent on Makayla's Indigeneity and whether her refusal might represent, in particular, a collective Indigenous sovereign claim. Nevertheless, this is very much how it was variously received, both in the mainstream media and by

Indigenous groups who were vocal in their support of Makayla and her community. At first, we might be tempted to say that Makayla's is a struggle for recognition in a classical liberal sense, in the terms set forth by Hegel and echoed in the UN Declaration. In Hegel's dialectic between the lord and the bondsman—sovereign master and subjugated slave—the bondsman accedes to lordship and recognizable personhood in a struggle to the death with the lord. Here, according to Hegel's system, at first individuals are un-self-reflexively "submerged in the being of *Life* [*in das Sein des* Lebens]—for the object in its immediacy is here determined as Life [*als Leben*]. They are, *for each other*, shapes of consciousness [*versenkte Bewußtsein*] which have not yet accomplished the movement of absolute abstraction, of rooting-out all immediate being."[57] Not yet self-conscious, the "I" is overdetermined by "Life," which must be wielded, wagered, and in some respects sacrificed in order to accede to sovereign freedom. The immediacy of consciousness—*versenkte Bewußtsein*—is submerged, sunk, in Life, and this relation must be severed in an "absolute abstraction," a "rooting-out," before the self-certainty of the "I" can realize its truth as universal. The individual "I" therefore must act and must demonstrate that it is "not attached to any specific *existence*, not to the individuality common to existence as such, that it is not attached to life." The bondsman thus accedes to lordship through mortification, "not [fear] of this or that particular thing or just at odd moments," Hegel writes, but when the subject's "whole being has been seized with dread; for it has experienced the fear of death, the absolute Lord."[58]

And indeed, Makayla does not cling to life at all costs, she risks death, and yet she does not stay alive, as in Hegel's narrative, to enjoy any recognition she has won in this struggle: death, real death, cruelly "cancels both the truth that was to result from it, and therewith the certainty of self altogether."[59] To anticipate the argument that follows, Nancy will characterize the Hegelian system as one in which "the individual can be the origin and the certainty of nothing but its own death."[60] Makayla's refusal is, then, neither claimed nor won for an individual "I," but, we might say, is articulated—and yet not quite claimed—in the name of her family, her community, her people, who stand with and alongside her, and in whom she lives in death. But this latter does not mean that *they* have won recognition, collectively, through surviving and holding her death.

If it is truly sovereign, the Canadian state cannot grant the recognition of a competing sovereignty, within its territory, without ultimately undermining its own. If the terms of this struggle are forcibly founded in a recognition-based (identity) politics, it will terminate in an impasse, in the contest of two phantasmatic sovereigns without end, a standoff waged by no "one," while abiding hegemonies persist or even metastasize. But this impasse is based on a sovereign ruse, in my view, because the state is only *nominally* and *juridically* sovereign; rather, in practice it is a biopolitical and neoliberal apparatus, spreading and amortizing the risks of those it makes live, while allowing others to die. I'm interested here in the ways that life emerges as *other* than mere survivorship, *other* than the lord's sovereign negation or sublation (*Aufhebung*) of death, and conversely, in death as *other* than the extinguishing of bare biological life in bondage. Specifically, I'm interested in disaffirming the biopolitical economies of a medico-legal regime that would keep Makayla alive on *its* terms, where the biopolitical power to make live banks on the canceling or inclusive exclusion (*Aufhebung*) of those it lets die in other ways. In this respect, Makayla's Indigenous "sovereign" claim (if it is read as such) is thus doubly unrecognizable because there simply is no state sovereign to bestow recognition (the state is biopolitical and the CAS is not truly sovereign), and because under a biopolitical power that makes live, death itself is disavowed and unrecognizable. As much as death is furtively produced, biopolitically it is canceled/sublated (*aufgehoben*) by "life itself."

Despite the repeated and widespread use of the term "sovereignty" in this case, I cannot read Makayla's claim as sovereign in the conventional politico-theological sense, nor do I understand her life and death in the tradition of a liberal politics of recognition. The divergent temporal modalities of sovereignty and biopolitics expose for us the sovereign ruses of biopolitics, its false or parasymbolic majesty. And, between past and future temporizations, they also render unspeakable the present moment, the instant of one's death. Attending to this instant and its significance, I argue, calls for a properly temporal argument, one that would interrupt the biopolitical temporizations of life and life-time, its fictive "timeliness," as well as its sovereign phantasms. Such an argument must acknowledge that time is not a neutral or universal category, a punctuating succession of "nows," and that we do not live and die *in* the same time any more than we are born or die *at* the same time. And this, by virtue of different experiences of time; contrapuntal narrativizations, tempos, and temporizations; diverse histories and practices of memorialization; divergent beliefs about the persistence of the past; as well as singular openings onto the future, that is, distinct ontologies that constitute the phenomenology of time-consciousness through particular and situated retentions and protentions. The experience of duration is never the duration of experience in clock-time. I'm not the person to offer an account of Indigenous ways of knowing or temporalities,[61] and, hardly capable of accounting for my own, I nevertheless hope to unsettle settler-colonial time so as to be present *to* other ways of living and dying, in time, at this instant, and to hold open this possibility as an indispensable aspect of decolonial practice. Bataille writes, "If I envision the *instant* in isolation from a thought that entangles the past and the future of manageable things, the instant that is closed in one sense but that, in another, much more acute sense, opens itself up while denying that which limits separate beings, the instant alone is the sovereign being."[62]

Here, then, in the service of a temporal argument, Bataille bequeaths to us a radically different and original way of conceptualizing sovereignty, one that most emphatically does not capitulate to the traditional sovereignty of laws and states, to a failed politics of recognition, or to liberal-humanist paradigms of political subjectivity. Ultimately, this may also suggest another relation to a community of others, to nonhuman animals, to lands and waters, and the planet. But for my immediate purposes, Bataille offers foremost a temporal argument of the *instant*, one that I invoke here neither descriptively nor normatively: neither an *is* nor an *ought*, I'm hoping rather to disrupt the temporalities of my own—our—reading and reason, to enact a caesura, a rupture, a fissure. In Bataille's terms, this would be an "insurrection of thought," or rather, of the *conditions* for seeing and thinking. Bataille's critique of Hegel offers us, then, a generative reconceptualization of sovereignty that, in contemporary terms, both refuses liberal recognition-based politics *and* the hollow affirmations of biopolitical life. In Bataille's thought, sovereignty *cannot* be aligned with lordship because it is not a risking of death as Hegel conceives it. For him, Hegelian lordship is comedic: the master risks death but nevertheless—absurdly—lives. In Jacques Derrida's gloss on Bataille's critique of Hegel, "The notion of *Aufhebung* . . . is laughable in that it signifies the *busying* of a discourse losing its breath as it reappropriates all negativity for itself, as it works the 'putting at stake' into an *investment*, as it *amortizes* absolute expenditure."[63]

Already obsolesced, sovereignty cedes to the biopolitical tropes and tempos of busying, investing, amortizing. Bataille's burst of laugher at this burlesque scene is theorized as an excess beyond the dialectic, beyond pure reason: "a point where laughter that doesn't laugh and tears that don't cry, where the divine and the horrible, the poetic and the repugnant, the erotic and the funereal, extreme wealth and painful nudity coincide."[64] As Bataille states, "In the [Hegelian] 'system,' poetry, laughter, ecstasy are nothing. Hegel gets rid of them in a hurry: he knows no other end than knowledge."[65] Poetry, laughter, ecstasy irrupt as a certain nonknowledge into the regime of the known and knowable. Death, too. Blanchot echoes Bataille when he writes, "In the Hegelian system (that is, in all systems), death is constantly in operation, and nothing dies, nothing can die."[66] Totally other, it is *sovereign* laughter, in Bataille's particular sense of sovereignty—utterly unconcerned with meaning and historicity, with systematicity—that constitutes the sovereign relation with death. In Bataille's famous formula, "The sovereign is he who *is*, as if death were not."[67]

And so, against state medico-legal regimes, against technoscience, biopolitics, and the punctilious administration that makes live: the excess of anguished laughter, tears, ecstasy. In Derrida's words, "What is laughable [for Bataille] is the *submission* to the self-evidence of meaning, to the force of this imperative: that there must be meaning."[68] Bataille is abundantly clear that his understanding of sovereignty "has little to do with the sovereignty of States, as international law defines it." Rather, for him sovereignty is what we might call a (non)articulation around the figures of death and dying: "Let us say that the sovereign (or the sovereign life) begins when, with the necessities ensured, the possibility of life opens up without limit." The instant alone is the sovereign being: it is a life of pleasure or jouissance beyond utility, temporally immanent, "when nothing counts but the moment [*l'instant*] itself." Its temporality is neither "servile" nor utilitarian, it does not "employ the *present time* for the sake of the *future*, which is what we do when we work."[69] The instant of one's death is neither productive nor biopolitical. It signals, Bataille suggests, a sort of animal life, a natural order or law, unpossessed by possessive individualism: "Death might seem to be the complete opposite of a function whose purpose is birth . . . , but we shall see . . . that this opposition is reducible, and that the death of some is correlative with the birth of others, of which it [death] is finally the precondition and the announcement."[70] Making live and letting die are locked in ineluctable embrace, a general economy.

If, as Bataille writes, "life is a product of putrefaction, and it depends on both death and the dungheap," then we might say that biopolitics and technoscience seek to obscure this ineluctable embrace and to administrate that natural order, imposing a temporality and historicity that intervenes between the living and the dead—in the administrative right to an administrated life. For us, today, life and death are estranged, segregated, in the regulative economies of making live and letting die. Bataille's understanding of sovereignty, then, would spurn such world-historization, and he seeks to give voice to this sovereignty in a paradoxical (non)articulation. In a fascinating passage, he writes in the first-person singular: "I will rejoin abject nature and the purulence of anonymous, infinite life, which stretches forth like the night, which is death. One day, this living world will pullulate in my dead mouth."[71] It is the dead mouth that will speak, that will contain, and from which will burst forth—pullulate: spawn, breed, crawl or swarm with—a living world, in rot and putrefaction, in silent speech. If this disaffirmation is not quite a positive affirmation, not quite dialectical as much as a pullulation, a form-of-life that is postulated on death and decay, he acknowledges as much, adding "The inevitable disappointment of the expectation is itself, at the same time, the inevitable horror that I deny, that I should deny at all costs."[72] A denial that is, at the same time, denied, by death, which would itself speak here in his place, in that dead mouth, as "I." Bataille's is a distinctly temporal argument and vocation. Death becomes the present absence of the future—a future being-with that is grieved when we lose someone, exposing the counterfactuality of that future, and our servility to it, reducing to nothing a being who was, properly speaking, no thing. In this respect, death "cannot be assimilated, cannot be incorporated" into the coordinates of vulgar temporality. "Death destroys what was to be, what has become a present in ceasing to be."[73] Bataille's is a work of hearkening.

I opened this chapter with the "necessaries of life," reflecting on the ambivalence of its genitive "of," exploited by law, by medicine, biopolitically, as the ambivalent politics *of* life itself. I have argued that this turning and troping of life and politics is temporal, indeed temporizing, in and as it were affirmed from a counterfactual future. In the face of this: the instant, the instance, that disaffirms biopolitical life. Against the politics of life and its necessaries: the instant of death, "the pullulation of error—beyond a silence that gives us over to the worst."[74] In this "error" the ambivalence of the genitive "of" occurs as nonknowledge, the impossible possibility, "the *impossible coming true*, in the *reign of the moment* [de l'instant]";[75] neither timely nor untimely, it is "the moment [*l'instant*] that counts, the moment of rupture, of fissures. . . . The miraculous moment when anticipation dissolves into nothing."[76] If I am present at this moment, in this moment, I am not present to it; *hors de soi*, driven from any presence-of-self or being-for-self (Hegel's *fürsichsein*), my "I" is exposed to pullulations, another to an other who dies. Bataille writes, "If one sees one's fellow-being [*son semblable*] die, a living being can no longer subsist except *outside oneself* [hors de soi]. . . . Each of us is then driven from the narrowness of their person and is lost as much as possible in the community of fellow-beings [*semblables*]. It is for this reason that it is necessary for communal life to hold itself as *high as death* [*de se tenir à* hauteur de mort]."[77] Paradoxical claims such as these are surely vexing. They resist systematization and contravene our familiar temporal and sovereign grammatical orders—opening instead onto a sort of contretemps that would hearken the solicitudes of communal life, and a thinking beyond the impasses of liberal subjecthood and reason.

In the final section, I invoke the work of Blanchot and Nancy, which is in conversation with Bataille and likewise honors the instant of death as the temporal instantiation of communal life. Through this theoretical lens, I return to the question I posed at the outset: Are we (ever?) in a position to distinguish Makayla's voice from Ezekiel's? As I suggested, it is difficult to say with certainty that the Stephans—and with them, a host of anti-vaxxers, religious fundamentalists, and libertarians of all stripes—have no worldview and no moral right to live and to die according to that order of things that is theirs. Their views may be deemed incoherent in light of the time and timeliness of life constituted in and as law, biomedicine, and for the moral majority we call civil society. And so, too, it might be argued, for the Saults and for many other Indigenous families who "fail" to embrace the covenants of biopolitical "progress." But this thinking remains caught within the warp and woof of medico-legal and (bio)ethical tropes, of normative life and life-time. It asks us to adjudicate between the claims of each. And it presumes an unreconstructed line of reasoning that cares naught for death. In my invocation of Bataille, then, his radical reconceptualization of sovereignty permits us to interrupt our perspective and to hearken, if we can, the sovereign instant of death and the voices of those gathered in its momentous embrace. This would shift the tone and the tense of our discussion away from a liberal recognition-based politics fixated on the individual, and turn our faces toward the possibilities of communal life in death.

## Communal Life in Death: Fragments

The necessaries *of* life, the politics *of* life: a genitive possession conjugated in and as relentless discourse, the resolute and full-throated avowals of law, medicine, public morality. The work of such writing, such speech, so pervasive that these tropes now virtually underwrite and sanction all normative writing and speech—it is this that fashions the political in our time.

Biopolitical tropes and absolutions conjoin identity and politics, ostensibly recognizing and affirming divergent identitarian masses—"human beings," Nancy writes, "defined as producers (one might even add: human beings *defined* at all), and fundamentally as the producers of their own essence in the form of their labor or work."[78] Any rejoinder must not simply re-join; it must rupture from within this conjugation, and refuse to do its work. Death fragments.

In stark contrast to biopolitical tropes, then, the presentiment of another order of discourse: *désœuvrement* (unworking), "the interruption of the incessant," "fragmentary writing," the "effects of passivity," a "life escaped from itself," to interpose just a few of Blanchot's phrases in debt to Bataille. Blanchot writes, "It is upon losing what we have to say that we speak—upon an imminent and immemorial disaster—just as we say nothing except insofar as we can convey in advance that we take it back [*que nous le dédisons*], by a sort of prolepsis, not so as finally to say nothing, but so that speaking [*le parler*] might not stop at the word [*la parole*]—the word which is, or is to be, spoken, or taken back [*dite ou à dire ou à dédire*]. We speak suggesting that something not being said is speaking."[79]

The speaking *of* loss, the speaking *of* the unsaid: de-composition, dis-ease, dis-integration: as dis-avowal, dis-possession, dis-affirmation. Against the conjugations of making live and letting die, and against the necessaries *of* life, the politics *of* life: the paratactical writing *of* disaster, un-writing, dehiscence. "The disaster is the time when one can no longer—by desire, ruse, or violence—risk the life which one seeks, through this risk, to prolong."[80] The "sort of prolepsis," for Blanchot, figures as the temporizing *instant* of one's death, a future event that speaks as if death had already elapsed—a speech that begins after death. "Dying means: you are dead already, in an immemorial past, of a death which was not yours, which you have thus neither known nor lived, but under the threat of which you believe you are called upon to live."[81]

Death: the identity of the subject is lost in/to this instant, and the present lost, too, from the flow-of-time. Blanchot writes, "'You die and yet you do not die and yet: thus, in a time without present, the dying that defers [*qui diffère*, also 'that differs'] speaks to you.'"[82] Speaking here in the time without present, dying for now deferred, the *instance* is the "time" of writing (*l'écriture*), a vow to the unavowable, an unspeaking (*dédire*), in the temporality of prolepsis, both imminent and immemorial. "'To die [*Mourir*] is not declined.'—This inert infinitive, agitated by an infinite neutrality that could not coincide with itself, infinitive without present.'"[83] As with death, writing cannot be declined—its obligation is death's inclination, too, a finitude that cannot be refused, but also grammatically, without declension, "to die" is neither the subject nor the object of a verb (either transitive or intransitive). It is neuter, neither singular nor plural, spoken by a subject who is *hors de soi* (in abyss and ecstasy), outside, ex-posed. "Thus the gift of speech, the gift of a 'pure' loss that cannot make sure of ever being received by the other, even though the other is the only one to make possible, if not speech, then at least the supplication to speak which carries with it the risk of being rejected or lost or not received."[84]

To write of Makayla's death, and to speak of her voice—as supplication, obligation, and in the desire to do justice to her—is to write and speak of justice in her time, not mine or "ours." But this desire risks reconstituting a certain sovereignty in which my desire for her all too easily morphs into the adjudication of which or whose communities ought to be granted recognition. In the solitude of my fragmentary writing, here and now, to write and to hold a death, in *its* time, now singular, now plural, is a certain madness. The time of my writing, of these words, is neither mine nor Makayla's. To write, to incline or ex-pose: the ever-broken time of mourning, perhaps. But my words are not quite the "work" of grief: "It is not grief that works: grief keeps watch."[85] How, then, in the language of metaphysics, in its sovereign grammars, and in its "life," to hold open what is unavowable, disastrous—to hold and to be held *by* it, so as to hearken, to disaffirm, or simply forbear? There is no time for dying, just the dead time of mad writing, a dead letter, supplication, obligation. I'm aware, too, that I impose on my reader's time—a reader who is other to this text and to its differing/deferring time: "To give is to give living and dying not at my time but according to the time of the *other*."[86]

And it is the instant of Makayla's death, in her time, that is perhaps much more difficult for us to hold than Ezekiel's, as much as I also desire to do justice to him. We might say that Ezekiel represents a problem *of* our times,[87] yet we nevertheless share this normative life-time with him. He is perhaps easier for us to recognize. Makayla, by contrast, is a problem *for* our time. Her voice, dying and in death, is much more difficult to (con)temporize. We have no time for her death, forgetting that time is neither ours to give nor for her to receive: "To write is to know that death has taken place though it has not been experienced, and to recognize it in the forgetfulness that it leaves—in the traces which, effacing themselves, call upon one to *exclude oneself from the cosmic order* and to abide where the disaster makes the real impossible and the desire undesirable."[88] My desire for Makayla—surely a racializing colonial trope—cannot be desirable. But how might we expose the sanctum of our colonial cosmic order, its command, its program, in a "dis-closure" that would not force a terrified retreat into the "safety" of the biopolitical enclosure?

My invocation of Bataille,[89] in these pages, is an occasion to reflect on death and community in my relation to Makayla, to Ezekiel, and ultimately, to that time which we call "ours." Both Blanchot and Nancy invoke the key Bataille passage cited above, namely, "If one sees one's fellow-being die, a living being can no longer subsist except *outside oneself*." Nancy does so in his essay "The Inoperative Community" (*La communauté désœuvrée*),[90] and Blanchot soon after in his response to it, *The Unavowable Community* (*La communauté inavouable*). In the latter, we read a reformulation of Bataille: "What, then, calls me into question most radically? Not my relation to myself as finite or as the consciousness of being before death or for death [*d'être à la mort ou pour la mort*], but my presence for another [*à autrui*] who absents himself by dying [*en tant que celui-ci s'absente en mourant*]."[91]

Such self-questioning is foremost a question of community, constellating around my presence-to and being-for the other who dies. This would wrest me, most radically, from the future-time of biopolitics in which the other, and I too, would be made to live. Indeed, it may well oblige me to attend (to) the deaths of those others who are allowed to die, when I remain, in time, my own livingness conjugated with their dying. Nancy declares, "Death is indissociable from community, for it is through death that that community reveals itself—and reciprocally."[92] If this is a lesson in community, it is difficult to hear and our biopolitical sensibilities will affirm quite the inverse: that life instead is indissociable from community, and that it is through life that community reciprocally reveals and affirms itself. Making live, after all, is biopolitical work, and those others who biopolitics lets die (also indissociable from its "work") amount to acceptable losses in its vocation, opportunity costs. In Nancy's terms, such livingness does not and cannot constitute a community; rather, it signals little more than a "society" ("by agreement" and "reason," to recall Rousseau, contracted for the "preservation" of one's life).[93] A society has no being-in-common and is not at all the same as a community. Society "is a simple association and division of forces and needs,"[94] concerned with the necessaries of life and their provision.

However, if we grant that death and community are in a reciprocal relationship of revelation, we must not forget that this occurs "*around the 'loss' (the impossibility) of their immanence* and not around their fusional assumption in some collective hypostasis." Said another way: "The death upon which community is calibrated [*est ordonnée*, also 'enjoined'] does not *operate* the dead being's passage into some communal intimacy, nor does community, for its part, *operate* the transfiguration of its dead into some substance or subject."[95] And yet, this is precisely the vocation of biopolitics: fusional assumption, collective hypostasis, and the operationalization of the dead as vital substance. The biopolitical state was not present to Ezekiel Stephan's death, even as the Crown instrumentalized his dead life as a phantasmatic "voice" that would speak in the name of life itself, and in the name of the state, to reaffirm the necessaries of life. Meanwhile, Ezekiel's parents and their supporters hardly invoke him: publicly, his fate is merely the occasion for a battle over parental rights and self-sovereignty—a demand for a certain way-of-life that must remain silent on his death lest their politics of life come undone in death's disaster. In the case of Makayla Sault, the biopolitical state initially seized on her life, to make live, and although it soon ceded this power and this future (for reasons we may never learn), Makayla continued to be instrumentalized across popular discourses, in life as in death, to shore up the pious biopolitical prattle—and the commonsense truths—of "timeliness" and "making live" at all costs.

In the reading I'm advancing here, community is incommensurable with identity, with liberal recognition-based politics, with "the human" of human rights discourse, and with the metaphysics of the subject. Rather, community suggests a being-in-common despite, and not by virtue of, these mechanisms. "Community is calibrated on death as on that which it is precisely impossible to *make a work* [faire œuvre]."⁹⁶ The "calibration" is not projective calculation, and justice is not the application of an ordinance, is not ordained by one "ordained," by the rule or the norm, but is given as incalculable, inordinate. Nancy is clear: "Community cannot arise from the domain of *work*. One does not produce it, one experiences or one is constituted by it as the experience of finitude [*on en fait l'expérience (ou son expérience nous fait) comme expérience de la finitude*]."⁹⁷ Against neoliberal production and consumption, against the "servility" of work (Bataille), against the counterfactual futures of biopolitical work and making live, and against the self-fashioning that these imply, community emerges in and as an unworking or worklessness (*désœuvrement*). "Community necessarily takes place in what Blanchot has called 'unworking' [*désœuvrement*], referring to that which, before or beyond the work, withdraws from the work, and which, no longer having to do either with production or completion, encounters interruption, fragmentation, suspension."⁹⁸ This is the *instant* of one's death—a being out of time. The *instant* in no way implies a metaphysics of presence; it is not presentism or subjective synchrony. In Blanchot's terms, it is the inexorable experience of passivity, *attente*, patience.

I noted above that the Stephans appealed their 2016 conviction, which was upheld by the Alberta Court of Appeal in November 2017. However, the appellate court's ruling was not unanimous, permitting the Stephans to take their case to

Supreme Court of Canada, which in May 2018 ordered a retrial on the grounds that the original trial judge had erred in his instructions to the jury. In law's time, at the court-ordered retrial of the case in the summer of 2019, David Stephan, who represented himself, "told the judge he feels there were elements of prejudice against him and his wife because they were *sovereign citizens*—people who believe in common law and don't feel they are responsible to any government."[99] And it is precisely this "sovereign" claim, echoing Indigenous sovereign claims, that gives me pause. Indeed, we hear similar "nativist" posturings in anti-vaxxer, fundamentalist, and libertarian rhetorics alike. Despite their rhetorical similarities to Indigenous claims, I am suggesting that they are incommensurable when we consider the reciprocal relation between community and death. Not long after Makayla's death another little girl with the same diagnosis and from the same First Nation became the center of a court battle that ended with an explicit legal judgment, this time, in favor of her right to refuse chemotherapy and pursue traditional Indigenous therapies. The presiding justice argued that "a right cannot be qualified as a right only if it is proven to work by employing the western medical paradigm."[100] He further argued that to force chemotherapy on an Indigenous girl is to "impose our world view on First Nation culture." In an interview, he elaborated: "Even if we say there is not one child who has been cured of acute lymphoblastic leukemia by traditional methods, is that a reason to invoke child protection? . . . Maybe First Nations culture doesn't require every child to be treated with chemotherapy and to survive for that culture to have value."[101] This embrace of death was a controversial value claim contesting the perceived time and timeliness of "our" life-time. And it asks us if our normative embrace of biomedicine is necessary for "our" culture to have value.

To be clear, just as with Makayla and her kin, the "sovereignty" of David and Collet Stephan was never on trial, even if it was variously spun that way by them and their followers. A verdict of guilty would have made martyrs of the Stephans. But this was not to be, at least for now. At the retrial they were found not guilty, and although their acquittal occurred by sleight of hand, their victory was nonetheless championed by their followers. In a ruling that strikes me as truly bizarre, the judge decided that Ezekiel did not die from bacterial meningitis, as his autopsy states. Siding with the opinion of one defense expert witness, he concluded that Ezekiel had had *viral* meningitis. In his judgment, he writes, "There is no specific treatment that is effective for viral meningitis. It follows that the Crown did not prove medical attention *would* have saved his life or that . . . medical attention even *could* have saved his life."[102] Disregarding the Medical Examiner's testimony,[103] the judge further ruled that meningitis was not even the cause of death: instead, Ezekiel died from "lack of oxygen." And so, given this surprising new postmortem, the Stephans were deemed to have fulfilled their duty as parents because they did indeed seek medical attention "when Ezekiel stopped breathing." I note, however, that when the Stephans met the paramedics, Ezekiel is reported to have had no pulse and no neurological activity. The time and timeliness of their actions in the "untimely" death of their son figures nowhere in the judgment. At the time of writing, the Crown is set to appeal the acquittal of the Stephans, arguing that the judge committed numerous errors and made comments (apparently including racist slurs toward one key witness) that would lead to "a reasonable apprehension of bias."

While anti-vaxxers, fundamentalists, and libertarians may appear to resist biopolitical state power, they nevertheless tend to do so from a politics of identity, in terms obedient to a politics of life. Ezekiel's death *occasioned* David Stephan's sovereign rights claim to a particular way-of-life. And Ezekiel's death galvanized those who have financed David Stephan's legal costs—a society "by agreement" contracted for the "preservation" of its own "life." Ezekiel himself all but vanishes from this scene: he dies and then dies again for the "life" that they hope to make and to live. Ezekiel does not speak, he has no voice other than the one ascribed to him, phantasmatically, by the Crown. By contrast, Makayla's voice speaks in refrain across her community, which has long lived in the shadow of death and has long been gathered and constituted in the ongoing disasters of an immemorial, genocidal history. Not quite identity, substance, or subject, her voice has been speaking for generations—and *for* forgotten generations—conveying a presentiment of another other of discourse, an interruption, a life escaped from itself. As Nancy writes, "That which is not a subject opens up and opens onto a community whose conception, in turn, exceeds the resources of a metaphysics of the subject."[104] And indeed, settler-colonial peoples may hear ourselves named in Makayla's claim, as the fated beneficiaries of terrorizing histories, Indigenous death-warranting, and dispossession.

In this reading, anti-vaxxers, fundamentalists, and libertarians do not share the temporality or being-in-common that continue to inform Indigenous cultures historically riven by death. And if the rhetorics of anti-vaxxers, fundamentalists, and libertarians are meant to echo the sovereign claims of Indigenous peoples and to trade on a similar recognition, these are misinvocations, for their sovereign tropes are conventional, even trite. In contradistinction, I'm suggesting that the sovereign Indigenous claim might more productively be theorized non-conventionally, according to Bataille's radical reconceptualization of sovereignty, where community is always already, and immemorially, in a reciprocal relationship of revelation with death. My suggestion is that Makayla is in this instant something other than recognizable subject, other than fusional identity or sacrifice, either for the state, which in this rare moment recoiled, or, arguably, for her community in communion. Her death is haunting precisely, we might say, because it remains, neither quite transfigured nor sublated (*aufgehoben*).

To conclude, I would like to try to counter the criticism that this argument is bound to generate. It might be said that I'm parroting a now-fashionable white liberal humanitarian sentimentality, foolishly peddling in a collective guilt, trafficking in "primitivist" tropes of Indigeneity, or even exhibiting a white savior complex. But it has not been my intention to offer a romanticized or essentialized reading of Indigeneity by juxtaposing diverse Indigenous cultures with the rise of anti-vaxxers, fundamentalists, or libertarians—for these people, too, have good cause to be suspicious of the state. They sometimes do make a compelling case against state medico-legal power, particularly when they remind us of the state violence that has accompanied these technologies, from neglect and human experimentation to "tolerable" thresholds of death due to medical errors, as I mentioned above. Marginalized communities, undoubtedly, have been disproportionately subjected to this "vital" violence, and it is hardly surprising when Black, Indigenous, and other People of Color express an ambivalence toward medico-legal interventions, for they continue to experience worse medical and legal "outcomes" than white people. I am not, then, wittingly "romanticizing" Indigenous cultures—or death as such—so much as hoping to de-romanticize "our" attachments to the technologies of biopolitical life itself. Ultimately, Makayla and Ezekiel tell us more about "our" community than theirs. We seem bound to misrecognize them, not because we need more or better terms of recognition, but because the very frame of a liberal recognition-based politics leaves our delusions of self-sovereignty intact, right down to the artifacts of "autonomy" and "capacity." Makayla and Ezekiel return us to ourselves; they are foils by which we might better understand the biopolitical "timeliness" of our own life-time.

Bataille's radical reconceptualization of sovereignty in and as the instant of one's death, in and as a reciprocal revelation with community—this is not, I am suggesting, unique to Indigenous peoples. For me, the sovereign instant of one's death is less the signature of an Indigenous "exceptionalism" than an unexceptional fact of the human condition we all share as creatures born to die. It holds for Makayla and Ezekiel as much as for you and me. This is the annunciation of community. And yet we struggle to hearken such a death. Obedient to a biopolitics that "makes live," I work tirelessly to flee death, both my own and the deaths of those I let die. We seem to have lost the temporizing instant of death, its proleptic voice supplanted by the projective promises of biopolitics. In asking who holds Makayla, who holds Ezekiel, in death, we may well wonder, Who holds the deaths of those we let die, and who will one day hold mine?

I have argued in this chapter that life and life-time are discursive figures— biopolitical tropes—that operate as self-evident norms, where the presumed time and timeliness of life is implicit. And I have argued that death fragments, from within, and in an instant. The temporizing instant of one's death calls for open conversation on narratives otherwise, on ways of knowing and being-in-the-world—including ways of dying—that are perhaps irreconcilable with medico-legal regimes of evidence-based practice, randomized controlled trials, technoscientific advancements, and disease and risk management. For "us," what it means to live, to regard the time of one's life, outside of these normative regimes borders on the unthinkable—indeed, it may seem insufferable, intolerable, even cruel. And yet, this unthinkability becomes the unavowable time of one's life in the all too real proximity of death, where the linear promises of biopolitical time become—for Makayla, for the Indigenous suicide, for the cancer patient—an insufferable, intolerable, even cruel master. Biopolitical life is lived in the tense and temporality of "living in prognosis,"[105] to borrow Lochlann Jain's ominous phrase, where cancer and treatment impose their own colonial order, the biomedical time of disease, lived-out in hospital waiting rooms, parking lots, on gurneys, subject to pharmacotherapies, in moments measured by biopsies and meted out in test results. Living in prognosis is life in a future tense, by a subject to possibility, to temporal necessity, and the necessaries of life. Condemned to a biopolitical livingness, a patient (increasingly, "client") might find herself inducted into the "affirmative" consumer cultures of cancer's pink ribbons, wigs, and kitsch.[106]

Lapse, relapse, onco-politics: when biopolitics inevitably and ultimately becomes unaccountable, unable to provide the necessaries of life. "It is thus not simply as death at work that cancer seems so singular a menace," Blanchot writes, adding "It is as a moral derangement, a derangement more threatening than the fact of dying, and which gives that fact back its essential trait: its way of not letting itself be accounted for or brought to account."[107] Makayla's is not the petulant defiance or insubordination of an eleven-year-old girl at the nexus of colliding, collective hypostatizations—Christian, Indigenous, daughter, cancer patient, individual possessing legal "capacity," "Canadian girl," et cetera. In some small way, silently and unaccountably, perhaps, she un-writes, de-scribes, de-composes what is underwritten, inscribed, composed. She unworks, interrupts, fragments, and suspends, while neither ceding to the established conventions of sovereignty, from the past, nor embracing the promised futures of biopolitical life. Death in this instant is both a mortal and moral derangement, an opening that cannot be closed; it is decay, de-composition, rot, pullulation, fever.

The purported certainty, and the promises, of prognostic time—the predictive rationality of biomedicine and anatomopathology—do not and cannot map onto the time of a life. And this failure matters for Makayla, for the Indigenous suicide, for the cancer patient, and, I would argue, for each and every mortal creature. The anxiety, then, is perhaps less that "we" failed to make Makayla or Ezekiel live on "our" terms, but that these errant terms only anxiously, and failingly, make "us." In response to a failed biopolitics of recognition we must find ways to disaffirm the temporal hegemonies of biopolitics, of medico-legal time, and neoliberalism—toward and comprehending the mortal experience of other life-times, other deaths, including my own (which is always also other to me), whether these resound in the rhythms of lands and waters, the songs of ancestors, the call of the crow or the wolf, or arrive from distant constellations that destine us and keep time. Against an enforced livingness, and against its deceitful terms of recognition: the instant of death, whose murmuring claim must in time take hold, even as "life itself" would eclipse forever this black sun.

# 4

## Racism's Digital Dominion | On Hate Speech and Remediating Racist Tropes

In order to betray your race, you had first to imagine yourself as one.
—Saidiya Hartman

On July 9, 2017, a thirty-one-year-old man by the name of Jamel Dunn drowned in a Florida retention pond while five teenaged boys, reportedly between fourteen and seventeen years of age, watched—and video-recorded—the event. The low-resolution smartphone video lasting just two minutes and thirty-five seconds was soon posted to YouTube, circulating globally for a short while (as news cycles go) and generating heated commentary both on and offline.[1] Meanwhile, Dunn's family filed a missing person report on July 12, unaware that he had died three days earlier. Dunn's body was recovered on July 14 and funeral services were held on July 29.[2] Scores of online commentators—on YouTube, Facebook, and across various tribute sites, online news sources, and a GoFundMe[3] account set up by Dunn's sister—expressed incredulity and moral outrage that the teens did nothing to help the drowning man. The boys did not intervene, nor did they alert authorities. Instead, they taunted and mocked him: "We not gonna help yo ass!" And as the man cried to them for help, they laughed, mimicked his cries and cursed him: "Boo hoo!" "Ain't nobody gonna help you, you dumb bitch, you shouldn't a got in there!" As the man sank beneath the surface for what would be the last time, one boy remarked, "He not comin' back up. Damnnnn. . . . Buddy not comin' back up." And then, calmly, chillingly: "Yeah. He dead. Buddy gone. RIP."

This chapter curates the (re)mediation of Dunn's death, the murky details of which suggest the oral cultural dimensions of contemporary digital life: agonistic, postliterate, fragmentary, often contradictory, and sometimes conveying an ethos of fake news. It remains unclear how or why Dunn ended up in the pond on that day. He was reported as disabled, but his disability was not revealed until much later. And the ages of the teens who recorded his death were inconsistently reported across news media.[4] Indeed, the varying accounts of Dunn's death—together with a host of online commentaries, some loving, many hateful—blur the boundaries between constative and performative speech/acts, much as the video-recorded event does in its own right. In what follows, I'm less concerned with the disputable "facts" than I am in the media themselves, the messages they hold and their hold on us. That is, I home in on the *form* of the address rather than its purported content or facticity. Nevertheless, certain facts impose themselves: Dunn was a Black man, and the five teenaged boys who recorded his death were also Black. The news media were consistent in reporting *these* details, so much so that one might suspect these accounts of exploiting racial tensions, of providing clickbait for a certain scripted and racist reception, while caring nothing at all about the man who lost his life on that day. In this, they virtually reenact the recorded indifference to Dunn's death, and they contribute to its dissemination. From the boys behind the camera, to the various media accounts, to those of us who shared, "liked," and otherwise circulated the scene across our various media platforms—it is as if *saying* and *doing* become chiasmatic, reversible. At what moment does free speech become hate speech, and how might we disambiguate these within our digital media ecologies where such speech repeats in anonymous algorithmic perpetuity?

Following from prior chapters that variously theorize "resistance" across pandemic politics, prison hunger strikes, and claims to medico-legal sovereignty, this chapter is situated somewhat closer to home in the quotidian, apparently unsacrificial, and otherwise prosaic media ecologies of making live and letting die. While Mr. Dunn died senselessly at the margins of society, his death nevertheless adumbrates an anatomy of the new digital body biopolitic, its grammars of social existence, and our connective complicity in letting die. That is, Dunn died by neglect, and yet in a torrent of digital speech—discourse carried recursively on and across our digital devices, in and as our recurring biopolitical tropes. The teens speak, their voices digitally looped and reanimated. But does their speech *sentence* Dunn? His sobbing and their cursing, desperate crying and shameful laugher, coincide in this instant—his, theirs, and ours—turning between life and death and life: an instance of terror together with spree, gesturing to "the precariousness of empathy and the uncertain line between witness and spectator," to invoke Saidiya Hartman.[5] We, too, tread this uncertain line. We click and are ensnared in the enduring instant between saying and said. Alongside loving tributes to Dunn, we read online comments that reverberate in racist slurs (and worse), claiming that what the teens say and do is hateful, that the video itself is hateful, while some say that Dunn's life does not matter, or that the scene is "proof" of widespread Black-on-Black violence (with the express purpose of undermining Black Lives Matter). This chapter addresses this address—an address without address, we might say, a voice without obvious time or place, a voice carried recursively in and across our contemporary mediascapes.

The conveyances of biopolitics and racism call for a rhetorical and media theoretical approach if we take seriously Alexander Weheliye's trenchant critique of Michel Foucault and Giorgio Agamben on the biopolitics of race and racism. When it comes to race, Weheliye argues, Foucault exhibits a "truancy" across his oeuvre, while Agamben enacts a "disavowal" and a "philosophical *unseeing of racializing assemblages.*"[6] It is in this context that I turn to performative speech/ acts, revisiting debates from the 1990s over whether hate speech is illocutionary or perlocutionary—that is, whether hate speech is injurious as such and neces- sarily so (i.e., an illocution), or whether the injury, rather, follows as a non- necessary consequence or sequel of the speech act itself (i.e., a perlocution). In the late 1990s, according to Judith Butler among others, the distinct promise of the perlocution was that such speech can, at times and in time, be turned back against the speaker to subvert the speech/act and to undermine its injurious force. But as I argue below, times have changed, and renewed debate is exigent today given the increasingly widespread use of the internet and digital social media over the last two decades.

Consider Brexit in the United Kingdom in mid-2016, the global rise of the alt-right and white nationalism, and the burgeoning of racist hate groups—on- and offline—particularly since the US election of Donald Trump in 2016.[7] Trumpism itself is a socially mediatized and globalized phenomenon thanks in part to the temporal im/mediacy of digital media, their effects, and exhortatory affects—particularly in the identitarian social and political compliance they would seem to ordain from both the Left and the Right.[8] In the digital context, without the conceit of a sovereign voice and without a fixed "address," it is difficult to locate who speaks, where or when, or to whom we might return the injurious trope, whether as subversion or insubordination. When tropes travel in an instant, at the speed of light, and when they replay in an ever-present digital "now," it is dif- ficult to imagine the time and timeliness of a perlocution. The future is not what it once was; time itself is not what it once was. This chapter builds toward an argument that the master trope of the digital social media interface is chiasmus: the reversal or inversion, perhaps even the indifferent exchangeability, of freedom and hate, life-making and death-warranting. Rhetorically, I will argue, these ambivalences open onto a question of addressivity (further developed in the Refrain)—the ways in which we hail others and are ourselves hailed and tropologically constituted as popular subjects of biopolitical racism.

Digital social media do not simply mediate the social and the cultural, as if these were independent of their transmission, or as if technologies were simply tools or means to an end. And it is misleading to suggest that the internet is "weaponized" in (re)mediating death. Rather, like language, digital media *are* sociality, they *are* contemporary culture, no less real or deadly for their virtuality. The internet does not quite represent the individual's relationship to society; the internet *is* society hypostatized—an algorithmic deep state, an under-standing, that makes a social group real to the individuals that comprise it, a "social fact" (to use a term from classical sociology). From the Word of God to the words of human beings and now to technologies that speak—agentic devices, screens, social and political media platforms, robots, but also big data, dataveillant algorithms, intelligent systems, the circuits and switches of transactional capitalism—these, among others, constitute a vast media ecology in our societies of control. They are the incantatory manner in and modality by which we see and speak and act, performed in and as virtual wor(l)ds, according to the gospel of big data,[9] and by means of what Ed Finn has called algorithmic "sourcery."[10] Indeed, the "management" of modern populations has become inconceivable without digital media, politics impossible without tweets and identity mining and big data. The face-to-face is now, increasingly, interface, and the interface interfaces the face-to-face. Inasmuch as Jamel Dunn's life matters, it is interfaced as a posthumous matter through recursive online comments that appear in synchrony along with his death-in-replay.

In what follows, the mediatized event of Dunn's death is read as yet another occasion for digital hate speech, in a refractive and refractory address that allegorizes how our digital media ecosystem stands in a synecdochal relation to the distributed and distributing agencies, the refractile power, of neoliberal biopolitics. In the words of Alexander Galloway, "Today all media are a question of synecdoche (scaling a part for the whole), not indexicality (pointing from here to there)."[11] As racializing assemblages, social media networks are not simply a metaphor for biopolitics, I argue, but are the modality, the interface and protocol, by which neoliberal biopolitics is now propagated and normalized. Biopolitical tropes, software, and hardware—now indispensable to subjectivity—prop up the ruse of a virtual moral and political agency, an illusory "end-user," an "I" mapped along the polarizing and reifying coordinates of "race," "biology," and "identity." If, as I have argued, a sham sovereignty is one ruse of biopolitical power, I try to rethink the conditions of moral and political agency, as well as the possibility for a disaffirmation that might permit us to address—and perhaps ultimately begin to redress—the harms of hateful speech/acts, and moreover, the operant conditions for their effective curses and recursions. How might we disaffirm without merely disavowing the propagation of hate—for we must apprehend it—and do so without embracing or impulsively echoing the moral censoriousness of the liberal individual fashioned as unreconstructedly Eurocentric and white? Indeed, I will conclude below that the unreconstructed whiteness of the "I" is the principal *address* of making live—both its site of (re)production and its phantasmatic destination.

The epigraph that opens this chapter—"In order to betray your race, you had first to imagine yourself as one"—is a line plucked from Saidiya Hartman's *Lose Your Mother*, which documents the author's journey to Ghana and her struggle to reckon with "the afterlife of slavery and the future of the ex-slave."[12] Here pressed into service out of its particular context, the epigraph might be read as urging Hartman's reader ("your ... you ... yourself"), and me, to ask self-reflexively, Must I too betray my race, and if so, what would it mean first to imagine myself as one? Are these the conditions for speech and for hearkening, the conditions by which we might begin to address and redress racist speech/acts and racism? To betray means to be unfaithful, disloyal, or to double-cross, but it also means to reveal unintentionally, to expose, to lay bare, or to say. Those who claim that the video of Dunn's death is evidence of widespread Black-on-Black violence surely invoke betrayal in both senses of this term (i.e., the teens are disloyal to their race, which exposes some essential "truth" about *being* Black). But before understanding the betrayal of one's race, Hartman suggests that one must first imagine oneself as "one"—and here again meaning refracts. In the first instance, this could mean *of* "one race." But racial identity involves the process of racialization, which is not the work of a categorical self, of a sovereign subject or liberal individual. Race is social, constructed, and imaginary, even as the effects of racializing acts and assemblages are all too real. And in the second instance, one must, if one betrays, imagine oneself *as* "one"—a word that doubles meaning once again, as both singular and collective "ones": as a bounded, undivided, and self-same individual, on the one hand, and as a social subject who belongs to and is claimed as one by the collective singularizations of one's "race" on the other. The racist imaginary seems to ontologize along these intersecting axes.

Hartman's sentence invites us to reflect on the lived experience of racialization, and occasions as well a reflection on my own written speech/acts, here and now, as a white male scholar speaking in the context of Dunn's death and in the wider contemporary context of white nationalism and racist hate speech/acts. In the first-person singular, Hartman writes, "I am a reminder that twelve million crossed the Atlantic Ocean and the past is not yet over. I am the progeny of the captives. I am the vestige of the dead."[13] But there is no "oneness" to her "I": it is a reminder, unbounded, multiple, vestigial. What, then, of my text, my speech, that uses "I" in these pages? How might I write so that my speech/acts neither embrace nor echo the oneness of presumed moral agency, sovereign authority, or liberal subjectivity? What sorts of betrayals—of my race, of my *oneness*—might I vocalize and enact? What sort of doubling of my subjectivity? "Is it possible," Hartman asks elsewhere, "to tell a story about *degraded matter* and dishonored life that doesn't delight and titillate, but instead ventures toward another mode of writing?"[14] The critical race theorist Sharon Patricia Holland poses a similar question, in words that resonate for me: "In the shadow of a resurgence of mostly extremist, sometimes brutal, white masculinity, how does any white man move to speak against a subject position designed for him by the media?"[15]

Let us acknowledge that speaking *as* a white male—and by implication, authoritatively *for* this set of human beings (or indeed, any other)—is problematic, a paratactical simplification: it is an investment in an abstraction, or for some, an idealization, when in fact I am not one thing, and that oneness is multiple, intersectional, and vestigial. No matter: I'm hailed in this moment as an ethical being, not so much in or as the purported oneness that I am—for I am not—but by the force of this abstraction, or idealization, and the ways that this is mobilized in the subjugation and suffering of others. It is less important that I recognize myself in this mobilization than I recognize the *effects* of the hateful addresses it realizes through "me." My ethical responsibility must extend to these effects irrespective of the success or failure of my own self-identification, my own localization or self-critique or resistance. The name need not carry my signature. It is not just I myself I cannot live with, but the effects of this self "designed . . . by the media," as Holland phrases it.

Reflexively, despite myself, I cannot but conjure the word "complicity," and others like it, equally damning: "accomplice," "accessory" (to a crime or simply as an ornament), "compliance," "collusion," "abetting," "collaborating" (literally, working-with). And if silence in the face of injustice is tantamount to complicity, compliance, or collaboration, it strikes me nonetheless that the cherished liberal vocalization of incredulity and moral outrage also seems scripted, quietistic, and says nothing—a liberal "I" narcissistically preoccupied by its own avowals and disavowals. In Hartman's words, there is a "pleasure of indignation yielded before the spectacle of sufferance."[16] But as white male angst spills onto the street and spills blood, carrying tiki-torches with chants of "blood and soil," as marches and rallies are organized by the KKK, and emboldened white supremacists and neo-Nazis occupy our streets and campuses and legislatures, while some are democratically elected and enact legislation, spreading hate under the guise of free speech and civil liberties—what could it signify, here and now, for a white male—or for anyone—to remain silent? For, while anti-Black racism is a matter of terror and degradation for Black subjects, it is not least the effect *of* a certain white subjectivity, whether in complicit silent passivity or, more contemptuously, in the postures of white innocence and victimhood, or, more contemptuously still, as a violent counterinsurgency mobilized in defense of "traditional" American values and rights.

If the march of white nationalists implicitly demands white faith and loyalty—and whiteness is destined there as blessing, gift, covenant—is this not the moment for a white male to betray his race, here and now, and to refuse the imaginary by which he is "one"? On the Right, those who march rely, at the very least, on one's silent complicity. And from the Left, at times, would-be allies *also* demand a reverent silence, invoking an identity politics according to which one's speech is unsanctioned on identitarian grounds. In what time, in what place, can one speak and refuse in body and in voice? Late one night I glimpsed a tentative answer of sorts to Holland's haunting question. I was reading her blog, where critical race theory and personal reflections on the subjugation of Black lives share the screen with some of her favorite family recipes—a juxtaposition I experienced as a generosity peculiar to the informal blog form, an invitation to her table, to break bread and to dialogue. This moved me. In the long shadows of the 2017 marches on Charlottesville, Virginia, there Holland writes, "The voices of the undocumented, the ordinary people living their lives who dreamed and are forgotten to us. The power in resurrecting those unknown to us is life changing. This is perhaps what time at University is for—to place our stories next to those unknown to us."[17]

The simplest formulation harbors a desolating demand. I struggle to do this in recounting the death of Jamel Dunn, mindful that resurrection is impossible, and mindful too that I cannot quite "tell a story capable of engaging and countering the violence of abstraction."[18] Nothing sanctions my speech. Nobody could authorize or grant it. "I" am unaccountable; no identity claim can satisfy the demand, no politics of life. Speech would emerge from and respond to a certain nothingness in which I'm undone, and yet I am tethered, unfree to escape into nihilistic abstraction. I press Hartman's and Holland's words into service, I use them, I use Dunn's story, and I lay myself open to charges of appropriation, "woke" grandstanding, liberal self-righteousness and scripted indignation. My intentions don't matter: I don't trust them, nor should you. But my "use" matters because these stories matter for a shared future that disaffirms racist biopolitics and in which we are destined to search together, still, for justice and peace.

I wish that I could speak in such a way that my words would betray and unwork the biopolitical conditions that normally grant their meaning. I wish that my "use" (*chresis*) could become catachrestic, to ab-use and ex-pose so much that is taken for granted (I return to *chresis* and catachresis in the book's Refrain). What follows might be read as a full-frontal and self-reflexive attack on the liberal-humanist "I" addressed and tropologically constituted by biopolitics as its ruse. From the ruins of such a subject, "I," unsovereign, must reply, with Hartmann, that I too—from my own particular vantage and advantages—am a reminder that twelve million crossed the Atlantic Ocean and the past is not over yet, that I too am the "progeny" of this accursed social order and live by virtue of the vestigial dead—in moral filiation, damned, and as their "beneficiary." Jamel Dunn was unknown to me, and his story unknown. My story I thought I knew, but it cannot be written without his set alongside my own. There is even a silent complicity in storytelling, it turns out. And complicity, if this is the right word, in the story of how his story will end. The ontology of one is always multiple. Our consociation is biopolitical, his and mine, and it is in and from this cursed relation that we must speak out, fail, and speak still.


## Remediating the Drowning of Jamel Dunn


I watched and rewatched the video of Jamel Dunn's death. Far too many times. But isn't once already too many? I watched even in my sleep. It followed me everywhere, it watched me watching. And at first, I found myself tempted to turn away from the teens, to locate myself among those online commentators who expressed outrage and moral condemnation.[19] In this ready-to-hand way, I might then feel good about feeling bad,[20] and share in their ostensibly humane sentiments. And yet, a slightly closer reading of what "they" write in online comments sections—just as with the vile comments found in feeds below digital news media—hardly affords an easy identification. Along with moral outrage one is assailed by no small share of vitriol, hatred, and often shockingly racist and inhumane tirades against these young men, and Dunn himself. Witness to this society of hate and its instrumentalization of the video, I felt I could not simply demonize or dehumanize these teens, and instead I began to imagine my being-with or alongside them—for this is how their video positions me phenomenologically and, as I'll argue, ethically. This chapter represents that unfinished work toward another mode of seeing and writing. I began to wonder if their calm and cruel indifference—"Yeah. He dead. Buddy gone. RIP"—discloses, for these young men, what it might mean to remain resolute (*Entschlossen*) in the face of death.

Here, I purposely misinvoke Martin Heidegger, who understands authentic Dasein as "resolute" in one's own being-toward-death. Heidegger writes, "Resoluteness, as *authentic Being-one's-Self*, does not detach Dasein from its world, nor does it isolate it so that it becomes a free-floating 'I.'"[21] Perhaps it does not matter that the death they attend is not exactly their own; they nevertheless stand in relation to Dunn, their lives entwined with his death, here and now for a digital eternity. Might their resoluteness (if we can use this word) disclose for us the manner in which these young men experience their own everyday being-in-the-world, not as free-floating and sovereign, but as inexorably tethered, embodied, vulnerable? As Heidegger writes, "The Others who are thus 'encountered' in a ready-to-hand environmental context of equipment, are not somehow added on in thought to some Thing which is proximally just present-at-hand; such 'Things' are encountered from out of the world in which they are ready-to-hand for Others—a world which is always mine too in advance."[22]

Who speaks, in this scene, and who is addressed, if the video circuits in and through an abiding discursive regime? What kind of world is this being-with, this remediating *Mitwelt*? It is one I might gladly disavow, and yet it is one I inhabit all the same, mine too in advance. The video is no artifactual Thing, nor are these young men mere Things: "Even if we see the Other 'just standing around,' he is never apprehended as a human-Thing present-at-hand, but his 'standing-around' is an existential mode of Being—an unconcerned, uncircumspective tarrying alongside everything and nothing."[23] In an existential reading, then, we might imagine the many ways that these young men are always-already, not unlike Dunn in their video, dehumanized across our media ecologies. We might hearken back to countless other video-recorded scenes tacitly in commerce with and tarrying alongside this one—a veritable archive of quotidian deaths and kill-ings, whose bystanders and perpetrators are seemingly unconcerned and uncir-cumspective, chillingly and violently attesting that Black lives do not matter. As Susan Sontag has remarked, "to live is to be photographed,"[24] but to die too, for death is a whole manner of living, and all of life's a screen.

The interface interfaces the face-to-face, and I don't just mean high-profile events and court battles, the murder of unarmed Black civilians by the police, but also the subjugation in the casual and the commonplace—the heightened biometric surveillance of Black bodies,[25] racial profiling, slurs, stop-and-frisk, stand-your-ground, as well as a host of scarcely perceptible gestures in their (im)plausible deniability. In this *Mitwelt*, the video itself indexes the unspeakable origins of a violence that began long before the lives of these young Black men or the death of this particular Black man, Jamel Dunn, which is witnessed and video-recorded for a posterity of interminable witnessing and, perhaps, grief. As a speech act, the video is an event in its own right, akin to the event of death that it records and reanimates with each click. It "names," as it were, the lack of origin of speech, its anarchism an asignifying absence, and it performs this lack as a repeatable *différance*, in the (re)iteration of violence and Black death.[26] In this, the video obviates any clear sovereign agency or accountability, any free-floating "I": to say and to do (nothing) become intransitive verbs, just as killing and letting die become disarticulable as speech/acts. Seeing and seen, the video, the commentaries, and their digital afterlives gesture to an apartheid that is not at all apart from me, us; together, testifying with us and against us, the medium's message is, in the words of Jacques Derrida, "the archival record of the unnameable."[27]

Being-with and alongside these young men is so discomfiting because I must reorient myself in relation not just to this particular scene—it is and is not sin-gular—but also as a witness and silent accomplice to those innumerable prior scenes for which there is no final count or account of Black life and death. The short video is an accessory to these countless crimes, yet another artifact of what Hartman calls "the afterlife of slavery—skewed life chances, limited access to health and education, premature death, incarceration, and impoverishment."[28] As I watch the video, I find myself alienated and immobilized at innumerable turns, asking who sees, who is seen, in this regime of (in)visibility. *Mis-en-scène*, I'm haplessly hailed by a drowning man whose cries arrive too late for me and for him, but also by the young men themselves who speak and who watch, and watch themselves watching, as we do, silently remediated and filtered through those prior and enabling scenes of violence both unoriginal and as it were without origin, anarchic, unnamable. I watch these young men watching him, I occupy their gaze as a spectator absent of all but a vain and belated moral agency. Have I truly *witnessed* a death?

Despite my worldly co-belonging with them I'm aware that my own ethical frame is not universalizable. My ethical frame figures as "universal" only insofar as I inhabit the moral postures of an anonymous "they" (*das Man*), whoever they may be, on- or offline: it is authentically "mine" only inasmuch as it is "theirs" already in advance. No ethics, this. I begin to grow weary of "framing" discourse. For all I know, had the police been called, the actions of these young men may have been "framed" much differently (I return to "framing" below). It is only in looking away that I'm able to wonder how or why these young men do not share my sense of responsibility for the other's life, how or why they not only did nothing (can at least one of them swim? make a phone call?) but chose instead to video-record Dunn's death, finding something in this scene worthy of sharing on social media. It is only in looking away that I might hear some small remorse, some voice of conscience, some slim acknowledgment of guilt: "We saw buddy die. . . . We coulda helped his ass—didn't even try to help him." In watching, I'm there, time is gathered in that instant/instance.

And could it be that these young men, rather than *failing* to identify with Jamel Dunn—as if identification were the measure of ethicality!—identify with him all too much, and in an anticipatory resoluteness see in him their own being-toward-death somewhere between the drowned and the saved, to borrow Primo Levi's phrase? If they don't see what they do, could it be that they do—that they *are*—what they see? This, after all, is an existentialist maxim: "'One *is*' what one does."[29] Their cruelty is neither theatrical nor spectacular; its everydayness fashions violence as a virtual nonevent, the signature of a condensed durational field.[30] Amid their jeers and their taunting laughter, I'm struck most by the way in which this drowning man is already as good as dead to them, his death seemingly banal and unremarkable, not altogether unlike those faceless deaths conveyed in statistics and reports, the collateral damages of yet another war, the unnamed casualties of drone strikes, of gun violence, of COVID-19, or the victims of austerity who go hungry, whose illnesses go untreated, remediated and rent beyond recognizability, as if for some higher purpose, some edifying Truth, some form of nation-building, the consummation of a long-awaited Destiny. Isn't this, *our* everydayness, not itself sick and surreal, laughably absurd, singularly revolting? Yes, yes. And so, what then is left for these teens to stage for us or to mock!?

Might they have glimpsed the terrible lie in our pious "culture of life"? And would history serve us to trace dim lines "to the slipperiness and elusiveness of slavery's archive": "the manifests of slavers; ledger books of trade goods; inventories of foodstuffs; bills of sale; itemized lists of bodies alive, infirm, and dead"?[31]

Their video speaks and speaks back to an agency and agencies that are not and never were theirs, exposing the fragility of the social order, unnamable archives, hallowed institutions. It reduplicates unoriginal circuits of specular violence, where the banalization of Black death is no more than another disabling and perishing[32] feature of Black life, reflected here in their burlesque enactment. In the stilled time that gathers here, the eternal belatedness of my moral con-demnation underscores for me the cursed impotence of my own political agency, and I resist yet cling affectively to liberal moral sentiment so as to reclaim a symbolic distinction (at least) between those who have let a man die and me who has "merely" watched as someone "just standing around." A vain and vicious distinction, this: liberal postures of incredulity and moral outrage are lifelessly ready-to-hand. Liberal affects, too, betray their normative scripts; identities, their subsumption into the value chains of the neoliberal economy, which white out the black marks of visible, violent erasure. Many on the Left—increasingly a radicalized alt-left—are so fond of their rituals of public self-recrimination, ceremonials of symbolic purification, cleansing, "I"-saying. We, too, are wounded, they will say. But no. Fuck that. I'd rather my grief yield to cynicism and get the better of me. And it does. I can't sleep at night. And when I do, I'm watching still.

We are complicit in the remediating *Mitwelt*, in the biopolitical economies of making live and letting die that inform this video, the conditions of its making, and the recursive ways *it* makes *us* and limns in advance our potentialities-for-being across the circuits of moral condemnation as well as the material conditions in and by which Black lives might matter for us. In Foucauldian parlance, the video circumscribes a "conceptual field" or "field of battle"[33] in and across which life and death are played out: how life manifests in relation to death, and signifi-cantly—but not only—the material distinctions between simple survival and full flourishing. Must we (as we tend to do) embrace a biopolitical life that (we are told) fully flourishes as it supervenes on death, where death is simply collateral damage, solitary and speechless? Or does their video not instead enact a manifest *inversion* of priority: a life that is solitary and speechless, a life that simply survives despite or even by virtue of death, with death as life's organizing principle, in its everydayness and proximity? If my use of "we" here is provocative, it is less my desire to interpellate my reader than to confess my own interpolation into this topology, my own undoing. As Fred Moten writes, "We has no address, no loca-tion. We's general dislocation makes addressability a kind of pretense, a kind of performance, as the relay between enactment, embodiment, and indictment."[34] My pretense, my performance, is not to summon my reader in a localizing address, but instead hopes to conjure, somewhere in a frozen moment between call and response, the complexion of neoliberal biopolitics, its unreconstructed whiteness, its epidermalization, where biopolitics is, as Weheliye phrases it, an "alternative term" for racism.[35] The "I" that I conjure is the subject of biopolitics and always-already on the scene of address; my pretense, my performance, hopes to disaffirm the ways that this scene enacts, embodies, and ultimately indicts those of us, its popular subjects, who find ourselves there. (I return to the metaphysics of the address in the concluding section.)

Inasmuch as "we" speak in the name of life, I'm arguing here that biopolitics is our historical a priori, and it speaks as the sacred and loquacious site of our (self-)righteous political and moral interventions, "authorizing" that speech/act in advance. As Foucault notes, by historical a priori he means "not a condition of validity for judgements, but a condition of reality for statements"[36]—that is, rhetorical and ontological conditions, rather than epistemological ones somehow added on in thought. The rhetorical and ontological conditions of our speech/acts lend meaning and suture together a *Mitwelt* and some sick semblance of authenticity. And yet, these conditions cannot validate our judgments under the aegis of any unreconstructed "oneness" or "we." Recall that biopolitics is the power to make live, but it is consubstantially the power to let die—a death that is implicitly the resoluteness and resolution of biopolitical life. It fashions our consociation with the life and death of Jamel Dunn. Biopolitics is a rhetorical *and* material power: I refuse to disarticulate these. Words matter, make matter. From a biopolitical perspective, then, within our unreconstructed historical a priori, the video brings us face-to-face with letting die. What escapes our biopo-litical grasp and remains inassimilable in this scene is the easy manner, the seeming indifference, with which these young men speak death, and name it—death—as a loquacious force, rather than life. In this naming, life is solitary and speechless, rather than death—an inversion of "our" ontological priority, of addressivity.

If we can suspend for a moment the liberal coordinates of moral authority, rather than judge from this scene a moral failure on the part of these young men, we might instead apprehend the ways that their lives are always-already the waste products of biopolitical power, those disavowed beings who can speak death, as it were, because they have been marked for death, allowed to die, disclaimed as lives that do not matter, lives that are not quite living. In Hartman's words, "Waste is the interface of life and death."[37] Rather than an affirmative and fully flourishing life, then, here we might be compelled to assume a death that is proximate—death as an everyday manner of being-with, and Black life as survivability, as life that resolves to cheat death, to jeer and to laugh at it, to remain on the scene, and not to be apprehended by the police, when the camera stops recording. If we can read in this way, and beyond what the scene itself might "frame" for us (and what we might normatively project there within its borders), the discourse of these young men is less unconcerned and uncircumspective, less a callous transgression of "our" sacred norms, than an opening instead onto a field of battle in which life doesn't matter, or matters otherwise, because death is proximate and quotidian, anticipated, even normative.

We might glimpse here the deathly economies of biopolitical life. The boys cannot save Dunn inasmuch as he is already unalive and always was; they speak, but, in speech autogenous and unpremeditated, they do not sentence him, they neither name nor pass judgment. Theirs is what Ann Laura Stoler might call a "colonial script," a repetition, not quite "carnal" in her sense of this term, but virtual, digitally incarnated.[38] And it is this digital biopolitics that concerns me here, as I hope to add obliquely or in a small way to the vast literature that links racialized bodies to (social) death—well established across Black and postcolonial studies, by critical scholars of the prison-industrial complex, of police violence, public policy, history, literature, economics, actuarial science, medicine, and so on. Across our digital mediascapes in particular, the links between life/death and digital networks are not particularly new. Already in the 1950s the early cybernetician Norbert Wiener, in his ominously titled *The Human Use of Human Beings*, suggests that the organism is a message, and life itself an informational network: "[The] organism is opposed to chaos, to disintegration, to death, as message is to noise."[39] My concern here is the racist "message" and its strange life. The noise matters—static, interference, outcry—because the network itself conveys—and normalizes—chaos, disintegration, and death. The message is that some organisms will be used and used-up.

I'm advancing an ontological argument—about how it might matter to matter—rather than an epistemological one fixated on conceptual knowledge or judgments. This relocates ethics away from immaterial universals and situates ethics as rhetorical and relational, a question of addressivity. The implication here is that I must distrust my moral sentiments, my affects or "intuitions," as philosophers are wont to call them (wont, from *wonen*: to dwell). It will not do to dwell in (or on) the old Kantian maxim to act always in such a way that our actions be willed as universal, and willfully immaterialized in a kingdom of ends. From death's other kingdom, I'm privileging here what is existential, rather than categorical.[40] The universal is a ruse, a formal or categorical a priori that is incommensurable with the ways our historical a priori is lived-in and lived-out, subject to recursion and re-vision, and full of deathly noise. These young men are less subjects in an epistemological regime so much as objects of an ontological one. They curse as they are cursed. It is senseless, then, to ask, Why didn't these young men think like me and do as I would do, what (I think) I would have done? Quite simply, they *are* not me, and it may well be that they don't embrace that conceit "we" call our *episteme*. Indeed, they are the absent presence by which our *episteme* has been violently affirmed and deployed, recursively, along such intersecting *différends* as race, culture, socioeconomic status, dis/ability, education, and the moral orthopedics these have fostered. Against the pious positivities of biopolitical life, which constitute the conceptual field of our historical a priori, these young men are disavowed, left for dead— spoken *of* in the passive voice, mere noise—until such a moment as this, when something unbidden breaks into our horizons of Being, and speech begins after death, becomes death's work.

The video is a speech/act that begins after death, and a belated means to that end. This is an ontological, rather than simply chronological, claim. The video may well end, chronologically, with the death of Jamel Dunn, but ontologically it takes its orientation and its inception from this end, an incipient death that is never far from a police presence, never far from life-threatening violence, systemic racism, white supremacy. Its inception is prefigured by the reception of other hateful speech/acts—many also captured on video—in which Black lives and Black deaths fail to matter, and where video evidence less pixelated and less ambiguous than this fails to persuade grand juries keen to acquit white police officers of their heinous crimes. We as viewers are accomplices in the viewing, in the circulation and recirculation, of these scenes and their virtual addresses, positioned in some sense (not somehow added on in thought) as ontologically and materially prior, as enabling conditions for the recursion of systemic, racialized violence, and cruel spectatorship. The recursive curse is ours. The media infrastructure is a racializing assemblage, a feedback loop, a dopamine-driven compulsion to repeat. And the event of Dunn's death does not take place without us watching: according to the choreographies of social media, it is produced for us, reproduced by us.

I submit that these cycles of recursive violence and the digital t(r)opologies of hateful speech/acts constitute the historical a priori of the young men behind the camera, where racist and racializing tropes circulate in and as our digital *topos*. To recall Foucault's terms, this history is a "condition of reality" rather than a "condition of validity for judgements." In other words, it is a historical system of traces, disarticulable singularities, and heterogeneities that constitute a racist biopolitical onto-logic, a reality sustained with normative and regulative functions, remediating mechanisms, unnamable archives, and distributed strategies for its reproduction. Beneath the shrill and so often pious biopolitical proclamations that "All Lives Matter!"[41] the Dunn video replays and resituates the resolute violence of biopolitics—a violence that biopolitics constitutively disavows by fixing violent recursions (such as this one) as chronological, rather than ontological, as discrete and aleatory "events" in the past, and as constative rather than performative in their power to name, to conjure, and conjure away. In a critical reading, however, the video also tacitly avows and disaffirms as it were this violence as *our* biopolitical infirmity, *our* sickness unto death. In this, we might say, the video is thanatopolitical, an irruption of death into the sick and surreal life of biopolitics, and a rupture-with our resolute indifference to death. Heidegger once again: "Resoluteness 'exists' only as a resolution which understandingly projects itself. . . . Only in a resolution is resoluteness sure of itself."[42] Despite the low resolution of the video, in its pixelated and grainy going-under, if we cannot look away might we glimpse, if only briefly, and unsure of ourselves, the resolutions of biopolitics and its resolute devotion to letting die?

## Alt-Free Speech and Hate Speech 2.0

In watching the video of Dunn's death, I'm forced to reconstruct the face-to-face as the teens record and verbally interject, glossing Dunn's death, performing a certain toxic masculinity, we might say, according to the choreographies of social media. I'm forced to conjure a face and a race—to assign agency and blame, as many online commentators do, whether on the basis of a liberal ontology or a racist one—because I never quite *see* Dunn's distant and pixelated face, and I don't see the faces of the boys who video-record him. Nor do I see those countless other scenes of Black death, but I'm left to speculate how these might have informed or directed this scene, as it unfolds, or how these other scenes might have fed into the lived experience of Dunn and the boys behind the camera, as well as my own subjectivity as I watch them watching. If they "appear" for me, if I can "locate" body-subjects in this refracted and refractory scene of address, much is my own doing, a projective and protective mechanism by which I might easily and implicitly disavow the historicity of this scene and phantasmatically shore up the sovereign agency of the teens, as well as my own sovereignty as someone "merely" watching. But neither their speech nor mine occurs in a vacuum. In the words of the critical race theorist and legal scholar Charles R. Lawrence III, "The racist acts of millions of individuals are mutually reinforcing and cumulative because the status quo of institutionalized white supremacy remains long after the deliberate racist actions subside."[43] And today, the status quo of institutionalized white supremacy is increasingly digital, where racist speech/acts don't so much subside as perdure in their ever-present, sometimes viral, reanimation and replay.

Online speech is notoriously difficult, often nearly impossible, to regulate or contain, to prosecute or punish, let alone to categorize as definitively hateful or injurious. Digital interfaces and devices allow the easy propagation, the remediation, of online content, for the most part globally, while in the United States the First Amendment continues to protect "free speech," now in a digital world. In 1990, in a text published before the internet age, Lawrence would write, "Much of the argument for protecting racist speech is based on the distinction that many civil libertarians draw between direct, face-to-face racial insults, which they think deserve first amendment protection, and all other fighting words, which they concede are unprotected by the first amendment."[44] Lawrence argued that this distinction is problematic, and he drew largely on anti-Black racist speech/acts that take place—still—on university and college campuses. He troubled the liberal presumption that speech redounds on the preexisting identity of the speaker or audience, locating injurious agency in the deep historicity of words themselves. In addition to face-to-face speech, he examined other media forms, including racist leaflets and posters and graffiti, to argue that speech is conduct, that speech *acts*. This is the case, he argued, due to "the immediacy of the injurious impact of racial insults," which are "like receiving a slap in the face." "The injury is instantaneous," he continued. "There is neither an opportunity for immediate reflection on the idea conveyed nor an opportunity for responsive speech."[45] The intended effect of such speech is terror and silence; the rejoinder often figures, if it does at all, as mere noise.

Lawrence's argument was prescient and warrants renewed reflection today. The instantaneity of ubiquitous digital communication platforms—including "killer apps" like YouTube, Twitter, Facebook, Instagram, Reddit, and TikTok—pose a distinct and unanticipated challenge for advocates of free speech, while they are a seeming boon to those who propagate hate speech. The collapse of the face-to-face[46] and the rise of the interface leaves civil libertarians in a quandary because a straightforward politics of (preexisting) identity will not suffice to localize intentional agency or map the vectors of injurious speech/acts. Moreover, liberal theorists have little to say about how identity is *iteratively* constituted in and through such speech acts themselves; quite simply, in online speech it is difficult, indeed, often impossible, to index a prior and consenting subject, a possessive individual or "I" recognizable according to the coordinates of everyday spacetime. Lawrence's text was published the same year as Judith Butler's *Gender Trouble*, whose theory of gender performativity offered a groundbreaking vocabulary for understanding the power of performative speech on subjectivation. In an oft-cited passage, Butler writes, "Gender is the repeated stylization of the body, a set of repeated acts within a highly rigid regulatory frame that congeal over time to produce the appearance of substance, of a natural sort of being."[47] Butler's discussion on gender echoes Lawrence's understanding of race and racism, its institutionalization, its historicity, and the ways that speech/acts are normalizing and "framing," reinforcing and cumulative. Much like Lawrence, Butler seeks to deconstruct identitarian forms of gender and race, at times taking issue with the liberal tenets of possessive individualism. Yet Butler will ultimately reject Lawrence's impassioned call to regulate at least some forms of racist hate speech through legal means.

Perhaps calls for greater regulation were doomed from the start, not necessarily because such regulation would contravene the First Amendment (Lawrence argues that strictly speaking it would not), but because law remains wedded to a liberal paradigm that relies on a presumptive individuality and agency that, with its identitarian logics, is incommensurable with the ways that speech and conduct are coextensive. This is a constitutive failure of law, for if law were to admit the fundamental relation between speech and conduct, its own speech acts (judgments that are themselves conducts) would founder, and its foundational authority would be undermined, caught in a performative contradiction.[48] Law has a constitutive hauntological problem. Indeed, a phantasmatic sovereign authority continues to underwrite the operation and force of law, sometimes anxiously and violently (consider law's serial acquittal of white police officers who kill unarmed Black civilians—biopolitically "justified" as letting die in defense of life). It is just this state (and police) power that Butler was unwilling to shore up through the increased powers that come with legislation. And even if these measures *were* legislated, as Lawrence had advocated, they would be impossible to implement, especially today, in the context of contemporary digital media. This debate as it unfolded in the 1990s could not have anticipated the manner in which digital media would transform the problem of hate speech, obsolescing the subjectivity implicit in the face-to-face and displacing the "total speech situation," as Austin would say, in and as the interface.[49]

In 1997, Butler published *Excitable Speech*, a book-length study on performativity in the context of hate speech, which revisited J. L. Austin's distinction between illocutionary and perlocutionary speech acts. In Austin's terms, we might say that Lawrence understands hate speech as illocutionary—it performs or *does* what it says, a performative that relies on sociohistorical conventions, and, when certain conditions are met, such speech will prove injurious: "*in* saying $x$ I do $y$," to invoke Austin's formula. Butler, however, takes critical distance from the illocution, theorizing instead some more hopeful way that racist hate speech might be "restaged" or "resignified" (Butler's words), because it is not unequivocally under the control of a sovereign subject who speaks. Butler reframes racist speech acts as perlocutionary, and echoes Austin: "Whereas illocutionary acts proceed by way of conventions, perlocutionary acts proceed by way of consequences."[50] And Butler is surely correct to distinguish the temporal immediacy of the illocution from the temporal lag of the perlocution. The perlocution relies on a temporal gap or caesura between call and response in which performative "failures" and "faultlines" (Butler's words again) might be exploited, ushering in the promised future of the perlocution, when hate speech, at times and in time, might be turned back against the speaker to subvert that speech/act and to disrupt its injurious force. A favorite example from gender studies is the resignification or restaging of the word "queer"; in hip-hop culture, a more contentious example is the use of the N-word (where the speaker and the setting continue to be of paramount importance).

As I emphasized in chapter 2, there is no way to guarantee the successful execution of a perlocution precisely because, according to Austin, it often contravenes rather than relies on conventions; its success or failure is situational, sociohistorical, and does not come down to the intentionality or interiority of the speaker (even though Austin himself does not quite relinquish this liberal model of subjectivity). In Butler's reading, the injurious effects of hate speech are a matter of perlocutionary consequences or sequels, which suggests that these effects are non-necessary, or even non-causal: "*by* saying $x$ I do $y$," to invoke Austin again. This is much as Hayden White had argued when he wrote that the trope "swerves in locution sanctioned neither by custom nor logic."[51] The "swerve" (a spatial metaphor) of the perlocution is also temporal, and it potentially subverts the force of the trope because it moves here in uncustomary or illogical ways, which cannot quite be predicted. Whereas Lawrence would emphasize the historical conventions, customs, and institutionalization of hateful speech/acts, deeming them illocutionary, Butler would emphasize the ways that they are also susceptible to perlocutionary redeployment in the right context and if there is *time* for their restaging and resignification.

But time is the crux of the matter. Given the instantaneity, the re-iterativity, and ubiquitous "now" of the digital interface, the *temporality* of hate speech collapses and its historicity is gathered in an instant/instance: there is often no wider context, no time and no place for a face-to-face response. This undermines one essential condition for the perlocution—namely, the temporal gap or caesura, the time for an effective restaging or resignification. Hypertextualized and caught in a digital repeat cycle, that subversive future increasingly is foreclosed, while the past becomes increasingly ontologized, condensed and suspended in the ever-present digital now. It is not that digital hate speech is without history; rather, its historicity is gathered in the instant/instance, decontextualized and potentially intensified. I propose calling this its *hyperhistoricity*, an attention deficit disorder that is constitutive of the digital interface itself and that is often strategically mobilized in digital hate speech.[52] It is the ultimate framing device. Here, we lose sight of the trope's *deep historicity*, the wider t(r)opologies of its turns and re-turns, in time and as time.

In the digital context, some twenty-odd years after this heady high theory surrounding free speech and hate speech, I'm therefore much less sanguine about the futures of the perlocution, its liberatory promise, or the fungibility of the racist trope. In the late 1990s, a younger and more idealistic me had felt hopeful for the righteous proliferation of perlocutions—resignifications that might at last spell the end of a sovereign speaker. If the speaker was no longer sovereign over a hateful trope, then in theory that trope could be repeatedly and multiply restaged and subverted. And at this time (just before tech bubbles, dot-com booms, rampant deregulation, and venture capitalism run amok), many of us believed that the internet would play a perlocutionary part in this "democratization," and perhaps (to echo contemporary parlance), in anti-racist and decolonial tactics. Alexander Galloway summarizes the conception of sovereignty that is transformed by virtue of our digital networks: "Sovereignty and power are defined in terms of verticality, centralization, essence, foundation, or rigid creeds of whatever kind. . . . Thus the sovereign is the one who is centralized, who stands at the top of a vertical order of command, who rests on an essentialist ideology in order to retain command, who asserts, dogmatically, unchangeable facts about his own essence and the essence of nature. This is the model of kings and queens, but also egos and individuals."[53] Vertical models of power, long critiqued by poststructuralism, have been structurally displaced in the digital context. But if the racist trope is no longer vertically oriented, if its power is no longer centralized, if it is networked and rhizomatic, it is for all that no less pluripotent. Quite to the contrary, in our case study the digital distribution of horrific death is played and replayed across YouTube and social media, turning and re-turning across heteronomic fields of spectatorship that are reticulate, networked, anarchic, rather than vertical or centralized or essential. Here, the topology itself—the interface, virtually without time or place—may be incommensurable with conventional conceptions of sovereignty, but far from freeing us it heralds new iterations of racist biopolitics and new tactics of white power.

To apprehend the video of Dunn's death is always already to have entered into commerce with countless other scenes (its deep historicity), which arrive in *après-coup*—as an aftershock—to choreograph the execution and reception of this digital "event." We can't quite say that any of the actors on this scene enjoy a sovereign agency. Their actions are themselves the perlocutionary consequences or sequels of racist tropes, speech/acts that are mirrored and reactivated by each hateful comment post, each click, each "like." There is no face-to-face, no meeting of ostensibly sovereign subjects positioned to "debate" or "disagree" in the liberal public sphere. And so, the eternal re-turns of Dunn's death muddy these waters and force us to rethink the sovereign agencies, and the localization—the scene and scenography—of the racist trope.

If the racist trope was once localized and authorized in the sovereign subject's speech/act, and if that speech/act once constituted the scene—the time and the place—of racism's conventional execution and uptake, what, then, are the sovereign conceits of the *digital* racist trope, when execution and uptake are simultaneous, when time and place are constitutively displaced, off-scene, in an address without address? In Galloway's terms, it is a "reticular fallacy" to assume that "given the elimination of such dogmatic verticality, *there will follow an elimination of sovereignty as such.*"[54] Sovereignty is no longer vertical: and yet it persists as the ruse of the network itself, a hyperhistorical agency that is now horizontal (but not democratic), crowdsourced, distributed, reticulate, machinic, and molecular.

The racist trope itself retains the sovereign power to name and to harm—but by virtue of the network, which is neither quite localized nor localizing. "I" watch a man drown, "I" watch the boys watching, watch myself watching them watching, and "I" find myself unable to arrest the motion, to locate a sovereign agent or singular doer, in a cruel and recursive spectatorship that is as much mine as it is theirs or his or ours. And if there is anything so fanciful as *popular* sovereignty in this instance, we are all to blame, each of us, popular agents of aggressive order, aggressive agents of popularity, from curated profiles to memes, the lifeblood of our social media ecologies.

If tropes themselves exercise a sham sovereignty by virtue of the digital scene, if we are subject to them, our participation in these networks merely affords us a sort of sovereignty by proxy, and an illusory self-sovereignty over them. Apprehending a death untethered from its own deeply historical time and place, we perform a sovereign conceit with each click, stopping the motion, fixing the meaning, and resituating ourselves as "merely" watching. It hardly matters if we are "for" or "against" what we see; either way, our sense of self relies on this social network, shored up iteratively and enacted repeatedly, whether we "merely" watch or join in some digital campaign that assents to or dissents from what we see. Our digital platforms become indispensable because they traffic in a phantasmatic sovereignty, where the self-possessed individual, the "I," is the very ruse by which our connective networks hold sway and cultivate a subjectivity that is docile and easily manipulated. They feed us a profoundly false sense of agency and freedom, which is repeated and validated by our newsfeeds.

Ostensibly sovereign individuals may be unwittingly complicit, or indeed, may *intend* in this context to do the opposite of what they nevertheless freely do. To offer one example, in her research on white supremacy and the phenomenon of cloaked websites, Jessie Daniels cites the example of several websites that emerged following Hurricane Katrina—websites with domain names such as Katrina-Families.com and ParishDonations.com, which appeared to offer a legitimate platform to help victims of the disaster. As Daniels's research shows, however, web traffic from these particular sites was redirected to InternetDonations.org, which was registered to a member of the neo-Nazi National Alliance, who was sued by the state of Missouri in 2005 "for violating state fund-raising law and for 'omitting the material fact that the ultimate company behind the defendants' websites supports white supremacy.'"[55] Without a great deal of sleuthing, and a fair degree of technical skill, those who out of kindness donated to "Katrina victims" via these websites could not have known they were not only doing nothing for those in need, but were supporting a neo-Nazi and his empire. Writing in 2009, Daniels notes that these particular websites were no longer active, but that this individual "continues to maintain a number of other websites, including the overtly anti-Semitic JewWatch.com and the cloaked site American CivilRightsReview.com."[56] As I write nine years later, the former is still active, while Google searches indicate that the latter was active until recently, and is cited by other websites (some overtly racist) and even as a legitimate source by a handful of peer-reviewed academic articles. Those innocently searching the internet for information on civil rights might until recently have found themselves on a website driven by a very different—and cloaked—ideology.

Cloaked websites, as Daniels explains, are not blatantly racist or hateful, they make no sovereign decree, but instead offer "an *alternative* way of presenting, publishing, and debating ideas"[57] about race, racism, and racial equality. The stealth sovereignty of the racist trope is built into the interface itself, and it's difficult to account for its perlocutionary sequels and consequences. Another example beyond race, but surely intersecting with it, includes websites that masquerade as legitimate sites about reproductive health but are in fact cloaked sites run by pro-life groups.[58] These represent a veiled form of propaganda conveyed less—or less explicitly—by epistemic content than by rhetorical form, thus concealing their ideological and political purposes. Daniels's use of the term "alternative," above, is chillingly prescient: Donald Trump and his supporters exploited these covert networks, embracing the "alternative facts" that helped propel the alt-white/right. Once-trusted sources of information, including bona fide news outlets, were decried regularly by Trump and his administration as "fake news." And in recent years, cloaking has gone viral with trolls and "sockpuppets"—fake or "bot" accounts on social media platforms, including Twitter, Facebook, Instagram, and the like.[59] These accounts appear to belong to real people but are used to spread spam or support political propaganda, often to drown out political dissent or to discourage voter turnout. They were used extensively in the 2016 American election, to support Marine Le Pen in France, Brexit[60] in the United Kingdom, and beyond.[61] This is how propaganda is disseminated—and cloaked—across big data media ecologies in the digital age. And even as I write, these examples are surely quaint and out of date.

Social media on the whole, not unlike the mediatized event of Dunn's death, are highly participatory and demand at least a passive complicity in their propagation. "Consumption" is a misleading term here, for it falsely presumes an agentic consumer, a liberal subject; indeed, subjectivity is produced *through* the very process of "prosuming" (producing + consuming) media content and curating one's digital public self. It is well known that social media platforms, such as YouTube, Facebook, TikTok, and Twitter, produce little to no content of their own: it is user-generated. In this neoliberal business model, with nothing tangible to sell, corporate profits rely on the exploitation of users' data, which are technologically amassed (big data), monetized, and sold to advertisers and political campaigns. This puts a new spin on what the early media theorist Marshall McLuhan once characterized as "cool" media, where the user is the content. Extending McLuhan's understanding of "cool" for the age of social media and biopolitics helps us to take account of cool networks, cool content, and our chilling relations with them—relations that are highly participatory and that blur the distinction between active producer and passive consumer.

McLuhan's distinction between "hot" and "cool" media is deceptively straightforward: "A hot medium is one that extends one single sense in 'high definition.'"[62] In other words, "hot media do not leave so much to be filled in or completed by the audience. Hot media are, therefore, low in participation, and cool media are high in participation or completion by the audience."[63] Written in the 1960s, McLuhan's examples of hot and cool media will strike contemporary readers as unintuitive. For McLuhan, television in the 1960s was a quintessentially "cool" medium, a "depth experience," because early television images were low-resolution: "The mosaic form of the TV image demands participation and involvement in depth of the whole being, as does the sense of touch."[64] The "whole being" suggests a synesthetic experience, one that marshals multiple senses simultaneously, blending them, even reversing them. Today, our HDTVs are high-resolution, a frenzy of hot visual surfaces, rather than cool depths. However, while they extend the sense of vision, they nevertheless constitute eminently cool networks of (re)production and networked subjectivity, especially given the confluence and interdependency of multiple media technologies and platforms (internet, streaming service, device, app, social media, advertising, etc.).

The "consequence" or "sequel" of an intended perlocution is therefore easily flipped, as we saw with cloaked websites and racist tropes. These "flips" or reversals are a racist tactic of the alt-right and alt-light.[65] They seem to understand the stakes as a battle for identity and affective attachment. McLuhan remarks, "When a community is threatened in its image of itself by rivals or neighbours, it goes to war. Any technology that weakens a conventional identity image, creates a response of panic and rage which we call 'war.' Heinrich Hertz, the inventor of radio, put the matter very briefly: 'The consequence of the image will be the image of the consequences.'"[66] "Hertz's Law" is formulated as a familiar chiasmus, a media trope that demonstrates the inherent reversibility of all media, here inverting the "image" and the "consequences" to trouble their causal relation, to suspend any certainty over which term is consequent, which antecedent. This intermediation is difficult to grasp, as N. Katherine Hayles writes more recently: "The contemporary indoctrination into linear causality is so strong that it continues to exercise a fatal attraction for much contemporary thought. It must be continually resisted if we are fully to realize the implications of multicausal and multilayered hierarchical systems, which entail distributed agency, emergent processes, unpredictable coevolutions, and seemingly paradoxical interactions between convergent and divergent processes."[67] McLuhan's background in rhetoric,[68] I believe, allowed him to anticipate these structures and to theorize media as a reversible relation between "figure" and "ground."[69] If the "consequences" of a mediatized image include demonstrable effects and affects, it is no less true that these figures constitute at the same time and in their own right an "imaginary" field, an environment or ground, that in no small way (pre)conditions the meaning and the force of the "consequences." Image and consequence, figure and ground, stand in the same reciprocal relation as medium and message, because "the 'content' of any medium is always another medium"[70] and "because it is the medium that shapes and controls the scale and form of human association and action."[71] In the context of digital media, the chiasmus is the master trope.

The global electric telecommunication network, as McLuhan called it, is a stunning synecdoche for biopolitics: it permits a diffuse yet immanently connected digital tribalism without individuals, a system in which nobody "acts" as such, and nobody is "acted upon."[72] The video of Dunn's death-in-replay is a chilling synecdoche in this regard: life and death play out without us ever seeing the teens or their handheld device, yet their device is that by virtue of which we see, along with our own devices and the digital service networks that join us to them across space and time in an instant. In letting die, nobody, strictly speaking, causes Dunn's death or kills him; letting die is a social media effect, codes and conventions in commerce with prior and enabling scenes of subjection, refracted through a racializing prism. Digital code, racial coding, and racist "moral" codes and protocols are woven into the interface. Distinct from speech or writing, code is "executable" language and "is addressed both to humans and intelligent machines."[73] Old binaries are destabilized, even obsolesced: subject and object, active and passive, antecedent and consequent, human and machine. Together, it is this racializing assemblage that calibrates human "agency," much as it does for those teens whose viewing and recording practices that day cannot be understood apart from the digital t(r)opologies that situate them in relation to Dunn and to us. It should be said that none of this is to exonerate the teens for what they do and fail to do, but it begins to expose an ontology and a world that we share with them, and by virtue of which the question of our own address must surface in Jamel Dunn's pixelated going-under.

## The Address of the "I"

In one of the conspicuously few texts in which Foucault discusses race and racism, he argues that it is in the early nineteenth century—along with the birth of biopolitics—"that racism is inscribed as the basic mechanism of power, as it is exercised in modern States."[74] I must leave to the side my concerns with Foucault's notion of "inscription" here, which has been addressed by other scholars (e.g., if racism is *the* basic mechanism of biopolitics, then why so little mention of it in Foucault's oeuvre, and moreover, where did biopolitical racism come from if, as Foucault claims, racism had already been in existence "for a very long time"?).[75] My interests here are decidedly more rhetorical, focusing on addressivity in the context of racist biopolitics. I would like to home in on what Foucault characterizes as the two "functions" of biopolitical racism.

The so-called first function, in response to the question "What in fact is racism?" is that racism, in fact, "is primarily [*d'abord*] a way of introducing [*le moyen d'introduire enfin*] a break into the domain of life that is under power's control: the break between what must live and what must die."[76] Racism is thus a breaking mechanism that sets in motion making live and letting die; it is "a way" of operationalizing biopolitics. In the original French text, it is the means or medium (*le moyen*, also "the average") "introduced," here, "finally" or "at last" (*enfin*), as if biopolitics had long sought the means of mediatizing and propagating itself. And while the word *enfin* is omitted from the English translation, it is worth noting the symmetry that Foucault's auditors would have heard, between means and (finally) ends: *le moyen* and *enfin* sound very much the same as *le moyen . . . en fins*, "means . . . into ends." The homonym suggests that the means of racism are (finally) its ends, that means and ends are reversible or chiasmatic.

Indeed, two short paragraphs above Foucault had introduced a parallel structure, also described as a function, asking "How will the power to kill and the function of murder operate in this technology of power, which takes life as both its object and its objective?" We might say that, functionally, the object of racism is its objective, means and ends, speech and act, locked in illocutionary im/mediacy. Foucault concludes this paragraph in summary: "That is the first function of racism: to fragment, to create caesuras within the biological continuum addressed by [auquel s'adresse] biopower."[77] The transitive function is figured as rhetorical: an address, and indeed, a racializing address that speaks in and as biopolitical power, and in speaking, fragments and creates caesuras, as if now suddenly it is not biopolitics that had long sought racism as its means or its vocation, but quite the inverse, that racism had finally found *its* means, *its* voice, in the performative address of biopolitics. This chiasmatic ambiguity of means and ends, objects and objectives, leaves us unable to grasp any causality or chronology, and Foucault is no help here, whether intentionally or symptomatically.

The address becomes central as we read Foucault's "second function" of racism. Here his third-person account shifts to appear in the form of a direct address, to a *you*, spoken first in the second-person plural (the polite *vous*), and then, abruptly, in the second-person singular, in familiar form (*tu*): "Racism has a second function. Its role is, if you like [*si vous voulez*], to allow the establishment of a positive relation of this type: 'The more you [*tu*] kill, the more deaths you [*tu*] will cause" or "The very fact that you [*tu*] let more die will allow you to live more [*toi tu vivras*].'" The "positive relation" of making live (more) and letting die, the interface, figures here in quotation marks as a direct and familiar address that cuts across collective will (*vouloir: si vous voulez*) to suggest a rhetorical meaning-making, a speaking (*vouloir-dire*). Who speaks with such familiarity, addressing the listener in the intimate singularity of the *tu* rather than, more politely and conventionally, as *vous*? And who, moreover, is hailed as the imagined addressee? After stating that the racist relation was originally a relationship of war, Foucault says that its function is now "completely new," neither military, nor warlike, nor a political relationship, but a biological one—or more precisely, a "biological-type relationship."[78]

The "newness" of biologized race suggests yet another caesura, a break with the past, and an ahistoricity (even a nascent hyperhistoricity) in and as the biological body itself. But not for long, and not only. Here the biologized/racialized body is quickly displaced and doubled once again as a distinctly rhetorical function, whose "positive relation" is stunningly assumed, *grosso modo*, by the "I" in the first-person singular. And so, from the third-person to the second-person address, we now read a truly remarkable and rare *self*-address—direct speech once again suspended in quotation marks: "The more inferior species die out, the more abnormal individuals are eliminated, the fewer degenerates there will be in the species as a whole, and the more I—as species rather than individual—can live, the stronger I will be, the more vigorous I will be. I will be able to proliferate." "I" am hailed and hail myself in the name of biopolitical life. "I" am consigned, licensed to kill. The "I" becomes one with the species or, rather, subspecies or race or population (here also mortifying "abnormal individuals" and "degenerates," biological threats, threats to my "purity"). We must not forget that this is (in Foucault's words) a "biological-type relationship" on a "biological continuum" "that appears to be a biological domain."[79] In this respect it is a cultural racism (also seizing on abnormals and degenerates), the cultural inscription of a reified biology that "appears" and is typologized by the biological imaginary—much as "blood"[80] has always traveled between culture and biology, and as "life" has come to figure as both a molecular and a moral calling, the duplicitous signature of biopolitics, as I have argued throughout.

Whose voice does Foucault apostrophize in these lines? Who speaks in this manner? Who is spoken, hailed? These are perhaps misleading questions, for they presume a sovereign power and vocation, and a sovereign addressee in the frame, a "who." If biopolitics operates in and as the caesura, it figures here as an ontological gap, rather than an expressly temporal one (as with the perlocution). And yet the racializing caesura is nevertheless constituted rhetorically, in and by an address. My claim here is that biopolitics is a performative speech act, but this speech is not sovereign: it has no clear time or place, and much like discourse within our digital media ecologies, its speech is diffuse, refractile and refractory. Nobody speaks, but rather, life itself speaks in the tropes of timeliness and life-time, from the counterfactual futures of making live. Life as it were instates the regime of addressivity by virtue of which the "I" speaks, ensuring in advance its addressability and its executive power *to* address, to summon, to sentence, to kill. The ruse of biopolitical power is the "I," the "one" (to recall Hartman), whose life and whose purity are (or will be) at risk. "I" am addressed biopolitically as a "one" and "oneness," here and now. "I" speaks "as species rather than individual," and this "specificity," this consocation, is, Foucault says, a question concerning technology: "The specificity of modern racism, or what gives it its specificity, is not bound up with mentalities, ideologies, or the lies of power. It is bound up with the technique of power, with the technology of power."[81]

It is, we might imagine, the abstract voice of biopolitical racism, in which means and ends, antecedent and consequent, matter little in their priority. This voice, and indeed not just this voice, but its addressee, are constituted—un-self-reflexively, technologically, and ontologically—as white. It is precisely this presumption, this self-evident oneness, that is performed in and as the address, in and as the voice of life itself, arriving as a projective force, and duping us into mistaking the effect as the cause. As Moten writes, "What it would be to have an ontological status, and know it, is what it would be to be a white person."[82] Today, the technologies of this biopolitical address could find no better metaphor, no better mechanism, materially or morally, than our digital networks—racism's contemporary means and its medium. To understand this scene of address permits us to chart the t(r)opographies of white power, by which ontological status is granted or withheld, and it returns me to myself as a situated subject who speaks and who writes from this scene.

Powerless as I am, by any means or in any medium, to address Dunn or the boys who recorded his death, I'm left with the profound question of what it could mean to apprehend[83] this scene, but also to forbear it—to endure it, and to hold and hold open my biopolitical consociation with them. In my effort to hold and hold open, I'm indebted to Fred Moten and Stephen Harney for their theorization of "the hold," in which they invoke the Black activist critic and poet Frank B. Wilderson III: "Uncertainty surrounds the holding of things and in a manner . . . in which the algorithm generates its own critique, logistics discovers too late that the sea has no back door."[84] The hold, in an obvious sense, is the hold of the slave ship—one remediating technology of historical racism, a "container" governed by logistics in a globalized economy. But perhaps it is also the "hold" of digital phantasy and projection, and the algorithmic authority of the remediating tropes in which we are held, apprehended, but also, paradoxically, *by* which we are called to hold, apprehend, and *through* which we are destined: "Modern logistics is founded with the first great movement of commodities, the ones that could speak. It was founded in the Atlantic slave trade, founded against the Atlantic slave."[85] I'm indebted as well to Christina Sharpe's theorization of the hold, in its multiple historical meanings, which she cites from the *Oxford English Dictionary*: "Hold—a large space in the lower part of a ship or aircraft in which cargo is stowed . . . ; continue to follow (a particular course); keep or detain (someone); a fortress."[86]

Sharpe argues that we are held "in the wake" of the Atlantic Slave Trade, and she reads (and we read) the Middle Passage together with scenes of Black life and (social) death in contemporary America, alongside the plight of those who survived the Haitian earthquake of 2010, and alongside the fate of African migrants who continue to cross the Mediterranean Sea, where human cargo— once again, ever still—is thrown into the sea, dead or drowned, and where those who survive the journey face profound hate/speech and a life of extreme precarity on European shores and beyond. Sharpe does not allow us to forget that history is not relegated to the past, that our globalized economy continues to rely on the fungibility of human lives. These multiple scenes are not for her discrete; they assail us from her text—means and ends, antecedents and consequents, become fluid in the wake. And she asks, "What does it look like, entail, and mean to attend to, care for, comfort, and defend, those already dead, those dying, and those living lives consigned to the possibility of always-imminent death, life lived in the presence of death; to live this imminence and immanence as and in the 'wake'?"[87]

Sharpe's strategy for "seeing and reading otherwise . . . reading and seeing something in excess of what is caught in the frame"[88]—and for care-fully countering a "deeply atemporal"[89] yet abiding racism—involves what she calls "Black annotation and Black redaction," which she understands as "ways to make Black life visible, if only momentarily, through the optic of the door."[90] This polyvalent "wake work," as she calls it, involving its own reversals and ana-grammatology,[91] seeks to shift what we might call our frames of reference. In writing, I have been mindful of the risks of reframing violence, only to reduplicate it, in recounting Dunn's story. Doors also have frames. And as I'm unable to perform Black annotation and Black redaction, I have tried to demonstrate how duplicability is itself an essential element of the digital t(r)opologies of racist hate/speech, part of its deep historicity reenacted across its hyperhistorical instantiations, of which I myself am a part. Thus, any strategy must include temporization—locating oneself in the depths of historicity's hold—and to counter the hyperhistoricity of digital hate/speech, which is "deeply atemporal" (Sharpe), virtually extemporaneous.

Given my discussion on digital media and the temporality of the perlocution, above, I find myself compelled to argue against contemporary "framing" discourse and against strategies that would "reframe" racist speech/acts. In the digital context, those frames—whether framings or reframings—are all too easily caught in a condensed durational field, a hyperhistorical and hypertextual "now." The sea has no back door. Consider for a moment the many theorist-activists who turn to a discussion of art and creativity—poetry, song, dance, fine art, literature, et cetera—in an effort to escape the biopolitical enclosure, to see and to read and, indeed, to live otherwise. This turn is a humanizing trope, yet often with little account of the onto-logics or prior politics of humanization. And if this is the work of reframing—annotating and redacting—it seems to place great faith in the power of the perlocution, the promise of another form of address, another means and medium, and a reckoning with irrecuperable loss beyond the labors of mourning. In Butler's terms, we "must repeat those injuries without precisely reenacting them."[92] And, with cautious optimism, Achille Mbembe writes, "If there is one characteristic trait of artistic creation, it is that, at the beginning of the act of creation, we always rediscover violence at play, a miming of sacrilege or transgression, through which art aims to free the individual and their community from the world as it has been and as it is."[93]

This work is of course vital: I devote my teaching to it, and my students' engagement with it always teaches me to think otherwise. But with my own words, here, at best I can only hope to begin to unwork, for I'm no artist, no poet, and because I don't know how to adjudicate the aesthetic, political, or even revolutionary value of art—however brave or beautiful—and to distinguish these works from the digital artifact of Dunn's death, which holds me close, overpowers me, but which is also variously aestheticized and politicized, streaming as terror and vile entertainment across our digital media. It is crass, I realize, to consider this grisly video alongside works of artistic creation, and I would not wish to negate what Butler calls the "democratic value of being offended" by art that disturbs our scripted and familiar frame(s) of reference.[94] Yet, my worry persists, and I recall Charles R. Lawrence III's argument: that it is not only old liberal lawmakers or those who defend the First Amendment who disagree on where to draw the thin line between freedom of expression and hate speech. We, too, are at a loss, particularly given the im/mediacy of a digital culture dominated by memes, social media tropes, and the re-turns (and reenactments) that they convey. If I myself am framed, my power to reframe will never quite escape those wider frames in which I find myself. And these frames are so often, so easily, politicized. For example, does Dana Schutz's *Open Casket*—a 2016 portrait of fourteen-year-old Emmett Till's mutilated dead body after he was lynched by two white men in 1955—reduplicate the violence of racialized terror and death? Does it "merely" trade in the event it depicts? Is it indexical? Or does it promise a critique and open for us an aesthetic space of potential perlocutionary reparation and justice, or even just auspicious rage? Who can say, and with what authority? The same questions have emerged more recently over the presence—and fate—of Civil War and colonial statues. These debates permeate our cancel culture. In the classroom, a fearful silence settles in as some students are afraid to speak, terrified that they will offend, that they won't invoke the right language, that they'll be mocked or labeled or "canceled" by their classmates.

The turn to art—which itself is always multiply "framed"—invokes a sovereign power, a "one" (and oneness) who, we must imagine, is sanctioned to see and to speak from an authoritative frame of reference (unless of course we embrace a radical relativism). But this begs the question of identity and authority. The line between free speech and hate speech might once have been adjudicated in the courts (recall law's phantasmatic sovereignty) on the basis of First Amendment protections, as it was in 1999 with Chris Ofili's *Virgin Mary*, which was the subject of a racist censorship campaign and lawsuit led by New York City mayor Rudolph Giuliani (who lost his case, thankfully). But such outrage from the Right now seems so long ago, from another time altogether. By sharp contrast, less than two decades later the display of Schutz's *Open Casket* at the Whitney Biennial in 2017 was met with outrage this time from the Left—and with demands across social media to take down Schutz's work on the grounds that it appropriates and exploits marginalized people's suffering. Should some things remain unseen or ultimately unseeable, unspeakable? And for whom? Today, we are more likely to experience trial-by-media according to a certain digital populism, tweets in the court of public opinion. And more recently, Giuliani has been less likely to engage in court battles and more likely to take to social media to denounce Black Lives Matter as "racist" or speak on Fox News to defend Trump's egregious lies, collusion, and sociopathic behavior.[95] When questioned about the possibility of Trump's first impeachment, he declared, "The jury is the public."[96] This is, I suppose, a form of "direct" democracy. And to his credit, Giuliani has moved with the times; the political Right has to date proven nimbler than the Left.

"Older" conventional forms of racism and the Culture Wars of the 1980s and 1990s have yielded to a strange inversion of identity politics, thanks in large part to the internet and social media.[97] At this moment in history, then, perhaps we must problematize and unwork the a priori "condition[s] of validity for judgements," to invoke Foucault once again, and, rather than trade in categoricals, to focus instead on the "condition[s] of reality for statements."[98] Indeed, as we watch and rewatch Dunn's mediatized death, in the proliferation of competing accounts and commentaries absent of an authoritative frame, without definitive truth, it might be best to refuse the rush to scripted judgments and affectations, and to try to see and speak along other lines. In the classroom, I invoke the poetry of Claudia Rankine: "What if what I want from you is new, newly made / a new sentence in response to all my questions, / a swerve in our relation and the words that carry us, / the care that carries."[99] We must have these difficult conversations. It is not, then, a question of my power to address—or "reframe"—Dunn or the boys who recorded his death. In the end, this chapter is about their address to me, which calls for me to hold and to account for countless other scenes that variously summon—and indeed, frame—their addressability alongside my own. A new sentence, a swerve. It is death, not life, that hearkens me from this scene, in the care that carries so many deaths. There is, after all, no possible future, no "reframing," in which Dunn lives. This, too, must be held.

In the context of digital hate speech, the life that we are given to see is unseeable or is not a life or is not grievable; futurity is colonized, filled with terror, fearful silence. At the nexus of contesting media tropes, it will not suffice to say that the video recording uniquely "frames" the event of Dunn's death, nor am I in a position to "reframe" this or any other framing—not quite—for this would imply a kind of sovereign (re)interpretation, and my experience of watching devastates any sovereign sensibility I might have enjoyed. I cannot impose a regime of visibility or addressivity: the loss within the frame repeats in *après-coup* a history of unseeable and unsayable losses without, all returning me to myself and my nonsovereign complicity in their (re)production. In Derrida's terms, racism's last word inaugurates "a memory in advance,"[100] poisoning the promise of my perlocutionary reframing. Racism exploits this tense and this tension.

Can we imagine a future life in other than biopolitical counterfactuals? The temporal potency of the subversive perlocution, always yearning for a future or future anterior—a time when this or that word *will have been* injurious but is no longer—strikes me if not as messianic, then not least as an oblique disavowal of the past, a refusal to find ourselves in the wake, in historicity's hold, or perhaps even heralds a questionable reconciliation with it, a holding *of* it in what might well once again be a complicitous form. And it is this that haunts me. For lurking in that promissory subversion, the futures of the perlocution threaten to pervert this history and our ongoing relation with/in it, as it. Dunn's death is not quite a unique moment for us but turns on and re-turns to those of us who watch. The video is not cinema verité, is neither referential nor indexical, not exactly, but a communicative interaction in the recursive popular mode of reality TV, Facebook Live, Instagram, TikTok, and just as so many narcissistic and incendiary presidential tweets. We cower. We seethe. We participate. It is an address we have grown accustomed to.

In response to unjust and violent deaths—some labeled terrorism, others patriotic sacrifice—we are digitally inducted into the advance affectivity of a recursive self-address, a meme: "Je suis Charlie," "I am Trayvon," "I am Neda."[101] Here, now, the social choreographies of grief follow the circuits of social media with all the pageantry of the prêt-à-porter. "I am . . . ," I identify with the victims, I too am as it were victimized, and I temporarily occupy a position of universal victimhood. As Lauren Berlant writes, "Mourning can also be an act of aggression, of social deathmaking: it can perform the evacuation of significance from actually-existing subjects."[102] It is worth noting here that two-thirds of Americans get their news via social media[103]—Facebook, Snapchat, Twitter, et cetera—where news is recursively, algorithmically generated by "likes," subject to a populism that itself is difficult to dislodge from Google's and Facebook's news and "trending" algorithms, which not infrequently promote fake news and propagate alt-right messaging by those adept at reverse-engineering and exploiting the artificial intelligence of these algorithmic infrastructures. Across these scenes, Dunn's death has no address, and the scene's addressivity is co-opted and colonized as a memory in advance.

Indeed, biopolitically, death is always an address without address, a call without the possibility of response, one that arrives too late and has no ontological status— "I can't breathe"—because letting die is the condition of possibility for making live, perpetually reinaugurating and sustaining the biopolitical regime of addressivity, the "I," the "one," who speaks. And it is this "I" that I must, in disaffirming, betray. Even our mourning is suspect when it "takes place over a distance," in Berlant's terms, where distance and (re)mediation help to figure mourning as an act of aggression: "Mourning is an experience of irreducible boundlessness: I am here, I am living, he is dead, I am mourning. It is a beautiful, not sublime, experience of emancipation: mourning supplies the subject the definitional perfection of a being no longer in flux."[104] This is yet another sovereign conceit. But there must be another way to mourn from *within* the violent turmoil of flux, in the wake where shared painful feelings, rather than bolstering identity and self-certainty, would serve to disorient and discomfit, to open rather than to close off into circuits and slogans and disremembrance.

In the biopolitical context, is another address possible, another way of seeing and saying? To recall Hartman once again, who can "tell a story capable of engaging and countering the violence of abstraction"?[105] What language is to-hand? As Mbembe remarks of colonial violence, its "techniques were at once reticular and molecular. . . . This molecular violence even infiltrated language. Its weight crushed all the scenes of life, including the scene of speech."[106] Any perlocutionary "reframing" is liable to have been colonized in advance. I recall Holland's suggestion as well, "to place our stories next to those unknown to us."[107] And yet I'm always-already addressed by biopolitics, held in its deathly regime of addressivity, by which I will be known and have an ontological status, and by which Dunn will go under, in frame, again and again.

How could I address Dunn *otherwise* without first accounting for the ways that my own speech emerges on the same ontological scene as his, my own living with his dying? These frames may seem unrelated, even incommensurable, and yet they are profoundly co-constitutive—and it is this that I am given to hold. If biopolitics constitutes the very "I" I would disavow in these pages, I remain, unable to humanize Jamel Dunn or to claim him, posthumously, in the affirmative rhetorics of liberalism and human rights. But whether I speak or remain silent, his story nonetheless addresses my own addressability on the biopolitical scene, and it is he who claims me, in death, and quickens my sense of one coming undone.

# Refrain | And Who by His Own Hand?

And who by brave assent, who by accident,
Who in solitude, who in this mirror,
Who by his lady's command, who by his own hand,
Who in mortal chains, who in power,
And who shall I say is calling?
—Leonard Cohen

What absence—or whose—is addressed by Leonard Cohen's *who*, which is neither deictic nor quite interrogatory? In the stanza's last line, we might say that the address is apostrophic, hailing an unnamed and unknowable caller. Death. Cohen's song also speaks to those who, whether by accident or incident, have answered the call and who are no more. His words tremble and await an unspeakable absence. And in its oblique address to us, the grim living, it plays proleptically on our own future having-been, to which we too are destined—an absence we carry within us as the broken mirror of our survival and as the condition of any *who*, any call. A call is a call, an address, only because it might remain unanswered. To whom does this address belong; whose, the haunting apostrophization?

The trope of apostrophe, by convention, is either an address to another who is not or is no longer there, or an address to an anthropomorphized object, thing, or concept. Apostrophe should not be mistaken for prosopopoeia, which lays claim to and possesses on the basis of such absence—or more violently: through an elision, erasure, or annihilation that permits possession's conceits. The trope of prosopopoeia is a throwing-of-voice that Quintilian characterizes as "impersonation": "Nay, we are even allowed in this form of speech [prosopopoeia] to bring down the gods from heaven and raise the dead."[1] Prosopopoeia is, then, the projection of one's own voice attributed to someone or something as if it were speaking in its own name. But apostrophe is no such thing: it personifies without quite impersonating: it does not quite speak *for* or *as* the absent addressee who cannot reply in propria persona. Apostrophe addresses; it is neither projection nor possession. And its address is premised (however fictively) on dialogue, on call-and-response, where an anticipated answer, or at least its potentiality, subtends the call. We might say that the impossible possibility of the reply ontologically precedes the call, and calls-forth that call, hearkening in advance: the apostrophe is summoned (by the absent addressee), the apostrophe in turn summons, and we tarry in this space. The address is always in the eternal return of this refrain.

The difference that distinguishes apostrophe from prosopopoeia is paramount if we wish to understand the t(r)opologies of neoliberal biopolitics—and not least, if we seek possibilities for a critical response that might disaffirm biopolitics. For a disaffirmation must be something other than a mere negation spoken in the same rhetorical register. In many respects, then, the master trope of biopolitics is prosopopoeia, whether expressly in the service of making live or letting die. It is a voice that impatiently projects the response it wishes to hear. It impersonates, colonizes, owns. It refuses to wait; inattentive, it willfully mistakes the echo for origin.

In an essay that treats what she calls "prosopopoeic citizenship" in the case of Terri Schiavo, Megan Foley offers a fine reading of prosopopoeia. Schiavo, who for fifteen years had been in an irreversible persistent vegetative state, became for a short while the site of biopolitical vigils and vocalizations. Michael Schiavo, her husband and legal guardian, petitioned for Terri's withdrawal from life-support systems, saying that this would have been her wish. Terri's parents, however, disagreed with Michael and disputed Terri's medical diagnosis, petitioning for continued life-support. This bitter struggle resulted in no fewer than fourteen appeals in Florida courts, five suits in a federal district court, a judgment by the Supreme Court of Florida, federal legislation (S. 686, "For the Relief of the Parents of Theresa Marie Schiavo"), and four US Supreme Court denials of certiorari.[2] For those who sided with Terri's parents, she was figured as someone who "wanted" to live, and who expressed that apparent desire, evidenced largely through disquieting videos of her medical examinations. Schiavo could not speak. And so innumerable "experts" saw fit to speak for her: US legislators, pundits, bioethicists, doctors, lawyers, disability activists, and religious leaders, including Pope John Paul II.[3] Many others, meanwhile, held firm that Schiavo should be allowed to die and understood her as expressing *this* wish. Foley argues, "Prosopopeia [*sic*], the trope of giving voice to a voiceless body, rhetorically resecured the link between citizens' rights to life and liberty—that is, [this] voice rearticulated the biopolitical and sovereign status of democratic citizens."[4] For Foley, prosopopoeia in this case represents a sovereign projection on the part of American citizens, an attribution of *their* voices, ventriloquizing what they sought to hear *from* Schiavo.

I would like to expand on Foley's reading of prosopopoeia in this remarkable media spectacle—a scene I see less as the effect of Terri Schiavo's plight, and more as its rhetorical condition of possibility. We might say that those who spoke *for*—and indeed, *as*—Schiavo impersonated her by attributing to her their own particular understanding of life (and this was true of both the "make live" and "let die" camps). But the "democratic" and "sovereign" agency of these voices, their uses and usurpations, is not so clear, and has become muddier in years since, with the rise of nativist nationalisms, anti-vaxxer movements, and the "biological" racism of the alt-white/right. Across these discursive fields, we are not quite sovereign, and our voices are not quite ours to throw; indeed, our speech always-already betrays its (and our) situated "thrownness," to borrow a Heideggerian term. In Schiavo's case, and with the benefit of hindsight, today it is perhaps easier to conceive that these voices issued, rather, from the diffuse and anonymous turns of biopolitical tropes, which circulated with determined frenzy through public discourse, (social) media, law, and Congress itself. Schiavo was less the site of prosopopoeial projections than a prosopopoeial *echo* of competing cultural affirmations. That is, the projective voices of concerned citizens must themselves be understood as projections—vocal embodiments, conveyances—of the biopolitical discourses that animated them. There was a double displacement at work. Schiavo's "speech," her "will" to live or to die, belonged neither to her nor quite to those who projected them as coming from her: we, the living, become the vocative conduits of prosopopoeial production, speaking biopolitically *for* and *as* life itself.

Schiavo herself, meanwhile, was a biopolitical effect, the fetish object of contesting powers, and an easy one to claim—neither quite living nor dead. Vowing to uphold its sacred post-9/11 "culture of life," Congress was above all preoccupied with the punctilious project of making live,[5] even as these same elected representatives were content to do precious little—scarcely five months later—as Hurricane Katrina made landfall and claimed 1,833 lives.[6] The stark contrast between making live and letting die, between Terri and Katrina, is an object lesson in biopolitical logics, and in the moral calculus that determines whose lives must be saved at all costs and whose are disposable (i.e., poor lives, Black lives). This logic—the obscene congress and intertwined economies between making live and letting die—was lost on Schiavo's supporters no matter their prosopopoeial persuasion. I suspect, however, that this logic was not lost on Katrina's (and later, Maria's) victims and their kin.

In marked contradistinction to prosopopoeia, the trope of apostrophe, I'd like to argue, permits rhetorical insight into the biopolitical conjunctions between making live and letting die. Unlike prosopopoeia, discussed above, apostrophe *addresses* the dead—those biopolitics unceremoniously lets die—and it waits, but does not jealously guard or "raise the dead" to speak *for* or *as* them. Apostrophe assumes absence without quite standing in for it; it speaks only to find that the very conditions of that speech must attend the unrecognizable voices of the dead. Rather than speaking *for* or *as* (as in impersonation), it speaks *to*, conjuring a spectral presence in staged anticipation of a response, a conversation, and it does so abidingly (to invoke a Derridean term: *demeurant*, with its etymological echo, "undyingly"). As Jonathan Culler remarks, apostrophe is unlike other tropes: "It makes its point by troping not on the meaning of a word but on the circuit or situation of communication itself."[7] Calling attention to the rhetorical situation, apostrophe is concerned with the relation among the voices in play in making speech/acts. The speaker, the absent addressee, and the audience that "overhears" the address—much as we do in Cohen's song, a quasi-liturgical text[8]—are conjoined in the apostrophization.

Consider for a moment the biopolitical tropes secreted in the conjunction, "to make live *and* let die." I have suggested a kind of doubled prosopopoeia as the circuitous mechanism by which biopolitics makes live *or* lets die (disjunctively), while nevertheless securing—and indeed, relying on, cultivating—the disavowed conjunction between them, conveyed by that deceptively inconspicuous little *and*. Whose deaths are repudiated, unspoken and unspeakable, in the vocative project, the vocation, of making live? The elision of these deaths, and moreover, the elision of that elision—eliding dying's biopolitical conjunction with making live—occasions my rhetorical reflections on the critical force of apostrophe. The "turning away" (*apo-*) of this figure (*strophe*) carries within it a turning back, against, or down: catastrophe and going-under. And it is catastrophe that remains deflected and unvoiced in biopolitical tropes that privilege life itself. When, however, we apostrophize the biopolitical dead—summoning or convoking those we have let die—we attend (to) violent elisions in the name of life, in the name of an established order, and in our own names.

In apostrophe's speaking *to* and *calling*, the projective violence of prosopopoeia's speaking *for* or *as* is exposed, troping "on the circuit or situation of communication itself," as Culler phrases it. And as Catherine Malabou writes, "The Greek word *katastrophē* signifies first the *end* (the end of a life, or the dénouement of a dramatic plot and the end of the play), and second, a *reversal* or upset, the tragic and unforeseeable event that brings about the ruin of the established order."[9]

Speaking *for* or *as* merely registers an absence, constatively. And yet, the speaking *to* of apostrophe does not quite accomplish the inverse: it does not render the absent other present. As Derrida suggests, apostrophe "simultaneously puts him at a distance or retards his arrival, since it must always ask or presuppose the question 'are you there?'"[10] It waits, into the future to-come. And as Derrida says elsewhere, we are obliged *de laisser de l'avenir à l'avenir*—"to let the future have a future,"[11] or, "to leave some of the future to what is (still) to come, *à venir*" (my translation). We wait, abidingly, unless what is to-come is anxiously filled (as so often it is) by the biopolitical promises of making live, driven toward the counterfactual futures of technoscience, medicine, securitization, law. These futures are apparently namable, knowable, and for many, they are preferable tropes, propitious projections, possessions. Nobody likes to wait.

Given the surreal ambivalences of apostrophe, it is little wonder, then, that Culler characterizes apostrophe as an embarrassment: "Readers temper this embarrassment by treating apostrophe as a poetic convention and the calling of spirits as a relic of archaic beliefs." Making apostrophe "conventional" domesticates what is otherwise unwieldy, unworldly, and which threatens to upset an established order that convenes and conjoins. Apostrophe itself has been elided, Culler argues: "apostrophes are out of place in formal critical writing," "systematically repressed or excluded" as "that which critical discourse cannot comfortably assimilate." And isn't this its point, apostrophe's *punctum*, its punctuative power, for which it has been relegated to a "mere" poetic conceit? Culler continues: "What is really in question, however, is the power of poetry to make something happen."[12] He cites Auden's ironic quip that "poetry makes nothing happen," but immediately follows with Auden's claim about poetry, in contretemps, that "it survives, / A way of happening, a mouth."[13] It is this survival that seizes on the relation between a way of happening—an evental trope—and a mouth, speech. To recall Georges Bataille, "this living world will pullulate in my dead mouth."[14] Culler's gloss on Auden's lines is simple: "Apostrophe reflects this conjunction of mouth and happening."[15] Between the dissymmetry of the tropological powers that make live and let die—the power to speak and be spoken, to flourish and fade away—here, apostrophe opens onto a middle voice, neither quite a presence that speaks nor an absence that is spoken but an absence that haunts and inflects the scene of address, brings into relation one who speaks presently, one who is spoken absently, and those bystanders, perhaps us, who "overhear" the exchange only to be caught in its address ourselves.

However, when Culler asserts that poetic apostrophization amounts to the poet's own self-conceit, I must part company with him. Here, I believe he conflates apostrophe with prosopopoeia. Culler writes, "The vocative of apostrophe is a device the poetic voice uses to establish with an object a relationship which helps to constitute him." For Culler, apostrophe—ultimately "a device"—shores up the poet's own projective sovereignty over language: the voice calls in this way in order to "dramatize its calling, to summon images of its power so as to establish its identity as poetical and prophetic voice."[16] For this sovereign "device" to succeed, we must hear the prosopopoeial echo of the poet's voice but must imagine that it comes from elsewhere to address him (a classic example is Shelley's "Ode to the West Wind"). In contrast to Culler, I would suggest that the relationship that "constitutes" the speaker is the prior and abiding condition for his apostrophic address in the first place. In my understanding, then, the apostrophic call devastates any illusion of constitutive intent: the speaker is as it were deconstituted by apostrophe, unmanned, and agonizes in the *attente* knowing full well that any reply will be unspeakable. Indeed, its unspeakability demands our abidance, and apostrophe speaks abidingly but is never "used" or abided as mere instrumental device.

Here, Barbara Johnson's feminist reading of apostrophe is more faithful to the trope as I understand it, where the apostrophic address is an expression of "the desire for the *other's* voice: 'Tell me—*you* talk.'" In her reading of Baudelaire's poem "Moesta et Errabunda" (Latin for "Sad and Vagabond"), apostrophe becomes the poem's theme, Johnson argues, and not just its rhetorical device. Unlike Culler, Johnson grasps the trope's rhetoricity. The poem opens with an address to a certain Agatha, his absent lover (perhaps a prostitute), but ends with an address to "an abstract, lost state"—the lost liveliness, the time, of the poet's childhood, *un paradis parfumé.* "What the poem ends up wanting to know," Johnson writes, "is not how far away childhood is, but whether its own rhetorical strategies can be effective." Faced with the irrecuperable loss of childhood, mourning it, every self-conceit is undermined, every apostrophe a failed interpellation: the loss cannot be captured in the sovereign grammar of our logics. Such loss can only be addressed and enacted, as the poem does, performatively. It is the kind of question one might mournfully ask oneself—already anticipating the answer—toward the end of one's life. Life's term—whether a grammatical or a temporal consummation—is here interrupted poetically, punctuated by the lyrical de-termination of the foreboding address: "The final question becomes: can this gap be bridged? Can this loss be healed, through language alone?"[17]

Apostrophe, then, addresses an absent other, an addressee imbued with a power that, one imagines, exceeds the powers of both speaker and audience, transcending our usual spatiotemporal and logical coordinates. The apostrophization invokes that power, awaits a reply, and trembles, for this voice—should it reply—would be catastrophic. Indeed, the indeterminate wait itself suggests catastrophe, a rhetorical suspension of dialectical reason, the end of the world. Above, I contrasted apostrophe with prosopopoeia, arguing that prosopopoeia is less an address than a *projection* of voice: it speaks *for* or *as* the absent other, who is in a certain sense dispensed with, elided—one who is powerless to respond in one's *own* voice. It is the means by which we safeguard the dialectic, securing a certain epistemic closure rather than risking the ontological uncertainty of desire and indeterminate openness. And I argued that the life-itself that is conjured by biopolitics amounts to a prosopopoeial projection, a sham sovereignty, that would as it were secure the speculative futures of our livingness. Death, of course, is repudiated in this gesture, a sinister "silence behind speech" (to invoke Nietzsche), and so I wonder whether we might address *this* death apostrophically, and if so, how the attendant silence—the gap or refrain—might signify. What is the address of the dead? In her essay on apostrophe, Johnson's reading of Baudelaire's poem ends with "the fate of a lost child—the speaker's own former self—and the [rhetorical] possibility of a new birth or reanimation."[18] Johnson asks whether the poem's own rhetorical strategies can be effective to bridge this gap, and to bridge it through language alone. Before returning to this question—and indeed, before returning to this essay on apostrophe, which provocatively turns to the politics of abortion and the poetic apostrophizations of aborted children—I would like to stage a detour through another of Johnson's essays, one written some eight years later, and which offers a somewhat different perspective on, and a tentative reply to, apostrophe's "gap."

## Minding the Gap

In her essay "The Alchemy of Style and Law," Johnson opens with the story of Mary Joe Frug's last essay, "A Postmodern Feminist Legal Manifesto," published posthumously in the *Harvard Law Review*. Tragically, Frug was killed in the course of writing her essay, and Johnson was asked by the journal to write a commentary on Frug's unfinished work, which would be published by the journal as is. An essay that "concerns ways in which legal rules combine to maternalize, terrorize, and sexualize the female body so that heterosexual monogamy is a woman's safest life choice,"[19] Frug left the following sentence unfinished when she got up and went out for a walk and was murdered:

Women who might expect that sexual relationships with other women
could

In her commentary, Johnson refers to this incomplete sentence as "the lesbian
gap," asking "How does this gap signify?"[20] Faced with an absence of text, and
with the sudden and violent loss of Frug herself, Johnson does not claim that
these "gaps" can be bridged, the loss healed through language alone or by any
other means.

Not once in Johnson's essay does the word "apostrophe" appear, though there
can be little doubt that this essay is about the apostrophic address—Johnson's
address to the late Mary Joe Frug, Frug's posthumous address to Johnson and to
us, and the ways that the *Harvard Law Review* addresses both Johnson and Frug,
as well as its wider readership. The editors at the journal returned Johnson's
manuscript and amended her sentence to "What does this gap mean?" Johnson
protests: "This is not at all the same question. '*What* does this gap mean' implies
that it *has* a meaning, and all I have to do is to figure out what it is. '*How* does
the gap signify' raises the *question* of what it means to mean, raises meaning as a
question, implies that the gap *has to be read*, but that it can't be presumed to have
been intended." In her reply to the editors, Johnson refuses the erasure of her
address and its signification, but moreover, she refuses the erasure of Frug's
"lesbian gap," its reduction to some stable and namable "meaning." Nevertheless,
"In every successive revision that my text underwent, the *how* was changed to a
*what*." Stupidly, of course, the gap simply means that Frug was killed before she
finished writing her sentence. But *this* murder and the unbridgeable gap that it
represents is a question that remains open, figuring for us the ways that women's
bodies are terrorized and sexualized, in violence and unto death. Johnson wryly
concludes, "The ideology of law review style attempts to create a world saturated
with meaning, without gaps, and, indeed, doubtless without lesbians."[21]

Johnson's anecdote about the publication of Professor Frug's final essay punc-
tuates, as an open wound, the rest of her essay on legal rhetoric, which problema-
tizes the ways that the *Harvard Law Review*'s expected legal "style" would also
address Patricia J. Williams, by rejecting *her* style and *her* critical self-signification
as a Black feminist legal scholar. The journal was prepared to publish Frug's
unfinished essay—gaps and all—but not Williams's finished essay. Johnson
characterizes this differential decision as "an interactive editorial process through
which a living author participates in the progressive erasure of her own words
and a textual respect that can occur only if the author is dead." Not unlike the

tradition of idealizing dead women in Western (male) poetry, Johnson suggests, Frug's "lesbian gap" is a dead letter to be tolerated as long as Johnson "closes" that gap and lays it to rest in a neutral and impersonal commentary. And if Frug's death itself authorizes the posthumous appearance of this gap—albeit one that Johnson was expected to bridge—that erasure is fetishized and projected onto Williams with the demand for her to be logical, neutral, and impersonal, rather than lyrical and apostrophic. As Johnson writes, "Williams repeatedly documents the revisions, erasures, and displacements her writing undergoes in its encounters with the rules of legal style and citation." Law and legal scholarship—imagined as an "impersonal book," a book with *no* avowable style—would as it were disavow the gap between law and bodily life. It is for this reason that Johnson praises Williams's as "a breakthrough book for the possibilities of a fully conscious historical subject of discourse who does not coincide with—indeed, has been subtly or overtly excluded from—the position defined as neutral, objective, impersonal."[22] And as Williams herself says of her writing, "I am trying to create a genre of legal writing to fill the gaps of traditional legal scholarship."[23] Style is political; form is means.

Whether a procedural matter of legal "style," as the journal claimed, or a much more prickly matter of censorship, misogyny, and racism, Williams found her "active personal" voice had been edited into "the passive impersonal," and all mention of her Blackness—pivotal to her argument—had been removed in compliance with an editorial policy that bans mention, euphemistically, of "physiognomy." Williams writes, "What was most interesting to me in this experience was how the blind application of principles of neutrality, through the device of omission, acted either to make me look crazy or to make the reader participate in old habits of cultural bias," which is to say, the racializing habit of "fill[ing] in the gap by assumption, presumption, prejudgment, or prejudice." The editors simply tell her, "Any reader will know what you must have looked like."[24] The very personal style of Williams's prose poses a challenge for law and legal scholarship, or indeed, for the implicit *law* of legal scholarship that the *Harvard Law Review* sought to uphold as a matter of neutral form and high principle.

To offer one salient example of her style from *The Alchemy of Race and Rights*, Williams tells a "subway story" that she reports having told to her law students, who later complained to her dean that their professor was not teaching them law. It is a story about minding the gap, recounting her encounter with a dead home-less man on a New York subway platform:

His mouth hung open, and his eyes—his eyes were half closed, yet open.... They were the eyes, I thought, of a dead man. Then, I rationalized, no, he couldn't be.... I looked at the face of another man who had seen what I saw, both of us still walking, never stopping for a second. I tried to flash worry at him. But he was seeking reassurance, which he took from my face despite myself. I could see him rationalize his concern away, in the flicker of an eye. We walked behind each other upstairs and three blocks down Broadway before I lost him and the conspiracy of our solidarity. Thus the man on the subway bench died twice: in body and in the spirit I had murdered.

In her retelling, to her students and again in the pages of her book, and in the conspiracy of solidarity she invokes, with the silent unknown passerby, with her students, with her readers, and now, here, with me and mine, I'm uncertain whether this man did not die a third, a fourth, or innumerable deaths, or whether he is reanimated in the retelling, unable to rest in peace, and, in turning to us, suffers an uncanny rhetorical afterlife. I think it is probably all of these: "We, the passersby of the dispossessed, formed a society of sorts. We made, by our actions, a comfortable social compact whose bounds we did not transgress. We made a bargain of the man who lay dead. We looked at each other for confirmation that he was not dead; we, the grim living, determined to make profit of the dead."[25] And it is this determination, this profit, as comfortable social compact, that we, the grim living, enact and accept as a kind of universal law, perhaps even a moral one.

Williams stages a discomfiting relation between reader and text: How might we address the dead, the dispossessed, and how will their absence signify for us? Or, might we be forced to invert this question and concede that the dead, the dispossessed, also address us? "The echos [sic] of both dead and deadly others acquire an hallucinatory quality; their voices speak of an unwanted past, but also reflect images of the future. Today's world condemns those voices as superstitious, paranoid; neglected, they speak from the shadows of such inattention in garbles and growls, in the tongues of the damned and the insane." From those eyes, unseeing yet seen, or from those voices, unspeaking yet spoken, we find ourselves addressed. If the man is legally dead, this is not the end of his story. "Much of what is spoken in so-called objective, unmediated voices," Williams writes, "is in fact mired in hidden subjectivities and unexamined claims that make property of others beyond the self, all the while denying such connections."[26] But the legal tropes of property and possession, including law's investment in self-possessed individualism, become fragile in this moment: we are dispossessed by a dead homeless man (what legal claim could he possibly have?), himself multiply dispossessed, and the story does not and cannot belong *to* anyone because it exposes the deeply differential *conditions of* our possessive belonging, legal rights, and personhood.

In the opening pages of her book, in a section titled "Excluded Voices," Williams claims that she is "using an intentionally double-voiced and relational, rather than a traditional legal black-letter, vocabulary." She writes these lines, or more correctly, she speaks them—at Christmastime, as she sits at her parents' kitchen table and tells her sister what her book—the one I cite here—is about. We are invited into this familiar scene of belonging; we overhear their conversation. We glean something of her method, if that is what it is, or better, her approach to excluded voices—absences that she addresses in her book, refusing to "flatten and confine"[27] them in any traditional legal black-letter vocabulary. If her voice is doubled, it also doubles back again and again, constellating around innumerable absences—those of the lives (and deaths) she addresses in her text, but her own life, too, appears in a highly stylized way, and in a manner that is double-voiced, sometimes parodic, and refuses to be contained or totalized by loss.

To write is to reckon with one's own absence from one's text, a text destined for a reader who is not present in—or better, to—the writing of it. There is, then, the absence of Williams's reader, who will "overhear" her conversation with her sister (also absent to us), who will glimpse the scene of writing, but who does not constitute it and only arrives belatedly in the retelling that is reading, from the absented voice that addresses us across space and time. Tellingly, in this scene neither sister really hears the other ("My sister and I will probably argue about the hue of life's roads forever"),[28] and we wonder, as well, what we, her absent addressees, can truly hear in the hues of this exchange. We might venture the claim that all writing is apostrophic inasmuch as it addresses a host of innumerable absences, and awaits abidingly. In turning toward what writing writes *about*, writing cannot but turn away from the concrete lives of these things themselves in order to render them communicable, to sunder them from their own spacetime, to set them free in the text, and to destine them to future readers unknown and unknowable, who will nevertheless write and refer to this past in a present-historical tense: "Williams writes"—as if claiming a self-presence to a writerly past, unverifiable yet somehow continuous in the telling. And the writer's address, her apostrophizations, direct or indirect, explicit or implicit, conjure and risk such an addressee at the same time that they absent her, the writer, from a text whose transitivity she cannot control—and will not be present to—in that future from which she will be read. It might well be this risky refusal of epistemic clo- sure—indeed, this deeply differential *exposure*—that law and legal scholarship— ostensibly so "neutral," so "objective," so "universal"—finds so transgressive, a breach of law's social compact and (con)temporization.

In an effort to imagine absence *in* language itself, I return briefly to Johnson's earlier essay on apostrophe, titled "Apostrophe, Animation, and Abortion." This essay anticipates Johnson's subsequent reading of both Frug and Williams in their forcible—yet ostensibly "neutral," "objective"—erasure in the pages of the *Harvard Law Review*. But while this latter text concerns a troubling end-of-life (whether physically or rhetorically violent), and echoes the prosopopoeial contest over Schiavo's plight, we see in Johnson's earlier essay similar rhetorics playing out in the contest over when and how life naturally begins. ("Natural" beginnings and ends are discursively produced *as* natural by medico-legal discourses, as we see in the shifting markers of life's beginning—conception, viability, "born-alive"—and death—cardiac death, brain death, brainstem death.) Johnson therefore anticipates the recent spate of legal "personhood initiatives" and draco-nian legislation that restrict and regulate women's rights to pregnancy termination, and unsurprisingly, much of this legislation works to restrict the kind of speech that would permit one to formulate or to claim a right in the first place. These biopolitical proscriptions are also typically carried out in the name of life itself and they imagine themselves, rather prosaically, as giving "voice"—and hence political personhood—to what they refer to as "unborn" or "preborn" children who would (have) claim(ed) a right to life in their own name. These "unborn voices" are the prosopopoeial projections of law, rendered contemporaneous, just as they are in so much pro-life rhetoric, where they are deployed to well-known political ends, whether as a function of religious belief, political ideology, biology, citizenship, women's rights, men's rights, the rights of the unborn, and so on. Indeed, this is a battle over voice and persuasive possession.

And yet these dead children's voices also populate a genre of poetry written by women—mothers—who address, and who stage their own address *by*, the children they have aborted. Johnson distinguishes these voices not merely as projective occupations of a sovereign speaker (prosopopoeia), but as multilayered structures of apostrophic address. She cites, for example, Gwendolyn Brooks's poem "The Mother": "I have heard in the voices of the wind the voices of my dim killed children." Brooks's poem makes it well-nigh impossible to establish "a clear-cut distinction ... between subject and object, agent and victim." Earlier in the essay, while Johnson's treatment of Baudelaire's and Shelley's poems understood the apostrophic address as motivated by the (male) poet's loss of childhood against the horizon of his certain death to-come, here, by contrast, she argues that Brooks and others succeed in "rewriting the male lyric tradition, textually placing aborted children in the spot formerly occupied by all the dead, inanimate, or absent entities previously addressed by the lyric."[29] In another instance, Johnson cites the "refrain" from Anne Sexton's well known poem "The Abortion": "Somebody who should have been born / is gone." She reminds us that the archaic term for "refrain" is "burden," which is also "child in the womb." This refrain, which interrupts the poetic voice three times, "puts the first-person narrator's authority in question without necessarily constituting the voice of a separate entity." She then cites Sexton's final stanza: "Yes, woman, such logic will lead / to loss without death. Or say what you meant, / you coward ... this baby that I bleed." Johnson writes, "Self-accusing, self-interrupting, the narrating 'I' turns on herself (or is it someone else?) as 'you,' as 'woman.' The poem's speaker becomes as split as the two senses of the world 'bleed.' Once again, 'saying what one means' can only be done by ellipsis, violence, illogic, transgression, silence. The question of who is addressing whom is once again unresolved."[30]

If we take seriously the notion that the apostrophic address returns on us, in refrain, to address and apostrophize us, in turn, by echoing loss and betraying the terms of our speech—and if we hold open the possibility that the dead hold us in their own address—then we cannot in the end decide, nonviolently or with any certitude, on the "true" or "real" provenance of these voices. As with the inflections of the dead, the dying, and the dispossessed among this book's various case studies, we might ask, Are they my own willful projections, cases of straightforward prosopopoeia? Or are they apostrophizations that hold the power to turn back on me, from the dead themselves? Is one choice more logical than the other according to the apparently neutral and objective laws of reason, or according to liberal conventions of legal personhood and voice? Certainly. But it is precisely these conditions that I've sought to contest and that the poems that Johnson cites suspend. The self-conceit of prosopopoeial projection is that it slyly shores up the speaker's sovereign will, operating in a quasi-epistemic register. With prosopopoeia, the speaker presumably bestows personhood on, animates, and anthropomorphizes an inanimate object. (And as I've argued above, this is complicated by the fact that the prosopopoeia so often echoes the affirmations circulating in the wider biopolitical culture.) By contrast, apostrophe and its returns would shake the foundations of the speaker's agency, personhood, and self-sovereignty (as well as that wider biopolitical culture).

Hearing animate voices from inanimate objects may well resemble the calling of spirits and archaic beliefs (in Culler's words) or cross over into what others have called superstitious, paranoid, damned, and insane (in Williams's words). However, my suggestion here is that we must, for a moment, refuse to decide, and instead remain uncertain about the "true" provenance of voice or its knowability. This is apostrophe's rhetoricity. Unmooring us from our usual coordinates of liberal subjecthood, this would permit us to call into question *how* that voice signifies when it is severed—as it always is, to some extent—from an agentic, liberal subject imagined to possess her words and control their transitive uptake. We must reckon with absence, elision, and dispossession since we are incapable of rescuing these losses and bridging these gaps through language alone. Indeed, to write is to assume this absence, elision, and dispossession. As Johnson remarks, "It becomes impossible to tell whether language is what gives life or what kills."[31] These poems do not allow us to settle on the speaker's identity, whether as an "I" or a "you," and the provenance of the address, and its addressee, to whom the address is destined, become as ambivalent as the poems' understanding of life itself, which is never clearly defined because it is so tied to voice.

The sovereign grammar of liberal legal logic is unable to address such ambivalence, just as it fails to address rhetoricity, the ways that language acts within and from the historical, legal, and corporeal conditions of one's speech/acts. And it is only by plucking lines out of context that these poems could be deployed as "pro-life" arguments against abortion. (I hope as much for my own text here.) As Johnson makes clear, to see these poems "as making a simple case for the embryo's right to life is to assume that a woman who has chosen abortion does not have the right to mourn. It is to assume that no case *for* abortion can take the woman's feelings of guilt and loss into consideration, that to take those feelings into account is to deny the right to choose the act that produced them." So often, assumptions, presumptions, prejudgments, or prejudices race in with their certain violence to fill epistemic gaps. Johnson cites Carol Gilligan's book *In a Different Voice* (1982, published in the same year as Williams's *Alchemy*), which was an important early text in the feminist ethics of care movement. In relation to moral capacities, Gilligan's empirical psychological research demonstrated that men tend to respond to a more abstract ethic of individual rights and obligations underwritten by duty and justice, whereas women tend to privilege an ethic of care revolving around empathy, relationship, and responsibility—and thus women speak "in a different voice." Or, in Johnson's gloss, "Female logic, as [Gilligan] defines it, is a way of rethinking the logic of choice in a situation in which none of the choices are good." Gilligan's book focuses on a woman's decision to have, or not to have, an abortion. Johnson cites Gilligan: "Believe that even in my deliberateness I was not deliberate," adding, "Believe that the agent is not entirely autonomous, believe that I can be subject and object of violence at the same time, believe that I have not chosen the conditions under which I must choose."[32]

We are summoned to believe the (legal, medical, moral) conditions of nonchoice, which in Frug's words maternalize, terrorize, and sexualize a woman's body "through rules such as abortion restriction that compel women to become mothers and by domestic relations rules that favor mothers over fathers as parents."[33] And so, there is an essential ambivalence in her "choosing," which does not redound on a liberal political subject who merely exercises the freedom of "choice"—and this is so even as we must fight for a politics that would safeguard such freedoms. Politics is not ontology, even as biopolitics collapses this distinction and operates as a naturalized, biologized onto-logic.

In this context, the unfree conditions of "freely" choosing preclude a nonviolent resolution, and, as these poems attest, a subject can be the site of two contrapuntal affects at the same time, an opposition that is figured here rhetorically in the ambivalence of the apostrophic address. To invoke Williams's words, such speech is "double-voiced and relational." And while I would not wish to imply that Williams's experiences are commensurable with the various experiences of women who write about their aborted children, I believe they share a common understanding of language, of figurative speech, and of impossible "choice." The speaker is the site of competing—but not necessarily mutually exclusive—affects in which she understands that she is not autonomous, but interdependent with others both living and dead. When she speaks, it is within and from the complex structures of historical, legal, and corporeal address. There is no willful or definitive dissociation from this intersubjective situatedness; indeed, there can be no ethics of care without it.

In Williams's writing, too, it is practically a refrain, and a burden, that her subjectivity is doubled. At one point she describes herself as "a crazy island, a suspicious hooded secret," writing "I edit myself as I sit before the television. I hold myself tightly and never spill into the world that hates brown spills. I'm afraid that everything I am will pour out onto the ground and be absorbed without a word. I may disappear. So I hold onto myself because I still have much left to say."[34] Johnson glosses a letter of rejection addressed to Williams from yet another journal's editorial board that takes issue with Williams's style: "The editors expect certain things that are highly revealing: that calm is the opposite of engagement, that to be convincing about anxiety one must demonstrate a loss of control. What seems to bother the editors is the *combination* of control and panic. They almost *want* the panic. . . . What is unfamiliar is a black woman writing calmly about panic, situating her own discourse as intelligent, fashionable, feminist, and post-modern—having the kind of self-consciousness about style and reception, about genre and metadiscourse, that instates a *complex* narrative voice as something other than a symptom."[35] This, too, is writing "in a different voice," one that understands what it means to be both subject and object of violence, one that addresses the conditions under which any address might be heard, and one that performs these ambivalences in an address to absent readers. And yes, many of these readers may well repudiate their own interpolation onto this scene, demanding instead the pale paternalistic prose of neutral description or prosopopoeic projection, a writing in which the "marks" of race and gender have decisively been effaced, unaddressed— or, at long last, a writing without voice: no writing at all: dead silence.

## Use

Rather late in this project, I was somewhat taken aback when a colleague of mine casually remarked that, given my case studies, this is a book about suicide. But no, I countered: the individual intentionality and "sovereign" voluntarism of the suicide had struck me all along as problematic. Can one not be suicided by society? Biopolitical deaths are not sovereign acts of choosing, even when they are com-mitted by one's own hand. And if we tend to think of suicides as preventable, untimely, unnatural, or tragic, these words struck me as neoliberalizing, even banal. Why, I wondered, do we so rarely speak of preventable, untimely, unnatural, or tragic *life*—or, if we do, it is when those lives have already been given over, anointed, unto death, dying, dispossession? By what ruse should modern life appear for us stripped of death and death's mantle? If we cling to life because it is inherently sweet, as Aristotle once remarked, it is also at times no less stupid, malcontent, insomniac: a pitiless and relentless is-ness conveyed so hauntingly by Emmanuel Levinas's *il y a*—"there is"—in its anonymous, thrumming existence, its inertia and perdurance, within me, in spite of me.

By what ruse, then, does this "is" become an ought, a moral injunction that demands life's timeliness, naturalness, freely willed and chosen in the chirpy affirmations by which I "choose life"? If this moral order and its neoliberal value chains—also unchosen—prove a burden for some, an unanswerable demand, or even unlivable, why can this malcontent only be registered in a pathologizing discourse that deems it depressive or suicidal, symptomatic? I had hoped to disrupt these logics, and admit that I even found some nonmorbid hope, what Jill Casid calls a "melancholy joy,"[36] in these morbid places. Death speaks to life and livingness, it disrupts the temporality of timeliness and the moral injunctions to make live secreted in the promised futures of biopolitical life—futures that, for some, are surely a "cruel optimism," as Lauren Berlant phrases it.[37] Life is never necessary, timely, natural, and I can't quite conceive of the "right" to life in the sanctimonious terms gifted by liberal human rights discourse. Indeed, the impossibility of living is always the possibility of dying, where death is destined in life until that moment it outlives us in and for those others we leave behind to live out their own (un)timeliness in time.[38]

In his discussion on suicide, Maurice Blanchot describes a "strange project" that would believe in a double death: "There is one death which circulates in the language of possibility, of liberty, which has for its furthest horizon the freedom to die and the capacity to take mortal risks; and there is its double, which is ungraspable. It is what I cannot grasp, what is not linked to *me* by any relation of any sort. It is that which never comes and toward which I do not direct myself." Within this curious doubling of death, Blanchot situates suicide as follows: "To kill oneself is to mistake one death for the other; it is a sort of bizarre play on words. I go to meet the death which is in the world, at my disposal, and I think that thereby I can reach the other death, over which I have no power. . . . Suicide in this respect does not welcome death; rather, it wishes to eliminate death as future, to relieve death of that portion of the yet-to-come which is, so to speak, its essence, and to make it superficial, without substance and without danger."[39] I'd be hard pressed to find better words to describe the "suicidal" remit of biopolitics, its "bizarre play on words," its rhetorical "power" to defer and differ death, to "eliminate" death's futurity and its essential temporization, its substance, its mystery, and its danger. Despite its pious affirmations of life itself, biopolitics lets die in the name of a promised future that disavows the essence of a death ungraspable, over which we hold no power. What is more, biopolitics not only disavows those it lets die, but also the livingness of those it makes live, for these living lives have in a sense been robbed of death's orienting horizons. Biopolitical life is not oriented by—and does not derive its meaning in relation to—death, but is a life occupied in fleeing death. Here, then, to invert Blanchot's remarks, we might say that for biopolitics there is a strange *doubling of life*—one life that circulates in the language of possibility, of liberty, and so forth, and there is its double, whose truth in death is ungraspable. Stated simply, biopolitics would have us mistake one life for the other. And yet: "Death must exist for me," Blanchot will reply, "not only at the very last moment, but as soon as I begin to live and in life's intimacy and profundity. Death would thus be part of existence, it would draw life from mine, deep within."[40]

Two deaths, but just one; two lives, but just one life to live. There is, then, a strange doubling of the subject, and a gap between its (my?) uses of "I," which may or may not bleed into a "you," living or dead. I am "double-voiced and relational," to recall Williams, or in Johnson's terms, "I have not chosen the conditions under which I must choose." A mortal body that speaks, both apostrophizing and catastrophizing, "I can be subject and object of violence at the same time." Who addresses whom? "I address myself to you," Derrida writes, "somewhat as if I were sending myself, never certain of seeing it come back, that which is destined for me."[41] Rhetorically, then, there is also a strange doubling of my (own?) uses of voice in these pages: in my textual address to the dead, dying, and dispossessed—but no less to my presently absent yet living reader—across this book's case studies; in my "use" of these precious perilous bodies in sickness and suicide; in hunger, subjects of medico-legal power, of time and race and technology; and not least, in my "use" of theory, which (I hope) permits a critical reflection on the uses of "use." My "uses" are abuses notwithstanding my intent. A priori, one can never negate a prior violence. The language I use in my address itself emerges from a host of prior addresses—some violent, some beneficent—that have constituted me as an addressee occupying a certain recognizable place, alongside you in yours. My use of this language betrays my ability to use it effectively, and use (*chresis*) crosses into catachresis because I must abuse language, in address, and in a manner that *disaffirms* without inadvertently reaffirming the recognizable terms or places that you or I might seek distance from. As Andrzej Warminski remarks, catachresis is not mere negation: "The abuse of trope by catachresis is not a negation—it is an (improper) abuse symmetrical to (proper) use—but just its wearing away, wandering, *erring*: a permanent exile of sense from which there is no return to the transfers of sense in metaphor, metonymy, synecdoche, and the like."[42]

But what "symmetrical" account of one's "proper" positionality could ever permit one to address the dead, the dying, the dispossessed who themselves are the incalculable cost of one's very livingness and speech? The question itself is obscene. If "I" am not "one," I'm still one who speaks, irrecusable. Any "accounting" for the self is impossible, perennially inadequate, and perhaps only shores up the agency of a liberal subject entrusted to "balance the books," so to speak. The entire lexicon of Western liberal subjecthood—a legacy complicit with colonization, dispossession, death—needs to be reimagined away from sovereign subjecthood and grammars. If Wittgenstein is correct, and there are "countless" *uses* of language,[43] then there must be a way to say that we are unable to continue to abide these conditions, and for a speech and a politics that would strive to be emancipatory without being self-servingly exculpatory. This cannot be the solitary task of an individual but is nonetheless cultivated there when I meditate on my speech and identity coming undone, on my own conditions of subjecthood undermined in the face of so much death and devastation—real losses that must be "counted," certainly, but that cannot be reckoned by any final statement of account. This doubled subject, "I," the one who writes and addresses you, here, also cannot be flattened or confined by an identity that is never freely chosen. This is its rhetoricity. Even so, such unfreedoms don't absolve me from a responsibility for the benefits that have long accrued at the site of my contested or repudiated belonging. This is an ethical double-bind, the space from which one writes and risks exposure, neither to reclaim nor to repudiate but to reckon *with* without refuge.

To disaffirm biopolitics, then, we must neither concede nor mimic its terms in our effort to negate them. I have asked us to consider how our lives might be punctuated differently (from *punctum*: to aggrieve, interrupt, mortify, vex, prick), or held in refrain (as a burden), if the tropic force of apostrophe belonged also to the biopolitical dead—to those we have let die but who nonetheless summon us, apostrophizing us in turn, rendering us ghostly to ourselves. Insofar as this book addresses those who have been absented, elided, or erased, I have hoped neither to speak *for* nor *as* the dead, nor to speak *of* them as "mere" conjurations. My claim is that they have something to say to us, the grim living, their addressees. The voices of those who are absented and elided—and whose absence and elision are the social compact and bargain of biopolitics—dispossess me of my vital self-presence and possessive individualism. In this moment I may come to *recognize* myself as doubled, and my self-relation becomes a burdensome refrain. Apostrophe is not mimetic: the trope of apparent possession holds the power to dispossess the speaker, who is prepossessed by his possessions, and who is in speaking spoken. To use the trope is, then, at times, to be disabused of it; use yields to abuse, *chresis* to catachresis, and vocative agency or antistrophe yields to catastrophe, as the trope returns in refrain to dispossess us of ourselves and carry us under. Abandoned by our words, introjected, this would suggest a different ethical relationship than we tend to find in contemporary ethics scholarship, which presumes (or would shore up) self-identity and epistemic consent through an instrumentalizing use of self and voice. In response, how might we imagine a situational ethics for those situations that cannot quite be segregated or submitted to the binding closures of epistemic judgments?

To be the ethical subject of one's speech/acts calls for a particular relation to oneself, which Foucault examined in his late work on the ancient Greek *epimeleia heautou*, the "care of the self." Care in this context represents an ethical relation that bears on one's *ēthos* or "character"—"individuals' ways of doing things, being, and conducting themselves"[44]—distinct from one's *ethos* or "habit(s)." This is not an epistemic or propositional relation and bears little resemblance to the modern tradition of Cartesian self-doubt. Reading Plato's *Alcibiades I*, Foucault points to the Socratic conception of *epimeleia heautou* as the care of one's soul, rather than the care we might take of our worldly possessions, reputation, and so forth. Care of the soul is figured in the Socratic dialogues as a relation of *chresis* or "use"—what we do with the soul, how we "use" it. Foucault explains:

> So you see when Plato (or Socrates) employs this notion of *khrēsthai* / *khrēsis* in order to identify what this *heauton* [self] is (and what is subject to it) in the expression "taking care of oneself," in actual fact he does not want to designate an instrumental relationship of the soul to the rest of the world or to the body, but rather the subject's singular, transcendent position, as it were, with regard to what surrounds him, to the objects available to him, but also to other people with whom he has a relationship, to his body itself, and finally to himself.[45]

I'm doubled in this moment, where my "use" of the ethical self-relation is most emphatically noninstrumental. *Chresis* is not a relation of rational knowledge, nor is it simply the "use" of a tool or device. Foucault insists on a more polyvalent reading of *chresis*: an orienting attitude, a conduct, disposition, or comportment. This is not, then, the free agency of an autonomous liberal subject. Foucault's classical examples, drawn from Plato, take the "use" of the passions and of anger (*epithumiais khrēsthai* and *orge khrēsthai*). We do not "use" our passions for something, we do not "use" our anger; rather, we "give way" to them, somewhere between mastering and submitting to them, as the occasion and context demand. So, too, with the *chresis aphrodision*, the "use" of one's pleasures. So, too, when we "use" the gods: when we petition for some favor or blessing, we do so by knowing how to be a proper supplicant, knowing how to ask, what to ask, and when. And so, too, again, when we "use" a horse: good horsemanship requires that we listen, in a mutual relation with the horse. You cannot just do with it as you will. As Ludwig Wittgenstein has remarked (employing a fine catachresis followed by a simile), "I sit astride life like a bad rider on a horse. I only owe it to the horse's good nature that I am not thrown off at this very moment."[46]

For a long while I have conceived of the ethical self-relation in Foucault's late work as *rhetorical*, making "use" of apostrophic self-address, implicating us in a language game that is not purely mimetic, that does not obey a black-letter vocabulary, but that is tropological, lyrical and not purely logical.[47] A perennial question for itself, the doubled subject (re)mediated here offers insight into my rhetorical "use" of the dead—those I address in this book as they address me. Only months before his own death, and in failing health, Foucault devoted his last lectures at the Collège de France to reflecting on the "uses" of death: "Meditating death is placing yourself, in thought, in the situation of someone who is in the process of dying, or who is about to die, or who is living his last days. The meditation is not therefore a game the subject plays with his own thought. . . . A completely different kind of game is involved . . . a game that thought performs on the subject himself."[48] Foucault turned to the fabled death of Socrates before concluding his lectures with a hurried treatment of Cynic philosophy and the "true life" ("I am not able at present to lecture to you properly on this theme of the true life; maybe it will happen one day, maybe never").[49] Meditating death, Foucault offers an extended analysis of Socrates's last words. Famously, Socrates says, "Crito, we owe a cock to Asclepius. Pay my debt, don't forget."[50] Why, with death imminent, does Socrates demand a sacrificial offering to Asclepius, the god of healing? Foucault is unsatisfied with conventional interpretations that propose death as the instrumental "remedy" for the ills of life, arguing that in this way death could not be experienced *as* death. Expanding on Georges Dumézil's work, Foucault claims instead that Socrates and his disciples have been "cured" of the false opinions that make the soul sick and the self unable to care for itself—and it is for this reason that Asclepius must be honored. We see the debt as communal when Socrates speaks to Crito, saying "*We* owe. . . ." Foucault continues: "It is a feature which marks the dramatic art of all the Platonic dialogues that, whatever their subject, everyone ends up jointly committed to the undertaking of discussion."[51] Because Plato's texts are dialogues, they are not just pragmatic demonstrations of truth, but are performative, rhetorically recruiting the reader

in a joint undertaking, which they do here, iteratively, in Foucault's own deployment of them for us, and mine for you.

Foucault concludes his lecture on the death of Socrates with an uncanny
dramaturgical prefiguration of his own death: "As a philosophy professor one
really must have lectured on Socrates and the death of Socrates at least once in
one's life. It's done. *Salvate animam meam.*"[52] These words are not unironic, invoking the ritualized Latin words of the Christian confessional, *Dixit et salvavi
animam meam*, but here beseeching salvation from his audience instead. Foucault
says *salvate* (the second-person plural imperative—a direct address) and omits
*dixit*, which would refer to the illocutionary power of one's own speech in the
rites of confession and redemption. It is as if Foucault wishes to distance himself
from his own words. If the words are in part playful, they nevertheless tell us
that Foucault has fulfilled a serious duty, and they tacitly acknowledge that
duty, that debt, as part of a joint undertaking with his audience. It is worth
recalling that Foucault had opened his lectures by sharply distinguishing
Socratic truth-telling from the speech of the professor, whom he had characterized as a mere "technician": "Everyone knows," he quipped, "and I know first of
all, that you do not need courage to teach."[53] The irony is classically Socratic: it
hides a truth. It is not just speech that takes courage, but care, too, unto death.
"It is the mission concerning the care of oneself that leads Socrates to his death."[54]
And while we might say that the story of Socrates's death inaugurated Western
philosophy, it continues to animate philosophy across its iterations, including
Foucault's, in his last days—and in lectures he delivers despite being "ill, really
ill,"[55] "despite being in bad shape."[56]

Is it not true that death always takes the eternal form of a living question that
becomes our own, bringing us each into relation with ourselves? Death is not
merely what lies ahead, as I inch closer: it is our history, an "unwanted past"
(Williams), unvanquished and spoken in refrain. How, then, could we not yearn
for another history, one we could embrace with less suffering, sorrow, and ambivalence, to find ourselves in a different address? From this other timeline, we might
have awoken without that weight that presses in from all sides, without unanswerable demands that we atone, in their liturgical cadences, their wretched and
relentless newsfeeds, that set the rhythms of our living and dying breaths, keeping
time. From such a phantasmatic past, our hate-filled history would at last be
undone, our lost childhood restored, *un paradis parfumé.*

Foucault's last lectures mine Cynic philosophy as a sort of parallel history to
Western philosophy, the road not quite taken. It promises no redemption, no

erasure of an unwanted past, no paradise, but it may help us to imagine another future. Cynic philosophy has less to do with conventional philosophemes or doctrinal schemas, less to do with dogmatic teaching or some epistemic "content." Rather, Cynicism is about rhetorical form, the modality or manner by which I stylize my life and come to question it critically: "So it is neither the chain of rationality, as in technical teaching, nor the soul's ontological mode of being, but the style of life, the way of living, the very form that one gives to life." In reality, however, the "optics" of the Cynic are hardly noble: "The man in the short cloak, with the long beard, bare and dirty feet, begging pouch, and staff, who is found on the street corner, in the public square, and at the temple door questioning people and telling them some home truths."[57] The trope of animality and of the "dog" (the *bios kunikos*) characterizes the Cynic, who, like the dog, is "shameless" and "indifferent." Today, the Cynic might resemble Williams's dead man on the subway platform, someone homeless, poor, or otherwise dispossessed, whose presence alone contravenes social norms, customs, and values. Foucault returns here to Plato to provide a brief genealogy of these two divergent strands in the history of Western philosophy: one became hegemonic, the other we might call a cynical subjugated knowledge.

The first is familiar. The key philosophical text here is Plato's *Alcibiades*, a dialogue in which the Delphic axiom, "know thyself," Foucault renders as the ethical care of the self, a self-relation (*auto to auto*) that is characterized as a relation of *chresis*, as I discussed above. Significantly, in the *Alcibiades* this self-relation focuses on the soul (*psyche*), which will come to figure for us as a psychologized— and ultimately Cartesian and epistemological—relation of rational self-knowledge in opposition to the body (*soma*). Across Christian history, this psycho-somatic dualism became hegemonic and the *Alcibiades* would prove a foundational text in the history of that long psychodrama we call Western philosophy, Enlightenment, and liberal self-consciousness. In contradistinction, Foucault identifies a second strand of Western philosophy in another of Plato's dialogues, the *Laches*. This is the road not quite taken. And in the history of thought it is an early moment of what would later—and for a short time—become Cynic philosophy. In the *Laches*, the self's relation to itself is once again characterized as *chresis*, but ethical self-reflexivity redounds not on the care of the soul (*psyche*), as in the *Alcibiades*, but on the care of life (*bios*). Cynic philosophy would radicalize this understanding of the *bios* as "a test of life, a test of existence, and the elaboration of a particular kind of form and modality of life." In the Cynical life, "one risks one's life, not just by telling the truth, and in order to tell it, but by the very way in which one lives. In all the meanings of the word, one 'exposes' one's life." Here, remarkably, no division between *psyche* and *soma* can be presumed. Foucault refers to this ontology of the self as a *"tropos* of life,"[58] which in my reading is a distinctly rhetorical life, a performative speech/act whose remains, in refrain, are perhaps even non-instrumentalizable. The Cynics were part of this tradition, and as we know, they would not write our particular history; however, they would somehow persist, subjugated but not quite extinguished, as the repudiated counterpart to Western reason.

## Last Words

"I can't breathe." A grisly perseveration, and in recent years the last words of no fewer than seventy Black lives murdered by American law enforcement officers.[59] The trope of stolen breaths, stolen voices, stolen lives in the name of life itself. I write these final pages in the wake of yet another brutal slaying of an unarmed Black person at the hands of the police. The familiar, ritualized murder—a lynching, if we attend to the dictionary definition—of George Floyd by a small mob of Minneapolis police officers on May 25, 2020, sparked unprecedented worldwide protests decrying (once again) systemic racism, police brutality, state violence, and authoritarianism. In the early days of the still ongoing protests, the presence of George Floyd, and details of his public execution, were acutely felt: he was addressed, remembered, mourned—a name and an image depicted on murals, on T-shirts, on placards, and across countless online platforms—a name and a death that invokes innumerable names, innumerable deaths—a name that embodies sorrow and rage, the unending legacy of racial injustice and racialized violence unto death.

A name spoken, in refrain, and a history of incalculable loss, repeated by millions who never knew this man but who would take to the streets in protest. And at no small risk to their own lives: many were met with repressive violence—police and military (if these are still distinct), as well as armed far-right extremists and white supremacists (some goaded by vile presidential tweets)—a brazen and lawless violence not dissimilar to that which motivated their protests, justifying them once again, in refrain.[60] The horrors of violence (once again) filled our screens, while some protestors were subject to this violence firsthand. In the midst of the worsening COVID-19 pandemic, in many jurisdictions citizens defied shelter-in-place orders and laws against public assembly, some wearing masks but nonetheless putting themselves at heightened risk of exposure to an incurable, and potentially fatal, disease. This exposure mirrors, in some respects, the exposure of Black lives to state-sanctioned quotidian violence, but also the differential and racialized exposure to the effects of COVID-19 and its financial fallout, which we know to disproportionately affect Black, Indigenous, and People of Color[61] as the very compact, the bargain, the profit of biopolitics—a dispossession destined for those (once again, still) for whom there has never been a palliative.

I would like briefly to consider the protests—ongoing, and in places like Portland, escalating at the time of writing—as a form of *parrhesia* or "truth-telling," which in the ancient Greek tradition always involves a risk and a certain courage to speak. In Foucault's terms, "When you accept the parrhesiastic game in which your own life is exposed, you are taking up a specific relationship to yourself: you risk death to tell the truth instead of reposing in the security of a life where the truth goes unspoken."[62] Specifically, I would like to venture a reading of the current moment in the context of Cynic philosophy—and ultimately, revolutionary militancy—for the Cynics, much like the protestors, depart from the Socratic tradition of parrhesiastic truth-telling, which remains discursive, typically characterized as a *verbal* address to an individual who holds disproportionate power over the speaker. While the Socratic parrhesiast verbally calls into question the *ēthos* of his or her particular interlocutor(s), the Cynical parrhesiast nonverbally calls into question the *ēthos* of the established social order: "The Cynic battle is an explicit, intentional, and constant aggression directed at humanity in general, at humanity in its real life, and whose horizon or objective is to change its moral attitude (its *ēthos*) but, at the same time and thereby, its customs, conventions, and ways of living."[63] If the life of Socrates is figured in philosophy as the "touchstone" (*basanos*) of his truth-telling, his life itself is often figured as little more than a supplement to or guarantee of the *logos* in his speech—a verbal *parrhesia*. For the Cynics, by contrast, truth emerges in and as a life lived, and truth is incarnated in and as a style of life. The shift from the *logos* of Socratic *parrhesia* to a kind of parrhesiastic expression in and as the *bios* marks a distinct shift from *dire-vrai* to *vivre-vrai*: from truth-telling to "the true life, life in the truth, life for the truth."[64] This slide from speech to an aesthetics of existence—from speech to a life lived—is not anti-rhetorical despite the shift from *logos* to *bios*; it suggests, rather, an understanding of rhetoric not as epistemic but as ontological, for the risk of parrhesiastic truth-telling always begins (and sometimes sadly ends) in the fatal exposure of one's life as the ontological condition of telling or living the truth. In Foucault's terms, Cynicism "makes the form of existence a way of making truth itself visible in one's acts, one's body, the way one dresses, and in the way one conducts oneself and lives. In short, Cynicism makes of life, of existence, of the *bios*, what could be called an alethurgy, a manifestation of truth."[65]

These insights are not merely the heady insights of high theory resurrected from ancient philosophies. LeBron James, of the Los Angeles Lakers, had the following to say on racism and Black Lives Matter in the context of the ongoing protests: "Unless you're a person of color, you guys don't understand. I understand you might feel for us. But you will never truly understand what it is to be Black in America. . . . A lot of people use this analogy that Black Lives Matter is a movement. It's not a movement. When you're Black, it's not a movement. It's a lifestyle. . . . This is a walk of life. . . . I don't like the word 'movement' because unfortunately in America and in society there ain't been no damn movement for us." Reflecting on the political changes in the United States since Barack Obama's presidency, he added, "You know what's going on now. Is that progress? I think we can all say that's not progress."[66] In listening to this interview—and James's views on "movement" and "progress"—I was reminded of "Ideology and Terror," the final chapter of Hannah Arendt's *Origins of Totalitarianism*. Pulling Arendt's text from my shelf, I found the parallels oddly compelling. Arendt opens this chapter with a critique of modern philosophies of "progress" and development, represented by Hegel, Darwin, and Marx. "The 'natural' law of the survival of the fittest," she writes, "is just as much a historical law and could be used as such by racism as Marx's law of the survival of the most progressive class."[67] Arendt describes these world-historical views on progressive modernity and linear self-actualization as a metaphysics of "movement"—an ideology that drives social, political, economic, and even existential understandings of "progress," which form the ideological kernel of totalitarian forms of government. Totalitarianism, too, Arendt notes, relies on myths of a metaphysics of progress, of divine right, or manifest destiny. In these terms, totalitarianism shares a great deal with biopolitics and its ideological investment in progressive livingness.

This ideology is the hallmark of the "suicidal state" (as I argued in chapter 1), which in Arendt's words is "quite prepared to sacrifice everyone's vital immediate interests to the execution of what it assumes to be the law of History or the law of Nature." What is distinct about ideological "movement," Arendt argues, is that its logic is self-generating and hermetically sealed, rhetorically propagated by what I'd call a tropological regime. Totalitarian forms of government are characterized, she claims, by their investment not in being but in tropes of becoming, by their "emancipation" from empirical reality and their tendency to conspiracy and orders of secret knowledge, and finally, by basing their logical system on an axiomatically accepted "idea" from which all "facts" must follow. By way of example, she writes, "The word 'race' in racism . . . is the 'idea' by which the movement of history is explained as one consistent process." The "inhabitants" of totalitarian regimes are thus figured—and come to figure themselves—as (increasingly aggressive) agents of progressive order and destiny, each there "for the sake of accelerating its movement"; consequently, they are therefore neither guilty nor innocent, as such, because "they can only be executioners or victims of its [movement's] inherent law."⁶⁸ I found these passages chillingly contemporary, notwithstanding some of Arendt's other more problematic discussions on race and public protest.

Arendt's analysis, which I invoke all too briefly here, maps provocatively onto the teleological force of neoliberal biopolitics, as I've been describing it, with its affirmative and nominally democratic investment in the counterfactual futures of technoscience, medicine, "LAW AND ORDER" (to cite a repeated Trumpism), and "life itself." And as LeBron James suggests, "progress" and "movement" are rigged: there has been no "movement" for Black folk; instead, he asks us to imagine a "walk of life" or a "lifestyle" that does not quite cede to the world-historical terms of "progress"—or, in other words, he asks us to imagine a style of life that would disaffirm the usual tropes of biopolitical subjecthood and its ideological affirmations. Such a (non)movement—a "walk of life," a "lifestyle"—might be (non)volitional; it might emerge collectively, rather than from a self-actualizing liberal political subject. Or, as I have argued throughout, it might gather around the impossible possibility of death, rather than life itself—a thanatopolitics rather than a biopolitics (and it was in this spirit that James then returned to the fatal shooting of Breonna Taylor, yet another victim of police violence, in a demand for justice). This (non)movement would run counter to the productive and appropriative logics of neoliberal and biopolitical "progress," which we know to produce death and dispossession as their silent compact and cost. It might emerge in and from (a) life that is not beholden to the ideology of "progress," from those who have found themselves on the wrong side of progress, or perhaps from those who recognize this and see the injustice, or perhaps again from those who begin to reckon with their own long-standing complicity and complacency in an order that may privilege them but whose injustice is unlivable.

We should not be tricked into believing that the affirmations of an ostensibly affirmative or democratic biopolitics are either necessary or natural, laws of History or laws of Nature. They are no brave assent. Rather, they represent a craven acquiescence to a contingent tropological regime that prioritizes certain forms-of-life over others. We must not think that by saying yes to "life," one says no to power and to death; on the contrary (to continue borrowing on Foucault's phraseology), one tracks along the course laid out by the general deployment of biopolitics.[69] And yet, in the sanctimonious affirmation of my "life," biopolitics demands that I say No to death, that I possess my life by locating death elsewhere, producing it there clandestinely, outsourcing it, as the condition of my living-on. In the performative affirmations of affirmative biopolitics we may hear the distinct echoes and ambivalences of, for example, affirmative action and, more recently, affirmative sexual consent movements whose affirmations open to competing readings of the "affirmative" (as well as of "consent"). These movements tend to "affirm" (in a black-letter vocabulary, contractually) an epistemic "equality" and "progress" while nevertheless quietly reproducing structural inequalities, promising corrective or equalizing measures through dialogue and policy initiatives that do not always address, let alone redress, deeply entrenched historical structures of violence and oppression—and not least, attitudes and habits. The inherent hypocrisy in such "affirmations," of course, is irreducible to one's demonstrated purity of intent (which is repeatedly demanded); rather, in many respects affirmation silently succeeds in shoring up a (neo)liberal political subject, which is its rhetorical condition of possibility, the paradoxical condition of speaking at all. This is all packaged and sold as "empowering."

Liberal ideology and political structures have themselves had an invisible hand (to invoke Adam Smith's celebration of individualism and self-interested action) in long-standing *illiberal* structures of systemic violence and oppression, including slavery, racism, colonialism, genocide, sexism, homophobia, and transphobia—in the name of enlightened "reason" and under the aegis of innocence and freedom.[70] In Warren Montag's terms, this represents a necro-economy: "Death establishes the conditions of life; death as by an invisible hand restores the market to what it must be to support life."[71] Ostensibly free speech becomes power's ruse and its alibi, while staunchly ignoring—and often enough capitalizing on—existing hierarchies of power and the differential "rights" to public address, which have never been equal. As Blanchot has remarked, "dialogue" itself is a liberal conceit "founded upon the reciprocity of words and the equality of speakers." Buried in a parenthetical comment in his remarkable little text "A Plural Speech," Blanchot notes that all speech "is based upon an inequality of culture, condition, power, and fortune." He concludes, "All speech is a word of command, of terror, of seduction, of resentment, flattery, or aggression: all speech is violence—and to pretend to ignore this in claiming to dialogue is to add liberal hypocrisy to the dialectical optimism according to which war is no more than another form of dialogue."[72] This does not mean that we ought to cease speaking; there is often more egregious violence in one's silence. Blanchot suggests that we must strive toward a "plural speech"—a discontinuity and interruption of individual identity, riven by the apostrophic force of absence and death. Apostrophe is neither "reciprocal" nor a true "dialogue"; it is not "free speech" in the paradigm of liberal political philosophy. And insofar as the unprecedented protests and widespread civil unrest refuse to travel under a single discursive banner, they may well constitute a form of "plural speech."

Protestors are variously and paratactically in support of Black Lives Matter, but also anti-racism more generally, and sometimes anti-fascism; they call for justice, to #DefundThePolice and topple Confederate and colonial statues; they stand in solidarity against police brutality, systemic racism, racial inequality, the suppression of minority voters, inequalities in health and education, racist criminal justice and Immigration and Customs Enforcement systems, authoritarian government, and the militarization of police forces and of civic life more generally, including the use of high-tech weapons and "predictive policing" software to target and surveil a host of peaceful protestors (or simply, citizens) the president has dubbed "domestic terrorists." This list is only partial because racism affects every conceivable facet of social, cultural, economic, and political life. And only a fool would imagine that this animus hasn't also poisoned "privileged" souls. So far, the protests have not crystallized into a single sound bite perhaps because they emerge from what James calls a "walk of life" or, in the terms of a Cynic philosophy, "life as scandal of the truth," where "the bareness of life" is "a way of constituting the body itself as the visible theater of the truth."[73]

If Cynicism is the road not quite taken, if its promise has to date failed to materialize, it has nevertheless persisted as a parallel history: "Cynicism, the idea of a mode of life as the irruptive, violent, scandalous manifestation of the truth is and was part of revolutionary practice and of the forms taken by revolutionary movements throughout the nineteenth century." Foucault indicates three types of militancy with ties to the Cynic tradition: sociality (e.g., secret societies), established organizations (e.g., labor unions), and a third form, "militancy as bearing witness by one's life in the form of a style of existence." Such a militancy, he says, "must manifest directly, by its visible form, its constant practice, and its immediate existence, the concrete possibility and the evident value of an *other* life, which is the true life."[74] And indeed, the protests reach toward an *other* life,

even as counter-protests have arisen in support of Trump and the military suppression of peaceful protest, with armed vigilantes and would-be insurrectionists
who seek to exacerbate the chaos, to cast peaceful protestors in a negative light,
or to reaffirm old racial hierarchies along the alt-right/white supremacist axis,
including those in American militia movements, American neo-Nazis, the Boogaloo Boys,[75] the Proud Boys, and self-anointed "American freedom fighters," as
Steve Bannon calls them, in their quasi-evangelical efforts to Make America
Great Again and to foment the next civil war.

It is noteworthy that Foucault opened his last lectures on *parrhesia* with the
crisis of Athenian democracy—a crisis of decadence and of populist "truth," which
in many respects mirrors the systemic failures of our own democratic capitalist
institutions, where the ruins of political liberalism and liberal subjecthood are
manifest in the quickening of culture and race wars. In the Athenian context,
democracy became increasingly discredited as the privileged locus of *parrhesia*,
ushering in a kind of alternative or fake truth-telling characterized by "the freedom
for everybody and anybody to say anything, that is to say, to say whatever they
like." When this becomes the case, Foucault asks, "who will be listened to, approved,
followed, and loved?" His answer: "It will be those who please the people, say
what they want to hear, and flatter them. The others, those who say or try to say
what is true and good, and not what pleases the people, will not be listened to.
Worse, they will provoke negative reactions, irritation, and anger. And their true
discourse will expose them to vengeance or punishment."[76] It is perhaps with
such demagoguery in mind that Foucault, in his discussion on Cynic militancy,
claims—without evidence—that suicide terrorism is "a sort of dramatic or frenzied
taking of the [Cynical] courage for the truth ... to its extreme consequence": "The
problem of terrorism and the way in which anarchism and terrorism, as a practice
of life taken to the point of dying for the truth (the bomb which kills the person
who places it)."[77] Critics have remarked that Foucault is mistaken here. Daniele
Lorenzini writes, for example, that "we cannot effectively trace *any* sort of conti-
nuity between these two practices, since the parrhesiast never (physically) endan-
gers the lives of others—he only risks, at the limit, his *own* life." Cynicism is, he
adds, "essentially nonviolent, opening for others a space of *moral* risk, for it seeks
to rattle the unreflected certainties and habits that lend to everyday life its (apparent) stability, and can therefore result in significant *social* and *political*
consequences."[78]

Foucault's insertion of terrorism in this context is curious, though it might
not constitute an error; elsewhere, of course, he underscores the essentially

nonviolent nature of the Cynic's style of life, and so his own insertion here—not quite descriptive—takes on a normative valence. If suicide terrorism is not part of the Cynic tradition, as Foucault well knew, he nevertheless suggests that it is an "extreme consequence" or limit case, a perlocutionary effect, perhaps, that might make sense as an *other* manifestation of life and death, today, or that might serve as a warning against ignoring the parrhesiastic pact and the refusal to hear the truth. In our moment, this steadfast refusal is institutionalized as "truth," and it lets die, sometimes callously, sometimes self-righteously, and sometimes in prosaic hymns extoling life, law, and liberty. Indeed, as Michael Hardt has argued, Foucault's turn to the Cynics could be read as advocating a kind of "militant life" as a powerful rejoinder to neoliberalism.[79] And in the current crisis of liberal democracy—in the catastrophe, dénouement, or ruin of the established order, with inequities and injustices reaching a boiling point—the specter of terrorism must be taken seriously. For, one wonders: what happens when lives become unlivable and deaths institutionalized in scorched earth policies informed by old and abiding racisms, privileges, and economies that would be inoperable without them?

The protests, even if we entertain their extreme consequences—which may well prove necessary to effect lasting and real change—do not represent sovereign speech/acts, but are, rather, a kind of destitute sovereignty or self-dispossession, and an unworking of operant conditions. Indeed, with a gesture to Austin, Foucault says that the parrhesiastic speech/act is the "opposite" of a "performative utterance," and in a footnote his manuscript clarifies: "The performative is carried out in a world which guarantees that saying effectuates what is said"—that is, he underscores that the illocution relies on a set of social conventions that may not obtain or may be challenged by a parrhesiastic speech/act. *Parrhesia* calls on "a whole family of completely different facts [*faits*, also 'acts'] of discourse which are almost the reverse, the mirror projection of what we call the pragmatics of discourse."[80] In this, *parrhesia* is more akin to the perlocution,[81] the effects of which are in Austin's terms nonconventional and unpredictable, even risky. Indeed, with the perlocution words themselves may be extraneous or unnecessary,[82] and insofar as (a) life bears witness and "speaks" in and from its own exposure, in Foucault's terms the protests might well "reverse and invert the theme of the sovereign life (tranquil and beneficial: tranquil for oneself, enjoyment of self, and beneficial for others) by dramatizing it in the form of what could be called the militant life, the life of battle and struggle against and for self, against and for others."[83] Such a reversal or inversion of sovereignty, of (a) life "exposed" to death, recalls Bataille's radical reconceptualization of sovereignty in the reciprocal relation between death and community (see chapter 3).

In this way, and in their most auspicious moments, the protests shine a light on—and indeed, they further incite—the death-warranting of our established order. They refuse to uphold the broken liberal contract, its "free speech," its false equalities. "Such is the paradox of the Cynic life," Foucault says, "it is the fulfill-ment of the true life, but as demand for a life which is radically other." The expression of the "true life" (*alēthēs bios, alēthinos bios*) is a call, a demand, for "an *other* life and aspiration for another world (*un autre monde*)." Perhaps this call itself responds to—perhaps it has hearkened—death's address. For the *other* irrupts, as we have seen, in and from the places of (social) death, where the breath is stolen, silencing life and speech, and where we are called to "bear . . . witness to the true life by one's life itself."[84] An *other* life, and an *other* world, then, in which we might hold death, in refrain, rather than repudiate or forget death; a thanatopolitics that would disaffirm the malignant affirmations of biopolitics, its tropologies of life itself, its sunny and reassuring vistas, and the futures it portends. Neither truths nor lies, we might say, because the call does not occupy an epistemic *topos* so much as it informs a style of life. To say that the stakes of parrhesiastic protest are ontological is to situate the question of truth in and as *ēthos*, in and as (a) life that risks itself for an *other* life, an *other* world, in which neoliberal biopolitics would no longer operate as a normative truth-function. The "true life," then, is hopeful yet neither true nor untrue in any epistemological, logical, or constative sense. Its call, however, resounds in one's relation with the living and the dead—an ethical relation that would critically disaffirm our bio-political regime and would welcome not just an *other* life, but, before it is too late, an *other* world in which an *other death* will one day be possible.

# Notes

## Introduction

1. Michel Foucault, *Discipline and Punish: The Birth of the Prison*, trans. Alan Sheridan (New York: Vintage, 1977), 8.

2. Michel Foucault, *The History of Sexuality*, vol. 1, trans. Robert Hurley (New York: Random House, 1978), 136.

3. Michel Foucault, *"Society Must Be Defended": Lectures at the Collège de France, 1975–1976*, trans. David Macey (New York: Picador, 2003), 241.

4. Ibid.

5. In French, this is a common term often used in economic transactions: a direct debit or automated payment.

6. Foucault, *History of Sexuality*, 136.

7. Foucault, *"Society Must Be Defended,"* 246. The pronoun originally translated in this passage as "he" has been replaced by "one" and should be understood as nonexclusive (in French, the gender of the pronoun follows the grammatical gender of the noun).

8. Foucault identifies four kinds of "technologies," which together comprise what he calls "governmentality": technologies of (1) production, (2) signs or signification, (3) power and domination, and (4) the self. See Michel Foucault, *Dire vrai sur soi-même: Conférences prononcées à l'Université Victoria de Toronto* (Paris: VRIN, 2017), 31. On governmentality, see chapter 3 below.

9. Foucault, *"Society Must Be Defended,"* 249.

10. See Alexander Galloway and Eugene Thacker, "Protocol, Control, and Networks," *Grey Room* 17 (2004): 6–29.

11. Foucault, *History of Sexuality*, 155–56; the translation has been modified to correct its gender-exclusive pronouns.

12. Ibid., 159.

13. Lucretius, *Of the Nature of Things*, book 3, "Folly of the Fear of Death," trans. William Ellery Leonard (1908, rev. 2013), Project Gutenberg, http://www.gutenberg.org/files/785/785 -h/785-h.htm#link2H_4_0009.

14. Foucault, *"Society Must Be Defended,"* 248.

15. Numerous very good introductions to biopolitics are available. See, for example, Thomas Lemke, *Biopolitics: An Advanced Introduction*, trans. Eric Frederick Trump (New York: NYU Press, 2011); and Catherine Mills, *Biopolitics* (New York: Routledge, 2018). There is also a comprehensive anthology of biopolitical texts across history. See Timothy C. Campbell and Adam Sitze, eds., *Biopolitics: A Reader* (Durham, NC: Duke University Press, 2013).

16. My understanding of our "epochal" shift is more rhetorical than Foucault's. My thinking has been informed by my reading of Hans Blumenberg's *The Legitimacy of the Modern Age*, which first appeared in German in 1966 (the same year Foucault's *The Order of Things* appeared in French). While Foucault speaks of epochal "discontinuities" and "ruptures," Blumenberg will say "reoccupations" (*Umbesetzungen*, a military trope)—the rhetorical means by which perennial questions are answered differently from one epoch to the next, based on the shifting

plausibility of answer-positions. In a later text, Blumenberg clarifies: "The accomplishment and establishment of the reoccupation are rhetorical acts; 'philosophy of history' only thematizes the structure of this process, it is not the agency responsible for it" (Hans Blumenberg, "An Anthropological Approach to the Contemporary Significance of Rhetoric," in *After Philosophy: End or Transformation?*, ed. Kenneth Baynes, James Bohman, and Thomas McCarthy [Cambridge, MA: MIT Press, 1987], 451).

17. Blumenberg argued that the modern age is distinctly characterized by the concept of "self-assertion" (*Selbstbehauptung*) and self-legitimation.

18. Didier Fassin, *Humanitarian Reason: A Moral History of the Present*, trans. Rachel Gomme (Berkeley: University of California Press, 2012), 6.

19. Consider, for example, the ethics and economies of postmortem sperm harvesting for reproductive purposes—literally making life from the dead. A recent legal case involved the parents of a young man who had died in a skiing accident. A court gave his parents custody of his sperm and placed "no restrictions" on its use, "including its potential for procreative purposes." Lindsey Bever and Allyson Chiu, "A Cadet Died in a Tragedy. Now His Parents Can Use His Sperm to Create His Child, a Judge Ruled," *Washington Post*, May 21, 2019, https://www.washingtonpost.com/health/2019/05/21/cadet-died-tragedy-now-his-parents-can-use-his-sperm-create-his-child-judge-rules.

20. Michel Foucault, *The Order of Things: An Archaeology of the Human Sciences* (New York: Random House, 1970), 237.

21. Ibid., 235.

22. Ibid., 237.

23. See, for example, Colin Crouch, *Post-Democracy* (Cambridge: Polity, 2004); and Mark Blyth, *Austerity: The History of a Dangerous Idea* (Oxford: Oxford University Press, 2013).

24. Michel Foucault, *The Birth of Biopolitics: Lectures at the Collège de France, 1978–1979*, trans. Graham Burchell (New York: Picador, 2008), 242, translation modified.

25. Blumenberg, "Anthropological Approach," 456.

26. Michel Foucault, "Language to Infinity," in *Aesthetics, Method, and Epistemology*, ed. James D. Faubion (New York: New Press, 1998), 89–101; "Of Other Spaces, Heterotopias," *Architecture, Mouvement, Continuité* 5 (1984): 46–49, http://foucault.info/documents/hetero topia/foucault.heterotopia.en.html.

27. Paolo Virno, *A Grammar of the Multitude: For an Analysis of Contemporary Forms of Life*, trans. Isabella Bertoletti, James Cascaito, and Andrea Casson (Los Angeles: Semiotext(e), 2004), 81.

28. Timothy C. Campbell, *Improper Life: Technology and Biopolitics from Heidegger to Agamben* (Minneapolis: University of Minnesota Press, 2011), vii.

29. Michael Hardt and Antonio Negri, *Empire* (Cambridge, MA: Harvard University Press, 2000), 388.

30. Roberto Esposito, *Terms of the Political: Community, Immunity, Biopolitics*, trans. Rhiannon Noel Welch (New York: Fordham University Press, 2013), 110.

31. Roberto Esposito, *Bíos: Biopolitics and Philosophy*, trans. Timothy Campbell (Minneapolis: University of Minnesota Press, 2008), 157.

32. Nikolas Rose, *The Politics of Life Itself: Biomedicine, Power and Subjectivity in the Twenty-First Century* (Princeton, NJ: Princeton University Press, 2006), 211, 220.

33. See Crouch, *Post-Democracy*.

34. I owe a footnote to Giorgio Agamben, who must be situated in the negative camp. I have been inspired by Agamben's work, but on biopolitics I part ways with him precisely in his parting from Foucault. Agamben rejects Foucault's thesis of epochal rupture and sees

in biopolitics little more than an ancient and abiding sovereign power. He draws on Nazi "Crown Jurist" Carl Schmitt, whose definition of sovereign power is succinct: "Sovereign is he who decides on the exception" (Carl Schmitt, *Political Theology: Four Chapters on the Concept of Sovereignty*, trans. George Schwab [Chicago: University of Chicago Press, 2005], 5). With the sovereign exception, Schmitt had in mind a severe economic or political crisis that would call for the application of extraordinary measures, such as martial law in a time of war, where the rule of law might (temporarily) be suspended, paradoxically, ultimately to preserve law and order. Agamben, however, has argued that nominally democratic modern states have come increasingly to use the state of exception as a normal paradigm of governance and securitization. In his appeal to sovereign decisionism, then, Agamben doesn't quite see how biopolitics is, in Foucault's terms, both a making live *and* a letting die. For him, Foucault's distinction between sovereign and biopolitical power is "perfectly trivial" (Giorgio Agamben, *Homo Sacer: Sovereign Power and Bare Life*, trans. Daniel Heller-Roazen [Stanford, CA: Stanford University Press, 1998], 87).

35. See Fassin, *Humanitarian Reason*.

36. Nancy Fraser and Axel Honneth, *Redistribution or Recognition? A Political-Philosophical Exchange* (London: Verso, 2003), 74.

37. Blumenberg, "Anthropological Approach," 431.

38. Ibid., 437.

39. Ibid., 439.

40. Ibid., 452.

41. See, for example, "Bannon WarRoom—Citizens of the American Republic," YouTube, https://www.youtube.com/channel/UCWVvSbEwoimVIT8hiDcNgcQ. The YouTube page in question has since been taken down for violation of YouTube's terms of service. Readers can access an archive of the channel's landing page at https://web.archive.org/web/201906241 24849/https://www.youtube.com/channel/UCWVvSbEwoimVIT8hiDcNgcQ. For a discussion of Bannon's *War Room* in the far-right digital media context, see Tad Lemieux and Stuart J. Murray, "The Pandemic as 'Joke': Meme Culture, the Alt-Right, and Steve Bannon's 'War Room,'" *TOPIA: Canadian Journal of Cultural Studies* 41 (2020): 94–103, https://doi.org /10.3138/topia-012.

42. Benjamin R. Teitelbaum, *War for Eternity: Inside Bannon's Far Right Circle of Global Power Brokers* (New York: Dey Street, 2020); see also "Covid-19 Is the Crisis Radical 'Traditionalists' Have Been Waiting For," *The Nation*, Apr. 8, 2020, https://www.thenation.com /article/politics/covid-traditionalist-bannon-putin.

43. Elsewhere, I address the tactic/strategy binary in a critical counter-reading of Michel de Certeau's *The Practice of Everyday Life*. See Stuart J. Murray, "The Practice of Everyday Death: On the Paratactical 'Life' of Neoliberal Biopolitics," *Canadian Review of American Studies* (forthcoming 2022).

44. Stuart J. Murray and Tad Lemieux, "*Combat-Débat*: Parataxis and the Unavowable Community; or, the Joke," *Philosophy and Rhetoric* 52, no. 1 (2019): 79.

45. Elliot Ackerman et al., "On Justice and Open Debate," *Harper's*, Oct. 2020, 3, published online July 7, 2020, https://harpers.org/a-letter-on-justice-and-open-debate. This open letter—also known as "The *Harper's* Letter"—was signed by more than 150 prominent writers, artists, and scholars.

46. See Jared Stark, *A Death of One's Own: Literature, Law, and the Right to Die* (Evanston, IL: Northwestern University Press, 2018).

47. Cara Finnegan, "The Critic as Curator," *Rhetoric Society Quarterly* 48, no. 4 (2018): 405–10.

Chapter 1

For this chapter's epigraph, I thank Kordestan Saadi and Jaffer Sheyholislami. A transliterated version of the original Farsi text reads as follows: *Dar donyaa do chiz nadaarad seda, 'ybe ser-vatmand va marge geda.*

1. Mayor Jim Watson, Twitter, Mar. 15, 2020, https://twitter.com/JimWatsonOttawa /status/1239257579634786306. The argument that follows develops work previously published as Stuart J. Murray, "COVID-19: Crisis, Critique, and the Limits of What We Can Hear," *TOPIA: Canadian Journal of Cultural Studies*, "COVID-19 Essays" (2020): n.p., doi: 10.3138 /topia.2020.covid-19.05. Copyright © 2020, University of Toronto Press. Reprinted with permission from University of Toronto Press (https://www.utpjournals.press).

2. Dr. Vera Etches, "Statement from Dr. Vera Etches Medical Officer of Health on COVID-19 Situation in Ottawa," Ottawa Public Health, Mar. 15, 2020, https://www.ottawa publichealth.ca/en/public-health-topics/previous-statements.aspx.

3. In Canada, the majority of deaths have to date been women, who constitute the majority of personal care workers. Performing the immaterial labor of care, they are often racialized and work more than one job—a factor that contributed to the spread of COVID-19 among the elderly in long-term care facilities (Canada currently ranks first in the world in per capita deaths among the elderly, a veritable institutionalized culling.) In the US context, see Lazaro Gamino, "The Workers Who Face the Greatest Coronavirus Risk," *New York Times*, Mar. 15, 2020, https://nytimes.com/interactive/2020/03/15/business/economy/coronavirus-worker -risk.html.

4. Lauren Berlant, "Slow Death (Sovereignty, Obesity, Lateral Agency)," *Critical Inquiry* 33, no. 4 (2007): 754.

5. Ludwig Wittgenstein, *Philosophische Untersuchungen / Philosophical Investigations*, trans. G. E. M. Anscombe, P. M. S. Hacker, and Joachim Schulte (Oxford: Blackwell, 2009), 95.

6. Ibid., 198.

7. Ibid., 207.

8. Maurice Blanchot, *The Writing of the Disaster*, trans. Ann Smock (Lincoln: University of Nebraska Press, 1995), 51.

9. Ibid., 50.

10. See Antonin Artaud, *Van Gogh, le suicidé de la société* (Paris: K éditeur, 1947).

11. Blanchot, *Writing of the Disaster*, 29.

12. Michel Foucault, *"Society Must Be Defended": Lectures at the Collège de France, 1975–1976*, trans. David Macey (New York: Picador, 2003), 260. The argument that follows draws on Stuart J. Murray, "The Suicidal State: In Advance of an American Requiem," special issue "In the Midst of COVID-19," *Philosophy and Rhetoric* 53, no. 3 (2020): 299–305. Copyright © 2020. This article is used by permission of The Pennsylvania State University Press.

13. Foucault *"Society Must Be Defended,"* 260.

14. Ibid., 254.

15. Ibid., 255, 257, 261, 258, 260.

16. See, for example, Alexander G. Weheliye, *Habeas Viscus: Racializing Assemblages, Biopolitics, and Black Feminist Theories of the Human* (Durham, NC: Duke University Press, 2014), chap. 4.

17. Kendall Thomas, "The Eclipse of Reason: A Rhetorical Reading of *Bowers v. Hardwick*," *Virginia Law Review* 79, no. 1805 (1993): 1806–7.

18. Ruth Wilson Gilmore, "Race and Globalization," in *Geographies of Global Change: Remapping the World*, ed. Ronald John Johnston and Peter James Taylor (Malden, MA: Wiley-Blackwell, 2002), 261.

19. Jacques Derrida, "Autoimmunity: Real and Symbolic Suicides: A Dialogue with Jacques Derrida," in *Philosophy in a Time of Terror: Dialogues with Jürgen Habermas and Jacques Derrida*, ed. Giovanna Borradori (Chicago: University of Chicago Press, 2003), 108.

20. Giorgio Agamben, "The Invention of an Epidemic," *European Journal of Psychoanalysis*, "Coronavirus and Philosophers," Feb. 26, 2020, http://www.journal-psychoanalysis.eu /coronavirus-and-philosophers.

21. Giorgio Agamben, "Clarifications," *An und für sich* (blog), Mar. 17, 2020, https://itself .blog/2020/03/17/giorgio-agamben-clarifications.

22. Michael Schwirtz, "The 1,000-Bed *Comfort* Was Supposed to Aid New York. It Has 20 Patients," *New York Times*, Apr. 2, 2020, https://nytimes.com/2020/04/02/nyregion/ny -coronavirus-usns-comfort.html. In a similar vein, one of the temporary pandemic hospitals set up in the borough of Queens treated just seventy-nine patients at a cost of $52 million. Brian M. Rosenthal, "This Hospital Cost $52 Million. It Treated 79 Virus Patients," *New York Times*, July 21, 2020, https://nytimes.com/2020/07/21/nyregion/coronavirus-hospital-usta -queens.html.

23. Frances Robles and Sheri Fink, "Amid Puerto Rico Disaster, Hospital Ship Admitted Just 6 Patients a Day," *New York Times*, Dec. 6, 2017, https://nytimes.com/2017/12/06/us /puerto-rico-hurricane-maria-hospital-ship.html.

24. Christina Sharpe, *In the Wake: On Blackness and Being* (Durham, NC: Duke University Press, 2016), 44.

25. Ibid., 46.

26. Ibid., 50.

27. Sheryl Gay Stolberg, "Fauci Plans to Use Hearing to Warn of 'Needless Suffering and Death,'" *New York Times*, May 12, 2020, https://nytimes.com/2020/05/12/us/politics/corona virus-fauci-senate-testimony.html.

28. Michael D. Shear and Sarah Mervosh, "Trump Encourages Protest Against Governors Who Have Imposed Virus Restrictions," *New York Times*, Apr. 29, 2020, https://nytimes.com /2020/04/17/us/politics/trump-coronavirus-governors.html.

29. I am aware, too, that these ongoing protests have intersected in troubling ways with the global protests sparked by the murder of George Floyd on May 25, 2020 (I return to these particular protests in the Refrain). But I refuse to treat those protesting anti-Black violence and racism in the same breath as those protesting public health orders, even as both might be considered anti-state or anti-government.

30. Austen Ivereigh, "An Interview with Pope Francis: 'A Time of Great Uncertainty,'" *Commonweal*, Apr. 8, 2020, https://www.commonwealmagazine.org/time-great-uncertainty.

31. Anti-Defamation League, "The Boogaloo: Extremists' New Slang Term for a Coming Civil War," Nov. 26, 2019, https://www.adl.org/blog/the-boogaloo-extremists-new-slang -term-for-a-coming-civil-war. In protests some "Boogaloo Boys" are recognizable by their Hawaiian shirts: "boogaloo" has morphed into "big luau" to escape censorship on Facebook and other social media platforms. "Big igloo" is yet another homonymous variant, with its own symbology.

32. Andrea Salcedo, "Hundreds Without Masks Packed a Hasidic Wedding in Brooklyn. The Organizers Face a $15,000 Fine," *Washington Post*, Nov. 25, 2020, https://www.washington post.com/nation/2020/11/25/hasidic-wedding-fined-new-york.

33. For an example of worship as "peaceful protest" see Daniel Burke, "California Church Defies Public Health Orders, Holds Indoor Services for Thousands with No Social Distancing," CNN, Aug. 13, 2020, https://www.cnn.com/2020/08/12/us/pastor-macarthur-church -california/index.html.

34. Here is just one news story: Leah Asmelash, "Florida Sheriff Bans His Deputies and Office Visitors from Wearing Masks on a Day His County Broke Records for Covid-19 Deaths," CNN, Aug. 12, 2020, https://www.cnn.com/2020/08/12/us/sheriff-no-mask-ocala-trnd/index.html.

35. I thank my friend Roland Klos for this formulation.

36. See Stuart J. Murray, "Thanatopolitics: On the Use of Death for Mobilizing Political Life," *Polygraph: An International Journal of Politics and Culture* 18 (2006): 191–215.

37. Giorgio Agamben, *Homo Sacer: Sovereign Power and Bare Life*, trans. Daniel Heller-Roazen (Stanford, CA: Stanford University Press, 1998), 122, 142.

38. Roberto Esposito, *Bíos: Biopolitics and Philosophy*, trans. Timothy Campbell (Minneapolis: University of Minnesota Press, 2008), 10. Note that thanatopolitics is both a "culmination" and a "reversal." Esposito is typically more nuanced than this, thinking thanatopolitics through the paradigm of autoimmunity; however, inasmuch as he remains committed to an "affirmative" biopolitics, thanatopolitics is always for him an aberration, even if it becomes normative, as in Nazi policy.

39. Michel Foucault, "The Political Technology of Individuals," in *Power*, ed. James D. Faubion (New York: New Press, 2000), 416.

40. Achille Mbembe, "Necropolitics," *Public Culture* 15, no. 1 (2003): 11–40; more recently, see *Necropolitics*, trans. Steven Corcoran (Durham, NC: Duke University Press, 2019).

41. Achille Mbembe, *On the Postcolony* (Berkeley: University of California Press, 2001), 103.

42. Achille Mbembe, "*On the Postcolony*: A Brief Response to Critics," *Qui Parle* 15, no. 2 (2005): 18.

43. Foucault, "*Society Must Be Defended*," 247.

44. See Barbara Biesecker, "No Time for Mourning: The Rhetorical Production of the Melancholic Citizen-Subject in the War on Terror," *Philosophy and Rhetoric* 40, no. 1 (2007): 147–69.

45. See, for example, George W. Bush, "President Bush Signs Partial Birth Abortion Ban Act of 2003," *The White House, President George W. Bush*, Nov. 5, 2003, https://georgewbush-whitehouse.archives.gov/news/releases/2003/11/20031105-1.html.

46. Aaron Gregg and Yeganeh Torbati, "Pentagon Used Taxpayer Money Meant for Masks and Swabs to Make Jet Engine Parts and Body Armor," *Washington Post*, Sept. 22, 2020, https://www.washingtonpost.com/business/2020/09/22/covid-funds-pentagon; Coronavirus Preparedness and Response Supplemental Appropriations Act, 2020, H.R. 6074, 116th Cong. (2020), https://www.congress.gov/116/bills/hr6074/BILLS-116hr6074enr.pdf.

47. Derrida, "Autoimmunity," 108.

48. Quoted in James Risen and Tim Golden, "3 Prisoners Commit Suicide at Guantánamo," *New York Times*, June 11, 2006, https://nytimes.com/2006/06/11/us/11gitmo.html.

49. This was a familiar Nazi strategy used to domesticate hate and violence: "The 'Aryan' is 'constructive'; the Jew is 'destructive'; and the 'Aryan,' to continue his *construction*, must *destroy* the Jewish *destruction*. The Aryan, as the vessel of *love*, must *hate* the Jewish *hate*" (Kenneth Burke, "The Rhetoric of Hitler's 'Battle,'" in *The Philosophy of Literary Form* [Berkeley: University of California Press, 1974], 204).

50. In the years since, it has become clear that, on US soil, Americans are more likely to be killed by homegrown radicals than by jihadis. See, for example, Scott Shane, "Homegrown Extremists Tied to Deadlier Toll Than Jihadists in U.S. Since 9/11," *New York Times*, June 24, 2015, https://nytimes.com/2015/06/25/us/tally-of-attacks-in-us-challenges-perceptions-of-top-terror-threat.html.

51. Jacqueline Rose, "Deadly Embrace," *London Review of Books* 26, no. 21 (2004): http://www.lrb.co.uk/the-paper/v26/n21/jacqueline-rose/deadly-embrace.

52. Ibid.

53. In Iraq, this hinged on the existence of so-called Weapons of Mass Destruction and Saddam Hussein's ties to Al Qaeda. These were eventually disproven, and the invasion arguably helped to propel the rise of ISIS and the ongoing conflicts and humanitarian crises in Syria, Yemen, and beyond. In Afghanistan, the war was sold to Americans as a moral cause against the Taliban: to ensure the right of young women and girls to an education—the same young women and girls who have been abandoned, nineteen years later, as the Taliban are invited to the negotiating table and are set to form part of Afghanistan's government. If it was true that "we will not negotiate with terrorists," we are now either willing to do so or the Taliban have been reclassified as a legitimate political organization.

54. Gilbert Burnham et al., "Mortality After the 2003 Invasion of Iraq: A Cross-Sectional Cluster Sample Survey," *The Lancet* 368, no. 9545 (2006): 1421–28.

55. International Physicians for the Prevention of Nuclear War, "Casualty Figures After 10 Years of the 'War on Terror': Iraq, Afghanistan, Pakistan," Mar. 2015, http://www.psr.org /assets/pdfs/body-count.pdf. The Afghanistan body count was reported at 220,000 and the Pakistan count at 80,000. Meanwhile, US troop deaths in Operation Iraqi Freedom total 4,902 and 3,576 in Operation Enduring Freedom (Afghanistan). See "The Iraq Coalition Casualties Count," http://icasualties.org, retrieved Sept. 22, 2020. As the Watson Institute at Brown University notes, roughly half of these deaths are due to enemy attack, by improvised explosive devices, for example, while the other half include death by "vehicle crashes, electrocutions, heatstroke, friendly fire, and suicides in theater"—with cause of death often simply listed as "nonhostile." Moreover, the above counts do not include some 8,000 private contractors employed by the United States (the majority of whom were citizens of other countries, with many deaths unreported), as well as more than 110,000 coalition partners—uniformed Afghans, Iraqis, and other allies. See "Costs of War," Watson Institute of International and Public Affairs, Brown University, updated July 2021, http://watson.brown.edu/costsofwar/costs/human /military/killed. The US Department of Defense website is labyrinthine and seems to be designed to obscure the cumulative statistics of casualties. For a detailed survey of the different and divergent body counts in the global War on Terror, see Roger Stahl, *Through the Crosshairs: War, Visual Culture, and the Weaponized Gaze* (New Brunswick, NJ: Rutgers University Press, 2018), 137–41.

56. See Derek Gregory, "Dirty Dancing: Drones and Death in the Borderlands," in *Life in the Age of Drone Warfare*, ed. Lisa Parks and Caren Kaplan (Durham, NC: Duke University Press, 2017), 25–58; and Derek Gregory, "From a View to a Kill: Drones and Late Modern War," *Theory, Culture and Society* 28, nos. 7–8 (2011): 188–215; see also Grégoire Chamayou, *Théorie du drone* (Paris: La fabrique, 2013); Samuel Issacharoff and Richard Pildes, "Drones and the Dilemma of Modern Warfare," in *Drone Wars: Transforming Conflict, Law and Policy*, ed. Peter Bergen and Daniel Rothenberg (Cambridge: Cambridge University Press, 2015), 388–420; Lauren Wilcox, "Embodying Algorithmic Violence: Gender, Race and the Posthuman in Drone Warfare," *Security Dialogue* 48, no. 1 (2017): 11–28; Elke Schwarz, "Prescription Drones: On the Techno-Biopolitical Regimes of Contemporary 'Ethical Killing,'" *Security Dialogue* 47, no. 1 (2016): 59–75; and Lisa Parks, "Drones, Vertical Mediation, and the Targeted Class," *Feminist Studies* 42, no. 1 (2016): 227–35.

The Bureau of Investigative Journalism maintains a current, searchable database of US drone strikes and other covert actions in Pakistan, Afghanistan, Yemen, and Somalia (see http://www.thebureauinvestigates.com/projects/drone-war). *The Intercept's* "Drone Papers" documents the US military's assassination program in Afghanistan, Yemen, and Somalia, drawing on "a cache of secret documents" (see http://www.theintercept.com/drone-papers). More recently, *The Intercept* has documented 550 US drone strikes in Libya since 2011. See Nick Turse, Henrik Moltke, and Alice Speri, "Secret War," *The Intercept*, June 20, 2018, http://www.theintercept.com/2018/06/20/libya-us-drone-strikes.

57. Department of Defense, "Clearance for DoD Information for Public Release," Instruction 5230.09, Jan. 25, 2019, https://fas.org/irp/doddir/dod/i5230_09.pdf.

58. Brandon Bryant, "Letter from a Sensor Operator," in *Life in the Age of Drone Warfare*, ed. Lisa Parks and Karen Caplan (Durham, NC: Duke University Press, 2017), 321–22.

59. Ashley Gilbertson, "The Life and Lonely Death of Noah Pierce," *UTNE Reader*, Mar.–Apr. 2009, https://www.utne.com/politics/lonely-death-noah-pierce-ptsd-iraq-war.

60. Daniel Somers, "'I Am Sorry It Has Come to This': A Soldier's Last Words," *Gawker*, June 22, 2013, https://gawker.com/i-am-sorry-that-it-has-come-to-this-a-soldiers-last-534538357.

61. See Kent D. Drescher et al., "An Exploration of the Viability and Usefulness of the Construct of Moral Injury in War Veterans," *Traumatology* 17, no. 1 (2011): 8–13. Moral injury is "strongly" and "independently" correlated with suicide risk. See Donna Ames et al., "Moral Injury, Religiosity, and Suicide Risk in U.S. Veterans and Active Duty Military with PTSD Symptoms," *Military Medicine* 184, nos. 3–4 (2019): e271–78.

62. "Department of Defense Suicide Event Report: Calendar Year 2017 Annual Report," Defense Suicide Prevention Office, July 12, 2018, https://www.dspo.mil/Portals/113/Documents/2017-DoDSER-Annual-Report.pdf.

63. Quoted in Nadia Taysir Dabbagh, *Suicide in Palestine: Narratives of Despair* (Northampton, MA: Olive Branch Press, 2005), 200. Saeed speaks as a true Kantian subject of Enlightenment here: "If a man cannot preserve his life except by dishonouring his humanity, he ought rather to sacrifice it" (Immanuel Kant, *Lectures of Ethics*, trans. Lewis White Beck [New York: Harper and Row, 1963], 156).

64. Talal Asad, *On Suicide Bombing* (New York: Columbia University Press, 2007), 2.

65. This figure might be interpreted in Agamben's terms as the *Muselmann*. See Giorgio Agamben, *Remnants of Auschwitz: The Witness and the Archive*, trans. Daniel Heller-Roazen (New York: Zone, 1999).

66. Asad, *On Suicide Bombing*, 2.

67. Ibid., 3.

68. Talal Asad, "Agency and Pain: An Exploration," *Culture and Religion* 1, no. 1 (2000): 32.

69. Johns Hopkins University, Coronavirus Resource Center, "COVID-19 United States Cases by County," https://coronavirus.jhu.edu/us-map.

70. Devan Cole and Tara Subramaniam, "Trump on Covid Death Toll: 'It is what it is,'" *CNN Politics*, Aug. 4, 2020, https://www.cnn.com/2020/08/04/politics/trump-covid-death-toll-is-what-it-is/index.html.


Chapter 2


1. Michel Foucault and Claude Bonnefoy, *Speech Begins After Death*, trans. Robert Bononno (Minneapolis: University of Minnesota Press, 2013), 36–37.

2. Christian O. Lundberg, "Letting Rhetoric Be: On Rhetoric and Rhetoricity," *Philosophy and Rhetoric* 46, no. 2 (2013): 250.

3. Foucault and Bonnefoy, *Speech Begins*, 43.

4. Ibid., 40. This is no doubt one dimension of an "archaeology" of knowledge, the project to enter into the "historical *a priori*" or the "conditions of possibility" of another epoch, another culture. We begin to realize that we cannot will ourselves to think outside of our own *episteme*, but that this thought comes from outside, paradoxically, and transforms our relation to ourselves—also a form of death. Indeed, Foucault's admission here suggests that his "history of the present" is always premised on death. See Michel Foucault, *The Order of Things: An Archaeology of the Human Sciences* (New York: Random House, 1970), xxii.

5. Foucault and Bonnefoy, *Speech Begins*, 44.

6. Ibid., 66.

7. Ibid., 71.

8. Thelton E. Henderson, "Joint Request for Order Authorizing Refeeding Under Specified Conditions of Hunger Striking Inmate-Patients and Order Thereon," *United States District Court, Northern District of California, Case No. C01-1351 TEH*, Aug. 19, 2013, http://www.scribd.com/doc/161727249/Order-Granting-Joint-Request-Authorizing-Refeeding.

9. Paige St. John, "California Prison Officials Say 30,000 Inmates Refuse Meals," *Los Angeles Times*, July 8, 2013, http://articles.latimes.com/2013/jul/08/local/la-me-pc-ff-california-prison-officials-acknowledge-hunger-strike-20130708.

10. Solitary confinement functions extralegally as "administrative segregation." This bureaucratic and rhetorical sleight of hand reframes cruel and unusual punishment—which would otherwise invoke legal protections under the Eighth Amendment—as an administrative, rather than punitive, exercise. Similar obfuscations plague Canada's prison system.

11. See "Prisoners' Demands," *Prisoner Hunger Strike Solidarity*, Apr. 3, 2011, https://prisoner hungerstrikesolidarity.wordpress.com/the-prisoners-demands-2. For a statistical summary of the number of California inmates in solitary confinement at this time, see Sal Rodriguez, "How Many People Are in Solitary Confinement in California's Prisons?," *Solitary Watch*, Dec. 12, 2013, http://solitarywatch.com/2013/12/04/many-california-prisoners-solitary-confinement; Keramet A. Reiter, "Parole, Snitch, or Die: California's Supermax Prisons and Prisoners, 1997–2007," *Punishment and Society* 14, no. 5 (2012): 530–63. For a summary of the conditions of solitary confinement at Pelican Bay State Prison's Security Housing Unit (SHU), see "Prison Focus Newsletter," *California Prison Focus*, 2013, http://www.prisons.org /documents/CPF-41.pdf, retrieved Apr. 17, 2015; Amnesty International, *Edge of Endurance*, Sept. 26, 2012, http://www.amnestyusa.org/research/reports/the-edge-of-endurance-prison-conditions-in-california-s-security-housing-units, retrieved Mar. 14, 2021.

12. (1) Eliminate group punishment; (2) abolish the debriefing policy and modify active/ inactive gang status criteria; (3) comply with recommendations of US Commission on Safety and Abuse in America's Prisons 2006 regarding an end to long-term solitary confinement; (4) provide adequate food; and (5) provide constructive programs and privileges for SHU prisoners. See "Prisoners' Demands."

13. Jeffrey Beard, "Hunger Strike in California Prisons Is a Gang Power Play," *Los Angeles Times*, Aug. 6, 2013, http://www.latimes.com/news/opinion/opinionla/la-oe-beard-prison-hunger-strike-20130806-story.html.

14. By declaring invalid a prisoner's prior DNR directives, it was unclear whether this court order surpassed the authorization of force-feeding and might be interpreted as permitting intravenous rehydration.

15. "Policy 4.22.2: Mass Organized Hunger Strike (rev. 07/2013)," *Inmate Medical Services Policies and Procedures*, http://www.cphcs.ca.gov/docs/imspp/IMSPP-v04-ch22.2.pdf, retrieved Feb. 15, 2015.

16. Henderson, "Joint Request."

17. Giorgio Agamben, *The Coming Community*, trans. Michael Hardt (Minneapolis: University of Minnesota Press, 1993), 86.

18. See Reiter, "Parole, Snitch, or Die."

19. Colin Dayan, *The Law Is a White Dog: How Legal Rituals Make and Unmake Persons* (Princeton, NJ: Princeton University Press, 2011).

20. Colin Dayan, "Writing in a Belittered World," *Small Axe* 45 (2014): 182.

21. Early instances of the "right to life" in law are framed negatively (a freedom *from*), where life is not quite inalienable but subject to sovereign or juridical will. See, for example, the Magna Carta (1215), the Declaration of the Rights of Man and of the Citizen (1789), and the United

States Bill of Rights (1789), in which the Seventh Article states, "Nor shall any person ... be deprived of life, liberty, or property, without due process of law." More recent United Nations declarations frame the "right to life" more directly and positively (an inherent freedom *to*). See, for example, the Universal Declaration of Human Rights (1948) and the International Covenant on Civil and Political Rights (1966), where the latter states, "Every human being has the inherent right to life" (Article 6.1).

22. Following Giorgio Agamben, for whom biopolitics is an extension of sovereign power, Ewa Ziarek has theorized the hunger strike as the political resistance of "bare life." See Ewa Płonowska Ziarek, "Bare Life on Strike: Notes on the Biopolitics of Race and Gender," *South Atlantic Quarterly* 107, no. 1 (2008): 89–105.

23. The exception here is capital punishment, the last gasp of sovereign power, which has for decades been on a downward trend (see https://deathpenaltyinfo.org/executions /executions-overview/executions-by-state-and-year). Executions in the United States are increasingly controversial as states have in recent years found it difficult to obtain lethal drugs and have resorted to compounding pharmacies and more experimental formulas that have in some cases caused prolonged agony and slow death. See Erica Goode, "After a Prolonged Execution in Ohio, Questions of 'Cruel and Unusual,'" *New York Times*, Jan. 17, 2014, https:// nytimes.com/2014/01/18/us/prolonged-execution-prompts-debate-over-death-penalty -methods.html.

24. See, for example, Naoki Kanaboshi, "Prison Inmates' Right to Hunger Strike: Its Use and Its Limits Under the US Constitution," *Criminal Justice Review* 39, no. 2 (2014): 121–39; Don Sneed and Harry W. Stonecipher, "Prisoner Fasting as Symbolic Speech: The Ultimate Speech-Action Test," *Howard Law Journal* 32, no. 3 (1989): 549–62; and Gerard A. Hauser, *Prisoners of Conscience: Moral Vernaculars of Political Agency* (Columbia: University of South Carolina Press, 2012).

25. For an overview of the ways that hunger strikes are conventionally theorized, see Falguni A. Sheth, "Unruliness Without Rioting: Hunger Strikes in Contemporary Politics," in *Active Intolerance: Michel Foucault, the Prisons Information Group, and the Future of Abolition*, ed. Andrew Dilts and Perry Zurn (New York: Palgrave Macmillan, 2016), 123–40.

26. Foucault and Bonnefoy, *Speech Begins*, 40.

27. Ibid., 39–40.

28. See Michel Foucault, "The Thought of the Outside," in *Aesthetics, Method, and Epistemology*, ed. James D. Faubion (New York: New Press, 1998), 147–69. Below I cite from a slightly different translation, in which the essay appears as "The Thought from Outside." See Michel Foucault and Maurice Blanchot, *Foucault, Blanchot*, trans. Jeffrey Mehlman and Brian Massumi (New York: Zone Books, 1990), 7–60.

29. In addition to Suidas and Isocrates, Plato gives an account of events in the *Phaedrus*, praising Stesichorus for being so clever, calling him an intellectual rather than disparaging him with the title "poet." See Plato, *Phaedrus*, in *The Collected Dialogues of Plato, Including the Letters*, ed. Huntington Cairns and Edith Hamilton (Princeton, NJ: Princeton University Press, 1982), 243a–b.

30. Foucault and Blanchot, *Foucault, Blanchot*, 10.

31. Ibid., 13.

32. Ibid., 10–11. It is worth noting here that the "contentless slimness of 'I speak'" calls to mind Marx's definition of value, which he describes a "slight and contentless thing" because it is something purely social. For Marx, when two commodities are exchanged in the market, we must posit a third thing—a value that mediates them. Marx assigns a subjectivity, an *agency*, to value: it is "self-valorizing," the "dominant subject," and a "self-moving substance." It is telling, then, that Foucault echoes a certain Marxian language, suggesting that the currency of speech,

its value, is the socio-subjective or discursive agency that fictively props up the subjectivity of speakers in the spoken exchange. See Karl Marx, *Capital: A Critique of Political Economy*, vol. 1, trans. Ben Fowkes (London: Penguin, 1990), 255–56. I thank Barbara Biesecker for this insight.

33. Michel Foucault, "Language to Infinity," in *Aesthetics, Method, and Epistemology*, ed. James D. Faubion (New York: New Press, 1998), 90.

34. Ibid., 91.

35. J. L. Austin, *How to Do Things with Words* (Oxford: Oxford University Press, 1962), 26, emphasis in original.

36. Austin's example is marrying a monkey, which he labels a "mockery." Fearful of shifting social conventions, certain American conservatives campaigning against same-sex marriage mockingly invoked the marriage of sheep, goats, and chickens as the inevitable outcome of extending marriage rights. For them, the "biology" of human sexual difference is as timeless and immutable as trans-species differences, and "biology" here figures as the basis of rigid conventions that determine and authorize permissible speech acts. While biological differences may be codified in law, the conventions of which Austin speaks are mutable and emerge—like law—in dialogue with culture, history, language, and the sciences.

37. Austin, *How to Do Things with Words*, 99.

38. Ibid., 113.

39. Michel Foucault, *The Foucault Effect: Studies in Governmentality* (Chicago: University of Chicago Press, 1991), 11.

40. Austin, *How to Do Things with Words*, 148.

41. Ibid., 101; my emphasis is to show that perlocutions may but need not be executed with design, intention, or purpose behind them.

42. Ibid., 101–2.

43. "In speaking, I threatened you" is illocutionary, but it is incorrect to say, "In speaking, I intimidated you." Intimidation is an effect or consequence of my speech, not performed *in* it. The perlocutionary speech act is, then, "By speaking, I intimidated you." The intimidating effect of my speech is not contained in the speaking but may (or may not) be produced by it.

44. This insight should persuade (or convince, get, incite . . .) us to reevaluate rhetorical studies and what we mean by rhetorical invention, which commonly defers to a liberal "I" or "we" without taking account of the force of the perlocution.

45. Ibid., 110–11. Austin's scare quotes around "physical" are to distinguish it, I suspect, from speech, which is technically a physical activity—moving our vocal cords, et cetera.

46. Ibid., 111n2.

47. Foucault and Bonnefoy, *Speech Begins*, 65–66.

48. See, for example, Dave Holmes and Stuart J. Murray, "Censoring Violence: Censorship and Critical Research in Forensic Psychiatry," in *Power and the Psychiatric Apparatus: Repression, Transformation and Assistance*, ed. Dave Holmes, Jean-Daniel Jacob, and Amélie Perron (Farnham, UK: Ashgate, 2014), 35–45.

49. To invoke this "preauthorization" might be the most succinct definition of identity politics.

50. J. Heshima Denham, "A Day in the Life of An Imprisoned Revolutionary," *San Francisco Bay View*, May 8, 2012, http://sfbayview.com/2012/05/a-day-in-the-life-of-an-imprisoned -revolutionary.

51. Nicole Natschke, "Voices from Solitary: 'I Am Somebody's Daughter,'" *Solitary Watch: News from a Nation in Lockdown*, Feb. 24, 2015, http://solitarywatch.com/2015/02/24/voices -from-solitary-i-am-somebodys-daughter.

52. *Prison Hunger Strike Solidarity*, https://prisonerhungerstrikesolidarity.wordpress.com, retrieved Apr. 9, 2015.

53. NCTT Corcoran SHU, 4B-1C-C Section, Super-Max Isolation Unit, "Corcoran Prisoners Join Pelican Bay Hunger Strike," *Prisoner Hunger Strike Solidarity*, June 30, 2011, https://prisonerhungerstrikesolidarity.wordpress.com/voices-from-inside/corcoran -prisoners-join-pelican-bay-hunger-strike.

54. Zaharibu Dorrough, J. Heshima Denham, and Kambui Robinson, "Feeling Death at Our Heels: An Update from the Frontlines of the Struggle," *Prisoner Hunger Strike Solidarity*, 2011, https://prisonerhungerstrikesolidarity.wordpress.com/feeling-death-at-our-heels -an-update-from-the-frontlines-of-the-struggle.

55. Colin Dayan, "With Law at the Edge of Life," *South Atlantic Quarterly* 113, no. 3 (2014): 631.

56. Dayan, "Writing," 182.

57. Pelican Bay Prison–SHU Short Corridor Inmates, "Formal Complaint Issued to Prison Officials Before the Hunger Strike Began July 1st, 2011," *Prisoner Hunger Strike Solidarity*, Feb. 5, 2010, https://prisonerhungerstrikesolidarity.wordpress.com/formal-complaint.

58. Keramet Reiter, "The Pelican Bay Hunger Strike: Resistance Within the Structural Constraints of a US Supermax Prison," *South Atlantic Quarterly* 113, no. 3 (2014): 590–97.

59. Ibid., 590.

60. Cited in ibid., 600.

61. One outcome of this "conversation" was a set of promised reforms, which ended the 2011 hunger strike protest. By 2013, claiming the CDCR had reneged on its promises, the prisoners once again went on a hunger strike.

62. T. S. Eliot, "The Hollow Men" (1925), in *Poems, 1909–1925* (London: Faber and Faber, 1934), 123–28, available online at https://archive.org/details/poems19091925030616mbp.

## Chapter 3

1. "Alberta Parents Convicted in Toddler's Meningitis Death," *CBC News*, Apr. 26, 2016, http://cbc.ca/news/canada/calgary/meningitis-trial-verdict-1.3552941.

2. Criminal Code, Government of Canada, R.S.C., 1985, c. C-46, (215 (1)(a)), last updated Apr. 29, 2016, http://laws-lois.justice.gc.ca/eng/acts/C-46.

3. Bill Graveland, "Give Stephans Tougher Sentences in Son's Meningitis Case, Alberta Crown Urges on Appeal," *CBC News*, July 7, 2016, http://cbc.ca/news/canada/calgary /crown-appeals-sentence-toddler-meningitis-death-1.3669581.

4. Ibid.

5. Ivan Illich, *Medical Nemesis: The Expropriation of Health* (Toronto: McClelland and Stewart, 1976).

6. Martin A. Makary and Michael Daniel, "Medical Error: The Third Leading Cause of Death in the US," *BMJ* 353 (2016): i2139, https://www.bmj.com/content/353/bmj.i2139.

7. See World Health Organization, "International Statistical Classification of Diseases and Related Health Problems," 10th rev. (2016), http://apps.who.int/classifications/icd10 /browse/2016/en.

8. The ranking of cause of death is problematic because it is nearly impossible to say what a "natural" death is. Cancer and heart disease are "natural" if we ignore some of the wider socioenvironmental factors that might be causal, such as poverty, pollution, lack of health care, carcinogenic pesticide use, et cetera. However, even if death by cancer and heart disease is forestalled biomedically, we might still consider many of these deaths as "natural" occurrences—and in ordinary

language we might say that these people did not die "before their time." With ICD codes, however, we are presumed to have died of something other than natural causes or old age. Of the 2,626,418 deaths in the United States reported in 2014, by far the largest demographic is eighty-five and over, accounting for 826,226 deaths. "Old age" and "senescence" figure discreetly under "Senility" (R54), but this category is rarely used in reporting and is not listed as a separate statistic (old age / senescence is included within the total combined deaths for one hundred distinct categories, from R00–99, totaling just 32,242—under 4 percent of those who died at the age of eighty-five and over). On the whole, 5 percent of Americans reportedly died in 2014 from influenza and pneumonia, and these "causes" also ignore old age / senescence.

In contradistinction to these presumably natural causes of death, we might assume that death by medical error is preventable, or "unnatural," and we might say that these people died unnecessarily and "before their time." In 2014, total deaths due to "complications of medical and surgical care" are reported as only 2,540 (under 0.1 percent) with an additional 7,130 due to infection by *Clostridium difficile*. The report is silent on medical errors or otherwise "preventable" and "untimely" deaths. See Kenneth D. Kochanek et al., "Deaths: Final Data for 2014," *National Vital Statistics Reports* 65, no. 4 (2016): 1–120, http://cdc.gov/nchs/data/nvsr/nvsr65/nvsr65_04.pdf.

9. Michel Foucault, "*Society Must Be Defended*": *Lectures at the Collège de France, 1975–1976*, trans. David Macey (New York: Picador, 2003), 246.

10. Makary and Daniel, "Medical Error."

11. See Linda Qiu, "Trump Oversells New 'Right to Try' Law," *New York Times*, May 30, 2018, https://nytimes.com/2018/05/30/us/politics/fact-check-trump-right-to-try-law-.html.

12. Michel Foucault, "Life: Experience and Science," in *Aesthetics, Method, and Epistemology*, ed. James D. Faubion (New York: New Press, 1998), 474.

13. Ibid.

14. In 2019 the US pharmaceutical industry was valued at approximately $511.4 billion. See Matej Mikulic, "U.S. Pharmaceutical Industry Statistics and Facts," *Statista*, https://www.statista.com/topics/1719/pharmaceutical-industry, retrieved Nov. 9, 2020.

15. Michel Foucault, *Abnormal: Lectures at the Collège de France, 1974–1975*, trans. Graham Burchell (New York: Picador, 2003), 26.

16. Bill Graveland, "Faith in Natural Remedies 'Like a Religion,' Say Experts Watching the Lethbridge Trial," *CBC News*, Apr. 26, 2016, http://cbc.ca/news/canada/calgary/lethbridge-meningitis-stephan-religion-caulfield-1.3553197.

17. David Bell, "David Stephan Gets Jail Time, Collet Stephan Gets House Arrest in Son's Meningitis Death," *CBC News*, June 24, 2016, http://cbc.ca/news/canada/calgary/lethbridge-meningitis-trial-sentence-parents-toddler-died-1.3650653.

18. Ibid.

19. David Stephan, public Facebook post, Apr. 27, 2016, https://facebook.com/david.stephan.568/posts/10156836594445722.

20. Canadian Press, "Experts Say Appeals in Toddler Meningitis Death Case Could Drag on for Years," *CBC News*, Aug. 14, 2016, http://cbc.ca/news/canada/calgary/experts-appeals-toddler-meningitis-death-could-take-years-1.3720745.

21. Some of this discussion draws on and revises previously published criticism of the Makayla Sault case. See Stuart J. Murray and Tad Lemieux, "The Time of a Life: Ethics and Cancer Care in the Case of a Young First Nations Girl," in *The Ethics of Care: Moral Knowledge, Communication, and the Art of Caregiving*, ed. Alan Blum and Stuart J. Murray (New York: Routledge, 2017), 91–108. I thank Tad Lemieux for his contribution to what follows.

22. See Nahnda Garlow, "New Credit Child Resists Forced Chemotherapy Treatment," *Two Row Times*, May 7, 2014, http://tworowtimes.com/news/local/new-credit-child-resists -forced-chemotherapy-treatment. See also the video "Ojibwe Child Refuses Chemo, Wants Traditional Medicine Instead," YouTube, May 13, 2014, https://youtube.com/watch ?v=NrF5wWQ4hIU.

23. The likelihood of cure was inconsistently reported across the media, sometimes as high as 90 percent, and occasionally noting that prognoses are not based on Indigenous populations, who for genetic reasons may not respond as well to treatment. Makayla had been diagnosed with the "Philadelphia chromosome," which would have made treatment less effective. For the purposes of this discussion, I do not address the problematic meaning of a "cure"—typically five years of life—in the temporalities of cancer and its treatment. See, for example, Connie Walker, "Makayla Sault, Girl Who Refused Chemo for Leukemia, Dies," *CBC News*, Jan. 19, 2015, http://cbc.ca/news/aboriginal/makayla-sault-girl-who-refused-chemo-for-leukemia -dies-1.2829885.

24. Canadian Cancer Society, "Aboriginal Traditional Healing," http://cancer.ca/en /cancer-information/diagnosis-and-treatment/complementary-therapies/aboriginal -traditional-healing, retrieved May 8, 2016.

25. Jacques Gallant, "Owner of Florida Health Spa Treating Aboriginal Girls Ordered to Cease Practising," *The Star*, Mar. 5, 2015, https://thestar.com/news/gta/2015/03/05/owner -of-florida-health-spa-treating-aboriginal-girls-ordered-to-cease-practising.html.

26. Tim Alamenciak, "Coroner Will Look into Death of Makayla Sault," *Hamilton Spectator*, Jan. 22, 2015, A1. The provincial Office of the Chief Coroner announced that it would investigate Makayla's death. The results of this investigation are not publicly available, but we can presume nothing unusual because to date a public inquest has not been deemed necessary.

27. Child and Family Services Act, RSO 1990, c C.11, in force from Dec. 31, 2011, through Aug. 30, 2015, http://canlii.ca/t/ldxd.

28. See Joseph Brean, "Official in Makayla Sault Case Says Laws on Child Protection and Medical Consent are Conflicting," *National Post*, Jan. 21, 2015, http://nationalpost.com/news /canada/official-in-makayla-sault-case-says-laws-on-child-protection-and-medical-consent -are-conflicting.

29. Health Care Consent Act, 1996, S.O. 1996, c. 2, Sched. A, in force from July 1, 2010, through June 30, 2015, https://ontario.ca/laws/statute/96h02/v13.

30. The Children's Aid Society of Brant, "Position Paper on Diversity and Anti-Oppressive Practice," July 18, 2008, http://brantfacs.ca/files/3913/9464/4826/Position_Paper_Final _Copy_July_18_2008.pdf, retrieved Sept. 13, 2016.

31. In a 2009 Supreme Court of Canada case, the Court ordered a fifteen-year-old Jehovah's Witness to undergo life-saving blood transfusions against her will. For children under sixteen years of age, this implies a judgment of "maturity": the greater the significance of the decision, the greater the burden of "proof," and the more the state has a duty to intervene. See A.C. v. Manitoba, 2009 SCC 30, June 26, 2009, http://scc-csc.lexum.com/scc-csc/scc-csc/en /item/7795/index.do. There have been similar cases at the provincial level in Ontario.

32. Teri Pecoskie, "Forcing Chemo on Girl Will Incite 'Wrath': Expert," *Hamilton Spectator*, May 17, 2014, https://www.thespec.com/news/hamilton-region/2014/05/17/forcing-chemo -on-girl-will-incite-wrath-expert.html.

33. See Elizabeth A. Povinelli, *Economies of Abandonment: Social Belonging and Endurance in Late Liberalism* (Durham, NC: Duke University Press, 2011).

34. This was the "expert report" by Dawn Martin-Hill, chair of Indigenous Studies at McMaster University, who had tried (unsuccessfully) to "broker a deal" between McMaster Children's Hospital and the Sault family. See Pecoskie, "Forcing Chemo on Girl."

35. Michel Foucault, "The Subject and Power," in *Power: Essential Works of Michel Foucault, 1954–1984*, ed. James D. Faubion (New York: New Press, 2000), 341.

36. Ibid., 340.

37. Ibid., 334.

38. Heather Cleland, "Dear Makayla: I Endured Chemo. Trust Me, It's Worth It," *Globe and Mail*, May 22, 2014, http://theglobeandmail.com/globe-debate/dear-makayla-i-endured-chemo-trust-me-its-worth-it/article18791085.

39. "Proportion of Indigenous Women in Custody Nears 50%," Office of the Correctional Investigator, Dec. 17, 2021, https://www.oci-bec.gc.ca/cnt/comm/press/press20211217-eng.aspx.

40. See Gary Geddes, *Medicine Unbundled: A Journey Through the Minefields of Indigenous Health Care* (Victoria, BC: Heritage House, 2017).

41. "The Office of the Chief Coroner's Death Review of the Youth Suicides at the Pikangikum First Nation: Executive Summary," Office of the Chief Coroner, Ontario Ministry of Community Safety and Correctional Services, June 1, 2011, last modified Mar. 14, 2016, http://mcscs.jus.gov.on.ca/english/DeathInvestigations/office_coroner/Publicationsand Reports/PIK_report.html, retrieved May 12, 2016.

42. Martin Patriquin, "Canada, Home to the Suicide Capital of the World," *Maclean's Magazine*, Mar. 30, 2012, http://macleans.ca/news/canada/canada-home-to-the-suicide-capital-of-the-world.

43. Juliet Guichon, Ian Mitchell, Roxanne Goldade, and Victor Lew, "Makayla Too Young to Make Medical Decision," *Hamilton Spectator*, May 31, 2014, https://www.thespec.com/opinion/columnists/2014/05/31/makayla-too-young-to-make-medical-decision.html.

44. Terry Glavin, "Makayla's Death, but Our Disgrace," *National Post*, Jan. 22, 2015, http://nationalpost.com/opinion/terry-glavin-makaylas-death-but-our-disgrace.

45. Carl Schmitt, *Political Theology: Four Chapters on the Concept of Sovereignty*, trans. George Schwab (Chicago: University of Chicago Press, 2005), 5.

46. Georges Bataille, *The Accursed Share: An Essay on General Economy*, vols. 2 and 3, trans. Robert Hurley (New York: Zone Books, 1993), 239.

47. This is why the deconstruction or critique *of* biopolitics risks reduplicating sovereign structures: "Deconstruction or critique of biopolitics maintains the old relationship between the biological and the symbolic, the discrepancy, the separation that exists between them. This is what prevents such a deconstruction or such a critique from superseding the traditional or metaphysical approaches to life." And conversely, it is why the deconstruction or critique of sovereignty also ends up invoking the very sovereign that is its object: "The critique or deconstruction of sovereignty is structured as the very entity it tends to critique or deconstruct . . . reaffirm[ing] the theory of sovereignty, that is, the split between the symbolic and the biological." See Catherine Malabou, "Will Sovereignty Ever be Deconstructed?," in *Plastic Materialities: Politics, Legality, and Metamorphosis in the Work of Catherine Malabou*, ed. Brenna Bhandar and Jonathan Goldberg-Hiller (Durham, NC: Duke University Press, 2015), 39.

48. I thank Tad Lemieux, whose outstanding PhD dissertation has been central to my thinking. See Tad Lemieux, "Arctic Rhetoric and Inuit Sovereignty" (PhD diss., Carleton University, 2019).

49. Michel Foucault, *Psychiatric Power: Lectures at the Collège de France, 1973–1974*, trans. Graham Burchell (New York: Palgrave Macmillan, 2006), 47.

50. See Frantz Fanon, *Black Skin, White Masks*, trans. Richard Philcox (New York: Grove Press, 2008).

51. Glen Sean Coulthard, *Red Skin, White Masks: Rejecting the Colonial Politics of Recognition* (Minneapolis: University of Minnesota Press, 2014), 23–24. See also the special issue of

*Philosophy and Rhetoric* devoted to "The Rhetorical Contours of Recognition," and here particularly Sarah K. Burgess, "Exposing the Ruins of Law: The Rhetorical Contours of Recognition's Demand," *Philosophy and Rhetoric* 48, no. 4 (2015): 516–35.

52. Coulthard, *Red Skin, White Masks*, 22.

53. "Canada Officially Adopts UN Declaration on the Rights of Indigenous Peoples," *CBC News*, May 10, 2016, https://www.cbc.ca/news/aboriginal/canada-adopting-implementing-un -rights-declaration-1.3575272.

54. United Nations, "Declaration on the Rights of Indigenous Peoples," Article 3, Mar. 2008, http://un.org/esa/socdev/unpfii/documents/DRIPS_en.pdf.

55. Ibid., Articles 3–4.

56. Ibid., Article 46.1, emphasis added.

57. G. W. F. Hegel, *Phenomenology of Spirit*, trans. A. V. Miller (Oxford: Oxford University Press, 1977), 113. Elsewhere, I have written on the relationship between Hegelian recognition and biopolitics; see Stuart J. Murray, "Hegel's Pathology of Recognition: A Biopolitical Fable," *Philosophy and Rhetoric* 48, no. 4 (2015): 443–72.

58. Hegel, *Phenomenology of Spirit*, 113, 117.

59. Ibid.

60. Jean-Luc Nancy, *The Inoperative Community*, trans. Peter Connor, Lisa Garbus, Michael Holland, and Simona Sawhney (Minneapolis: University of Minnesota Press, 1991), 3.

61. See, for example, Mark Rifkin, *Beyond Settler Time: Temporal Sovereignty and Indigenous Self-Determination* (Durham, NC: Duke University Press, 2017). I would note, however, that Rifkin's formulation of Indigenous "temporal sovereignty" yields to the liberalized ruses of sovereign power and misses the lessons of biopolitics.

62. Georges Bataille, *The Unfinished System of Nonknowledge*, trans. Michelle Kendall and Stuart Kendall (Minneapolis: University of Minnesota Press, 2001), 187.

63. Jacques Derrida, *Writing and Difference*, trans. Alan Bass (Chicago: University of Chicago Press, 1978), 257.

64. Bataille, *Accursed Share*, 439n3.

65. Georges Bataille, *Inner Experience*, trans. Leslie Anne Boldt (Albany: State University of New York Press, 1988), 111.

66. Maurice Blanchot, *The Writing of the Disaster*, trans. Ann Smock (Lincoln: University of Nebraska Press, 1995), 45.

67. Bataille, *Accursed Share*, 222.

68. Derrida, *Writing and Difference*, 256.

69. Bataille, *Accursed Share*, 197–99.

70. Ibid., 79–80.

71. Ibid., 80–81.

72. Ibid.

73. Ibid., 216.

74. Ibid., 217.

75. Ibid., 211.

76. Ibid., 203.

77. Georges Bataille, *Œuvres complètes*, vol. 7 (Paris: Gallimard, 1976), 245, translation mine.

78. Nancy, *Inoperative Community*, 2.

79. Blanchot, *Disaster*, 21.

80. Ibid., 40.

81. Ibid., 65.

82. Maurice Blanchot, *The Step Not Beyond*, trans. Lycette Nelson (Albany: State University of New York Press, 1992), 107. See also "The Instant of My Death," a short story by Blanchot,

which appears alongside Derrida's commentary, "Demeure: Fiction and Testimony," in Maurice Blanchot and Jacques Derrida, *The Instant of My Death" and "Demeure: Fiction and Testimony*," trans. Elizabeth Rottenberg (Stanford, CA: Stanford University Press, 2000), 1–12.

83. Blanchot, *Step Not Beyond*, 107.

84. Maurice Blanchot, *The Unavowable Community*, trans. Pierre Joris (Barrytown, NY: Station Hill Press, 1988), 12. See also Derrida, who writes, "For there to be a gift event (we say event and not act), something must come about or happen, in an instant, in an instant that no doubt does not belong to the economy of time, in a time without time" (*Given Time I: Counterfeit Money*, trans. Peggy Kamuf [Chicago: University of Chicago Press, 1992], 17).

85. Blanchot, *Disaster*, 51.

86. Ibid., 89.

87. See, for example, Aleksandra Sandstrom, "Most States Allow Religious Exemptions from Child Abuse and Neglect Laws," *Pew Research Center*, Aug. 12, 2016, http://pewresearch .org/fact-tank/2016/08/12/most-states-allow-religious-exemptions-from-child-abuse-and -neglect-laws.

88. Blanchot, *Disaster*, 66.

89. Bataille's work on sovereignty and death, published only posthumously, represents his engagement with questions of community and communitarianism in the 1930s, written in the looming shadows of European fascism and its distinct biopolitical paroxysms. Nancy states that "Bataille has gone farthest into the crucial experience of the modern destiny of community," even though interest in Bataille's thought has been "meager and all too often frivolous." He continues, "What has not yet been sufficiently remarked is the extent to which his thinking emerged out of a political exigency and uneasiness—or from an exigency and an uneasiness concerning the political that was itself guided by the thought of community" (*Inoperative Community*, 16). And Allan Stoekl, in his commentary on Bataille's texts, writes, "It must be recalled when reading Bataille's writings from 1935 to 1940 that there is an assumption that democracy in the West is doomed; the choice is between some form of communism and fascism" (*Visions of Excess: Selected Writings, 1927–1939*, trans. Allan Stoekl [Minneapolis: University of Minnesota Press, 1985], 261). In these years, Bataille was, for a time, fatefully drawn to both excesses (see Nancy, *Inoperative Community*, 16–21). And yet, if the uneasy question of community is today as exigent as ever, our choice is no longer quite framed in Bataille's terms from the 1930s.

What would, in Bataille's time, soon prove a false choice "between some form of communism and fascism" is perhaps today best conveyed by the "rational"—but equally false—choice between biopolitics and fascism. The operative assumption is that biopolitics represents humanity's greatest hope for community freely chosen. Roberto Esposito goes so far as to say that while biopolitics poses a risk to democracy, this does not mean "that another kind of democracy is impossible, one that is compatible with the biopolitical turn" (*Terms of the Political: Community, Immunity, Biopolitics*, trans. Rhiannon Noel Welch [New York: Fordham University Press, 2013], 110). Between biopolitics and fascism, Esposito asserts that "affirmative" biopolitics is the only "democratic" option, the only form of communitarianism (if this is still the right word) that is viable today. I'm not persuaded by this "choice" and would invoke Blanchot's question: Are we still willing—by biopolitical desire, ruse, or violence—to risk the "life" that we seek, through this risk, to prolong? In answer to this question, we should pay heed to Bataille's false choice: Nancy reminds us that "fascism was the grotesque or abject resurgence of an obsession with communion; it crystallized the motif of its supposed loss and the nostalgia for its images of fusion. In this respect, it was the convulsion of Christianity, and it ended up fascinating modern Christianity in its entirety" (*Inoperative Community*, 17). Indeed, by the late 1930s, communism and fascism were ultimately conjoined. And I would recall Blanchot's description of the 1930s, when Bataille had become so deeply preoccupied with the question of community. At that time, Blanchot writes, there was "the premonition of what [was] already fascism but the meaning of which, and its becoming, elude[d] the concepts then in use" (*Unavowable Community*, 5). To what extent, then, is a "democratic" or "affirmative" biopolitics conjoined with a burgeoning (neo)fascism? And what concepts, today, what tropes, will elude our elusions and permit our own premonitions to speak?

90. Originally published in the journal *Aléa* 4 (1983), and republished as the first chapter in Nancy, *Inoperative Community*, 1–42.

91. Blanchot, *Unavowable Community*, 9.

92. Nancy, *Inoperative Community*, 14.

93. Jean-Jacques Rousseau, *The Social Contract*, trans. Maurice Cranston (London: Penguin, 1968), bk. 1, chap. 2.

94. Nancy, *Inoperative Community*, 9.

95. Ibid., 14–15. Pierre Joris's translation of *ordonnée* in this passage is "enjoined to death." "Calibrated" sounds too mechanical or calculated; to be given or "enjoined to death," *ordonnée*, is inordinate. See Blanchot, *Unavowable Community*, 10.

96. Nancy, *Inoperative Community*, 14–15.

97. Ibid., 31. An alternate translation might be "One does not produce community, one experiences it as the experience of finitude (or, its experience makes us)."

98. Ibid.

99. Bill Graveland, "'Bad Things Happen to Good Parents,' Defence Argues at Trial of Alberta Couple in Son's Meningitis Death," *CBC News*, Aug. 29, 2019, emphasis added, https://www.cbc.ca/news/canada/calgary/david-collet-stephan-lethbridge-meningitis -toddler-death-trial-1.5264901.

100. Hamilton Health Sciences Corp. v. D.H., 2014 ONCJ 603 (81), https://www.canlii .org/en/on/oncj/doc/2014/2014oncj603/2014oncj603.html.

101. The Honourable Justice Gethin B. Edward, quoted in Tom Blackwell, "Judge Says Forcing Aboriginal Girl to Stay in Chemo Is to 'Impose Our World View on First Nations Culture,'" *National Post*, Oct. 16, 2014, https://nationalpost.com/health/judge-says-forcing -aboriginal-girl-to-stay-in-chemo-is-to-impose-our-world-view-on-first-nation-culture.

102. R. v. Stephan, 2019 ABQB 715 (105), https://www.canlii.org/en/ab/abqb/doc/2019 /2019abqb715/2019abqb715.pdf.

103. Canadian Press, "Medical Examiner Tells Couple's Trial That Toddler Didn't Die from Lack of Oxygen," *CBC News*, June 11, 2019, https://www.cbc.ca/news/canada/calgary /stephans-toddler-death-trial-medical-examiner-1.5171360.

104. Nancy, *Inoperative Community*, 14.

105. Sarah Lochlann Jain, "Living in Prognosis: Toward an Elegiac Politics," *Representations* 98, no. 1 (2007): 77–92. See also S. Lochlann Jain, *Malignant: How Cancer Becomes Us* (Berkeley: University of California Press, 2013): "When Mary found that her cancer *had* spread (had, indeed, been spreading), her health status retroactively shifted. *I am alive. No, you are . . .* In one swift motion, the cancer prognosis detonates time, which scatters like so many glass shards" (28).

106. See Barbara Ehrenreich, "Welcome to Cancerland," *Harper's*, Nov. 2001, 43–53.

107. Blanchot, *Disaster*, 87.

Chapter 4

1. See http://youtube.com/watch?v=e3zD_Y2sGqY, posted on July 20, 2017, retrieved Nov. 19, 2020; the video has since been removed. The first newspaper account of the video is by Ariel Zilber, "'Oh, He Just Died!': Horrifying Video Shows Group of Teens Laughing

While Watching a Disabled Man Drown in a Pond," *Daily Mail*, July 21, 2017, http://dailymail .co.uk/news/article-4716516/Teens-filmed-laughing-watching-disabled-man-drown .html#video. The argument that follows draws on Stuart J. Murray, "Regarder le regard: Le racisme biopolitique et les propos haineux numériques," *Canadian Review of American Studies* 50, no. 1 (2020): 143–64. Copyright © 2020, Canadian Association of American Studies (CAAS), reprinted with permission from University of Toronto Press (https://www.utp journals.press).

2. Dave Berman, "Mourners Gather at Funeral Service for Drowning Victim Jamel Dunn," *Florida Today*, July 29, 2017, http://floridatoday.com/story/news/local/2017/07/29/mourners -gather-funeral-service-drowning-victim-jamel-dunn/518160001.

3. "Long Lived Jamel Dunn," Go Fund Me, July 17, 2017, http://gofundme.com/nd4cvm -long-lived-jamel-dunn.

4. One year later, the case was closed and no charges were filed. See J. D. Gallop, "No Charges for 5 Teens Who Mocked and Filmed Drowning Man, Jamel Dunn, in a Cocoa Pond," *Florida Today*, June 22, 2018, https://floridatoday.com/story/news/2018/06/22/no -charges-year-after-teens-mocked-drowning-man-prosecutors-rule-out-filing-charges/723 259002.

5. See Saidiya V. Hartman, *Scenes of Subjection: Terror, Slavery, and Self-Making in Nineteenth-Century America* (New York: Oxford University Press, 1997), 4. Hartman's historical analysis of racial subjugation resonates with this scene, and in particular her treatment of "diffuse" terror, "mundane and quotidian," enacted in the interchange between terror and enjoyment, witnessing and spectatorship.

6. Alexander G. Weheliye, *Habeas Viscus: Racializing Assemblages, Biopolitics, and Black Feminist Theories of the Human* (Durham, NC: Duke University Press, 2014), 56, 65.

7. See, for example, the Southern Poverty Law Center's "Hate Map," http://splcenter.org /hate-map, which at the time of writing is tracking a total of 917 hate groups in the United States. Since 2015, the SPLC documents a 197 percent increase in anti-Muslim hate groups. And they document "an explosive rise in the number of hate groups since the turn of the century, driven in part by anger over Latino immigration and demographic projections showing that whites will no longer hold majority status in the country by around 2040."

8. To offer just one example, consider how Facebook helped to fuel the ethnic cleansing of the Rohingya in Myanmar: "Facebook has become a breeding ground for hate speech and virulent posts about the Rohingya. And because of Facebook's design, posts that are shared and liked more frequently get more prominent placement in feeds, favoring highly partisan content in timelines." Megan Specia and Paul Mozur, "A War of Words Puts Facebook at the Center of Myanmar's Rohingya Crisis," *New York Times*, Oct. 27, 2017, http://nytimes.com /2017/10/27/world/asia/myanmar-government-facebook-rohingya.html.

9. Ian Bogost, "The Cathedral of Computation," *The Atlantic*, Jan. 15, 2015, https://www .theatlantic.com/technology/archive/2015/01/the-cathedral-of-computation/384300.

10. Ed Finn, *What Algorithms Want: Imagination in the Age of Computing* (Cambridge, MA: MIT Press, 2017).

11. Alexander R. Galloway, *The Interface Effect* (Cambridge: Polity, 2012), 8–9.

12. Saidiya Hartman, *Lose Your Mother: A Journey Along the Atlantic Slave Route* (New York: Farrar, Straus and Giroux, 2007), 107.

13. Ibid., 18.

14. Saidiya Hartman, "Venus in Two Acts," *Small Axe: A Caribbean Journal of Criticism* 12, no. 2 (2008): 6–7.

15. Sharon Patricia Holland, *Raising the Dead: Readings of Death and (Black) Subjectivity* (Durham, NC: Duke University Press, 2000), 141.

16. Hartman, *Scenes of Subjection*, 21.

17. Sharon Patricia Holland, "The Graveyard," *The Professor's Table* (blog), Aug. 31, 2017, http://theprofessorstable.wordpress.com/2017/08/31/the-graveyard.

18. Hartman, "Venus in Two Acts," 7.

19. In a classical sense, commentators act as the Chorus in a play, and the address as a parabasis. "The Chorus too should be regarded as one of the actors; it should be an integral part of the whole, and take a share in the action" (Aristotle, "Poetics," in *The Complete Works of Aristotle: The Revised Oxford Translation*, ed. Jonathan Barnes [Princeton, NJ: Princeton University Press, 1984], 1455b24–1456a32).

20. See Robert Meister, *After Evil: A Politics of Human Rights* (New York: Columbia University Press, 2011).

21. Martin Heidegger, *Being and Time*, trans. Edward Robinson and John Macquarrie (New York: Harper & Row, 1962), 344.

22. Ibid., 154.

23. Ibid., 156.

24. Susan Sontag, "Regarding the Torture of Others," *New York Times Magazine*, May 23, 2004, 28.

25. See, for example, Simone Browne, *Dark Matters: On the Surveillance of Blackness* (Durham, NC: Duke University Press, 2015); and Ruha Benjamin, *Race After Technology: Abolitionist Tools for the New Jim Code* (Cambridge: Polity, 2019).

26. On the notion of "evental rhetoric" as the "occurrence of discourse": "not the saying of the Event, not the inscription of the Event into language or into speech, but saying *as the* Event, saying as eventful and not as an eventuality" (Barbara A. Biesecker, "Prospects of Rhetoric for the Twenty-First Century: Speculations on Evental Rhetoric Ending with a Note on Barack Obama and a Benediction by Jacques Lacan," in *Reengaging the Prospects of Rhetoric: Current Conversations and Contemporary Challenges*, ed. Mark J. Porrovecchio [New York: Routledge, 2010], 19).

27. Jacques Derrida, "Racism's Last Word," *Critical Inquiry* 12, no. 1 (1985): 291.

28. Hartman, *Lose Your Mother*, 6.

29. Heidegger, *Being and Time*, 283.

30. On the ontology of duration as distinct from everyday "scientific" spacetime, see Henri Bergson, *Creative Evolution*, trans. Arthur Mitchell (Mineola, NY: Dover, 1998). See also Keith Ansell-Pearson, *Philosophy and the Adventure of the Virtual: Bergson and the Time of Life* (New York: Routledge, 2001); and Gilles Deleuze, *Bergsonism*, trans. Hugh Tomlinson and Barbara Habberjam (New York: Zone, 1988).

31. Hartman, *Lose Your Mother*, 17.

32. "*Dasien's* going-out-of-the-world in the sense of dying must be distinguished from the going-out-of-the-world of that which merely has life [*des Nur-lebenden*]" (Heidegger, *Being and Time*, 284).

33. Michel Foucault, *The Archaeology of Knowledge and The Discourse on Language*, trans. A. M. Sheridan Smith (New York: Pantheon, 1972), 126.

34. Fred Moten, *Black and Blur* (Durham, NC: Duke University Press, 2017), 242.

35. Weheliye, *Habeas Viscus*, 72.

36. Foucault, *Archaeology of Knowledge*, 127.

37. Hartman, *Lose Your Mother*, 115.

38. See Ann Laura Stoler, *Carnal Knowledge and Imperial Power: Race and the Intimate in Colonial Rule* (Berkeley: University of California Press, 2010).

39. Norbert Wiener, *The Human Use of Human Beings: Cybernetics and Society* (Garden City, NY: Doubleday, 1954), 95. N. Katherine Hayles offers a powerful critique of early cybernetics as a forgetting of embodiment; see *How We Became Posthuman: Virtual Bodies in Cybernetics, Literature, and Informatics* (Chicago: University of Chicago Press, 1999).

40. See Heidegger, *Being and Time*, 156.

41. On the analysis of "white lives matter," "blue lives matter," and "all lives matter," see Barbara A. Biesecker, "From General History to Philosophy: Black Lives Matter, Late Neoliberal Molecular Biopolitics, and Rhetoric," *Philosophy and Rhetoric* 50, no. 4 (2017): 409–30.

42. Heidegger, *Being and Time*, 345.

43. Charles R. Lawrence, "If He Hollers Let Him Go: Regulating Racist Speech on Campus," *Duke Law Journal* 1990, no. 3 (1990): 443.

44. Ibid., 436–37. See also Mari J. Matsuda et al., *Words That Wound: Critical Race Theory, Assaultive Speech, and the First Amendment* (Boulder, CO: Westview Press, 1993); and Catharine A. MacKinnon, *Only Words* (Cambridge, MA: Harvard University Press, 2002).

45. Lawrence, "If He Hollers," 452.

46. Even face-to-face encounters, such as public protests and events, are mediated by the interface, both explicitly and implicitly or stylistically: protestors view the protest through the lens of their mobile devices, uploading digital media content instantaneously, commenting, recirculating, and so forth. Increasingly, public face-to-face events seem to be hyperreal, made with social media and digital distribution in mind.

47. Judith Butler, *Gender Trouble: Feminism and the Subversion of Identity* (New York: Routledge, 1990), 45.

48. I thank Sarah Burgess for this formulation.

49. Although Butler's more recent work, *Notes Toward a Performative Theory of Assembly*, refers frequently to the use of social media in public protest, Butler nevertheless privileges an analysis of the freedom of assembly—*bodies* in the street, their right to appear (an Arendtian theme) and to be addressed in the face-to-face. Tellingly, the early working title for Butler's collection of essays was *Bodies in Alliance*. See Judith Butler, *Notes Toward a Performative Theory of Assembly* (Cambridge, MA: Harvard University Press, 2015), 24.

50. Judith Butler, *Excitable Speech: A Politics of the Performative* (New York: Routledge, 1997), 17.

51. Hayden White, *Tropics of Discourse: Essays in Cultural Criticism* (Baltimore: Johns Hopkins University Press, 1978), 2.

52. I distinguish between *hyperhistoricity* and *deep historicity*, extending Bernard Stiegler's distinction between *hyperattention* and *deep attention*. For him, *hyperattention* characterizes our care-less engagement in digital contexts, which he diagnoses as a "global attention deficit disorder." Bernard Stiegler, *Taking Care of Youth and the Generations*, trans. Stephen Barker (Stanford: Stanford University Press, 2010), 176–79. N. Katherine Hayles draws a similar distinction between "hyper reading" and "close reading." See N. Katherine Hayles, *How We Think: Digital Media and Contemporary Technogenesis* (Chicago: University of Chicago Press, 2012), chapter 3.

53. Alexander R. Galloway, "The Reticular Fallacy," *b2o: an online journal* (2014): http://www.boundary2.org/2014/12/the-reticular-fallacy.

54. Ibid.

55. Jessie Daniels, *Cyber Racism: White Supremacy Online and the New Attack on Civil Rights* (Lanham, MD: Rowman & Littlefield, 2009), 118.

56. Ibid.

57. Ibid., 119, emphasis added.

58. See Jessie Daniels, "From Crisis Pregnancy Centers to Teenbreaks.com: Anti-Abortion Activism's Use of Cloaked Websites," in *Cyberactivism on the Participatory Web*, ed. Martha McCaughey (New York: Routledge, 2014), 140–54.

59. Indeed, there are businesses that sell fake social media "followers" who will retweet and post automated responses: "Celebrities, athletes, pundits and politicians have millions of fake

followers." See Nicholas Confessore, Gabriel J. X. Dance, Richard Harris, and Mark Hansen, "The Follower Factory," *New York Times*, Jan. 27, 2018, http://nytimes.com/interactive /2018/01/27/technology/social-media-bots.html. On Facebook's "anti-social" social media influence, see Siva Vaidhyanathan, *Antisocial Media* (Oxford: Oxford University Press, 2018).

60. See Carole Cadwalladr, "The Great British Brexit Robbery: How Our Democracy Was Hijacked," *The Guardian*, May 7, 2017, http://theguardian.com/technology/2017/may/07 /the-great-british-brexit-robbery-hijacked-democracy.

61. See, for example, Jonathon Morgan and Kris Shaffer, "Sockpuppets, Secessionists, and Breitbart: How Russia May Have Orchestrated a Massive Social Media Influence Campaign," *Medium*, Mar. 31, 2017, http://medium.com/data-for-democracy/sockpuppets-secessionists -and-breitbart-7171b1134cd5; Eudaimo, "Trump, Sock Puppets and the Russia Strings on Both of Them" (three articles), *Medium*, Jan. 31, 2017, http://medium.com/@eudaimo/trump-sock -puppets-and-the-russian-tie-art-1-9407edff767. On the activities of Russian trolls in the 2016 American election, see Scott Shane, "How Unwitting Americans Encountered Russian Opera- tives Online," *New York Times*, Feb. 18, 2018, http://nytimes.com/2018/02/18/us/politics /russian-operatives-facebook-twitter.html; and Matt Apuzzo and Sharon LaFraniere, "13 Russians Indicted as Mueller Reveals Effort to Aid Trump Campaign," *New York Times*, Feb. 16, 2018, http://nytimes.com/2018/02/16/us/politics/russians-indicted-mueller-election -interference.html.

62. Marshall McLuhan, *Understanding Media: The Extensions of Man* (Cambridge, MA: MIT Press, 1994), 22.

63. Ibid., 23.

64. Ibid., 354.

65. See Jesse Singal, "Undercover with the Alt-Right," *New York Times*, Sept. 19, 2017, https://nytimes.com/2017/09/19/opinion/alt-right-white-supremacy-undercover.html.

66. Marshall McLuhan, *Letters of Marshall McLuhan* (Oxford: Oxford University Press, 1987), 387.

67. N. Katherine Hayles, *My Mother Was a Computer: Digital Subjects and Literary Texts* (Chicago: University of Chicago Press, 2005), 31.

68. McLuhan was influenced by Mansfield Forbes, F. R. Leavis, and I. A. Richards. See his PhD thesis from Cambridge University (1943), posthumously published as Marshall McLuhan, *The Classical Trivium: The Place of Thomas Nashe in the Learning of His Time* (Corte Madera, CA: Gingko Press, 2006).

69. See Twyla Gibson, "Double Vision: McLuhan's Contributions to Media as an Inter- disciplinary Approach to Communication, Culture, and Technology," *MediaTropes* 1, no. 1 (2008): 143–66, http://mediatropes.com/index.php/Mediatropes/article/view/3345/1489.

70. McLuhan, *Understanding Media*, 8.

71. Ibid., 9.

72. In earlier work, I argued that McLuhan's "Electric Revolution" resonates powerfully with the nineteenth-century paradigm shift that Foucault has charted, from sovereignty to biopolitics. The political dimensions of power and discourse, as understood by Foucault, are only intimated by McLuhan, while conversely, McLuhan's understanding of media helps to fill in lacunae in Foucault's analysis, since the rise of biopolitics is scarcely conceivable without an understanding of contemporaneous revolutionary advances in media technologies and telecommunications. See Stuart J. Murray, "Rhetorical Insurgents: Biopolitics and the Insur- rectionary Rhetoric of McLuhan's Cool Media," *Canadian Review of American Studies* 42, no. 2 (2012): 123–41.

73. Hayles, *My Mother Was a Computer*, 41.

74. Michel Foucault, "*Society Must Be Defended*": *Lectures at the Collège de France, 1975–1976*, trans. David Macey (New York: Picador, 2003), 254.

75. Foucault claims that although racism had already been in existence, "it functioned elsewhere [*ailleurs*]" (ibid.). For a critique of this *ailleurs*, again see Weheliye, *Habeas Viscus*, 54ff. See also Ann Laura Stoler, *Race and the Education of Desire: Foucault's "History of Sexuality" and the Colonial Order of Things* (Durham, NC: Duke University Press, 1995).

76. Foucault, "*Society Must Be Defended*," 254.

77. Ibid., 255.

78. Ibid.

79. Ibid.

80. See, for example, Paul Rabinow, *French DNA: Trouble in Purgatory* (Chicago: University of Chicago Press, 1999).

81. Foucault, "*Society Must Be Defended*," 258.

82. Moten, *Black and Blur*, 280.

83. With this term, and throughout this chapter, I'm grateful for my conversations with Tad Lemieux. See Stuart J. Murray and Tad Lemieux, "Apprehending the Death of Jamel Dunn," *Los Angeles Review of Books*, Sept. 18, 2017, http://thephilosophicalsalon.com /apprehending-the-death-of-jamel-dunn. "Apprehend" also echoes Judith Butler's use of the term in *Frames of War: When Is Life Grievable?* (New York: Verso, 2009).

84. Stephen Matthias Harney and Fred Moten, *The Undercommons: Fugitive Planning and Black Study* (Brooklyn: Autonomedia / Minor Compositions, 2013), 91. See also Rinaldo Walcott, *The Long Emancipation: Moving Toward Black Freedom* (Durham, NC: Duke University Press, 2021).

85. Harney and Moten, *Undercommons*, 92.

86. *OED Online*, cited in Christina Sharpe, *In the Wake: On Blackness and Being* (Durham, DC: Duke University Press, 2016), 68.

87. Sharpe, *In the Wake*, 38.

88. Ibid., 117.

89. Ibid., 5.

90. Ibid., 123.

91. "This is Black being in the wake. This is the anagrammatical. These are Black lives, annotated" (ibid., 77).

92. Butler, *Excitable Speech*, 40–41.

93. Achille Mbembe, *Critique of Black Reason*, trans. Laurent Dubois (Durham, NC: Duke University Press, 2017), 173–74.

94. See Judith Butler, "The Value of Being Disturbed," *Theory and Event* 4, no. 1 (2000): https://muse.jhu.edu/article/32568/summary.

95. See Megan Twohey, "Rudolph Giuliani Lashes Out at Black Lives Matter," *New York Times*, July 10, 2016, http://nytimes.com/2016/07/11/us/politics/rudy-giuliani-black-lives -matter.html; and Taige Jensen and Japhet Weeks, "Need a Lawyer? Better Call Rudy," *New York Times*, July 31, 2018, http://nytimes.com/2018/07/31/opinion/giuliani-trump-russia -defense.html.

96. Dan Berry, Benjamin Wiser, and Alan Feuer, "In Defending Trump, Is Giuliani a Shrewd Tactician or 'Untethered'?," *New York Times*, Aug. 27, 2018, https://nytimes.com/2018/08/27 /nyregion/trump-giuliani-lawyer-mueller.html.

97. Isaac Kaplan, "Don't Equate Today's Culture Wars to Those of the 1990s," *Artsy*, Dec. 26, 2017, http://artsy.net/article/artsy-editorial-equate-todays-culture-wars-1990s.

98. Foucault, *Archaeology of Knowledge*, 127.

99. Claudia Rankine, "what if," in *Just Us: An American Conversation* (Minneapolis: Graywolf Press, 2020), 11.

100. Derrida, "Racism's Last Word," 291.

101. Neda Agha-Soltan was killed in the Iranian election protests of 2009. See Nima Naghibi, *Women Write Iran: Nostalgia and Human Rights from the Diaspora* (Minneapolis: University of Minnesota Press, 2016), chap. 1.

102. Lauren Berlant, "The Subject of True Feeling: Pain, Privacy, and Politics," in *Cultural Pluralism, Identity Politics, and the Law*, ed. Austin Sarat and Tomas R. Kearns (Ann Arbor: University of Michigan Press, 1999), 51.

103. Angela Moon, "Two-Thirds of American Adults Get News from Social Media: Survey," *Reuters*, Sept. 8, 2017, http://reuters.com/article/us-usa-internet-socialmedia/two-thirds-of-american-adults-get-news-from-social-media-survey-idUSKCN1BJ2A8.

104. Berlant, "Subject of True Feeling," 51.

105. Hartman, "Venus in Two Acts," 7.

106. Mbembe, *Critique of Black Reason*, 164.

107. Sharon Patricia Holland, "The Graveyard," *The Professor's Table* (blog), Aug. 31, 2017, http://theprofessorstable.wordpress.com/2017/08/31/the-graveyard.


Refrain

1. Marcus F. Quintilian, *Institutio Oratoria*, trans. Harold E. Butler (Chicago: University of Chicago, n.d.), 9.2.31.

2. See Kathy L. Cerminara and Kenneth W. Goodman, "Key Events in the Case of Theresa Marie Schiavo," University of Miami, Apr. 7, 2015, http://www.miami.edu/index.php/ethics/projects/schiavo/schiavo_timeline, retrieved Apr. 19, 2015.

3. "The administration of water and food, even when provided by artificial means, always represents a *natural means* of preserving life, not a *medical act*" (Pope John Paul II, "Address of John Paul II to the Participants in the International Congress on 'Life-Sustaining Treatments and Vegetative State: Scientific Advances and Ethical Dilemmas,'" Mar. 20, 2004, http://w2.vatican.va/content/john-paul-ii/en/speeches/2004/march/documents/hf_jp-ii_spe_2004 0320_congress-fiamc.html, emphasis in original).

4. Megan Foley, "Voicing Terri Schiavo: Prosopopeic Citizenship in the Democratic Aporia Between Sovereignty and Biopower," *Communication and Critical/Cultural Studies* 7, no. 4 (2010): 382–83.

5. On March 18, 2005, Schiavo's feeding tube was removed by court order. The next day, the US Senate delayed its Easter recess in order to reach a compromise with the House on S. 686, "For the Relief of the Parents of Theresa Marie Schiavo." On March 19–20, the House returned from Easter recess to debate the bill and voted at 12:30 a.m. to suspend its rules and pass the legislation (203 yeas to 58 nays). It was signed into law by President George W. Bush at 1:11 a.m.

6. Richard D. Knabb, Jamie R. Rhome, and Daniel P. Brown, "Tropical Cyclone Report, Hurricane Katrina, 23–30 August 2005," National Hurricane Center, Dec. 20, 2005 (updated Sept. 14, 2011), https://www.nhc.noaa.gov/data/tcr/AL122005_Katrina.pdf.

7. Jonathan Culler, "Apostrophe," *Diacritics* 7, no. 4 (1977): 59.

8. Cohen's "Who by Fire" is a phrase taken from the *Unetanneh Tokef*, a liturgical poem traditionally chanted as part of Yom Kippur, the Day of Atonement. It, too, includes a litany of fates consonant with God's judgment: "Who will live and who will die; who will die after a long life and who before his time; who by water and who by fire, who by sword and who by

beast, who by famine and who by thirst, who by upheaval and who by plague, who by strangling and who by stoning."

9. Catherine Malabou and Jacques Derrida, *Counterpath*, trans. David Wills (Stanford, CA: Stanford University Press, 2004), 4.

10. Jacques Derrida, *The Politics of Friendship*, trans. George Collins (London: Verso, 2005), 173.

11. Jacques Derrida and Bernard Stiegler, *Echographies of Television: Filmed Interviews*, trans. Jennifer Bajorek (Cambridge: Polity Press, 2002), 85.

12. Culler, "Apostrophe," 62, 59, 60, 62.

13. W. H. Auden, "In Memory of W. B. Yeats," in *Collected Poems* (London: Faber, 1976), qtd. in Culler, "Apostrophe," 62.

14. Georges Bataille, *The Accursed Share: An Essay on General Economy*, vols. 2 and 3, trans. Robert Hurley (New York: Zone Books, 1993), 81.

15. Culler, "Apostrophe," 62.

16. Ibid., 63.

17. Barbara Johnson, "Apostrophe, Animation, and Abortion," *Diacritics* 16, no. 1 (1986): 30–31.

18. Ibid., 32.

19. Barbara Johnson, "The Alchemy of Style and Law," in *The Rhetoric of Law*, ed. Austin Sarat and Tomas R. Kearns (Ann Arbor: University of Michigan Press, 1994), 267.

20. Ibid.

21. Ibid., 267–68.

22. Ibid., 266, 263.

23. Patricia J Williams, *The Alchemy of Race and Rights: Diary of a Law Professor* (Cambridge, MA: Harvard University Press, 1992), 7.

24. Ibid., 48, 47.

25. Ibid., 27, 28.

26. Ibid., 144, 11.

27. Ibid., 6.

28. Ibid., 149.

29. Johnson, "Apostrophe," 32.

30. Ibid., 35.

31. Ibid., 34.

32. Ibid., 33.

33. Mary Joe Frug, "A Postmodern Feminist Legal Manifesto (an Unfinished Draft)," *Harvard Law Review* 105, no. 5 (1992): 1050.

34. Williams, *Alchemy*, 183.

35. Johnson, "Alchemy," 265.

36. See Jill H. Casid, "Thanatography: Working the Folds of Photography's Wild Performativity in Capital's Necrocene," *Photography and Culture* (2020): 213–38, http://www.doi.org/10.1080/17514517.2020.1754658.

37. See Lauren Berlant, "Cruel Optimism," *differences* 17, no. 3 (2006): 20–36.

38. I had had these conversations with my late friend and colleague Deborah Lynn Steinberg as she was dying from cancer. Our conversations remain with me, are echoed in these pages, and found their way into a posthumous coauthorship with the dead. See Stuart J. Murray and Deborah Lynn Steinberg (deceased), "To Mourn, To Re-imagine Without Oneself: Death, Dying, and Social Media/tion," *Catalyst: Feminism, Theory, Technoscience* 4, no. 1 (2018): 1–31, https://catalystjournal.org/index.php/catalyst/article/view/29632.

39. Maurice Blanchot, *The Space of Literature*, trans. Ann Smock (Lincoln: University of Nebraska Press, 1982), 104.

40. Ibid., 125.

41. Jacques Derrida, *The Post Card: From Socrates to Freud and Beyond*, trans. Alan Bass (Chicago: University of Chicago Press, 1987), 45.

42. Andrzej Warminski, *Readings in Interpretation: Hölderlin, Hegel, Heidegger* (Minneapolis: University of Minnesota Press, 1987), lv.

43. Ludwig Wittgenstein, *Philosophische Untersuchungen / Philosophical Investigations*, trans. G. E. M. Anscombe, P. M. S. Hacker, and Joachim Schulte (Oxford: Blackwell, 2009), 14.

44. Michel Foucault, *The Courage of the Truth: The Government of Self and Others II: Lectures at the Collège de France, 1983–1984*, trans. Graham Burchell (New York: Palgrave Macmillan, 2011), 33.

45. Michel Foucault, *The Hermeneutics of the Subject: Lectures at the Collège de France, 1981–1982*, trans. Graham Burchell (New York: Palgrave Macmillan, 2005), 56–57. I note that this passage stands in sharp contrast to the "use" of neoliberalism, which "involves extending the economic model of supply and demand and investment-costs-profit so as to make it a model of social relations and of existence itself, a form of relationship of the individual to himself, time, those around him, the group, and the family" (Michel Foucault, *The Birth of Biopolitics: Lectures at the Collège de France, 1978–1979*, trans. Graham Burchell [New York: Picador, 2008], 242).

46. Ludwig Wittgenstein, *Culture and Value*, trans. Peter Winch (Oxford: Blackwell, 1980), 36.

47. The apostrophic self-address in Foucault's late work serves, on my reading, as an ethical response to the self-address, the "I," of biopolitical racism discussed at the end of chapter 4.

48. Foucault, *Hermeneutics of the Subject*, 357–58.

49. Foucault, *Courage of the Truth*, 163.

50. Plato, *Apology*, 118a, qtd. in Foucault, *Courage of the Truth*, 96.

51. Foucault, *Courage of the Truth*, 109.

52. Ibid., 153.

53. Ibid., 24.

54. Ibid., 113.

55. Ibid., 1.

56. Ibid., 287.

57. Ibid., 144, 193.

58. Ibid., 127, 234, 144.

59. Mike Baker, Jennifer Valentino-DeVries, Manny Fernandez, and Michael LaForgia, "Three Words. 70 Cases. The Tragic History of 'I Can't Breathe,'" *New York Times*, June 29, 2020, https://nytimes.com/interactive/2020/06/28/us/i-cant-breathe-police-arrest.html.

60. See, for example, Jamelle Bouie, "The Police Are Rioting. We Need to Talk About It," *New York Times*, June 5, 2020, https://nytimes.com/2020/06/05/opinion/sunday/police-riots.html.

61. Ibram X. Kendi, "What the Racial Data Show," *The Atlantic*, Apr. 6, 2020, https://www.theatlantic.com/ideas/archive/2020/04/coronavirus-exposing-our-racial-divides/609526.

62. Michel Foucault, *Fearless Speech* (Los Angeles: Semiotext(e), 2001), 17.

63. Foucault, *Courage of the Truth*, 280.

64. Ibid., 163.

65. Ibid., 172, translation modified.

66. "LeBron James Speaks on BLM: 'When You're Black, It's Not a Movement; It's a Life-style,'" YouTube, July 23, 2020, https://youtu.be/T6CkKIObfws. I thank Sarah Burgess for bringing this interview to my attention.

67. Hannah Arendt, *The Origins of Totalitarianism* (New York: Schocken Books, 2004), 463.

68. Ibid., 461–62, 468–69.

69. See Michel Foucault, *The History of Sexuality*, vol. 1, trans. Robert Hurley (New York: Random House, 1978), 157. See also my brief discussion in the introduction, 5–6.

70. See Domenico Losurdo, *Liberalism: A Counter-History*, trans. Gregory Elliott (New York: Verso, 2011). I thank Firoze Manji for bringing this text to my attention.

71. Warren Montag, "Necro-Economics: Adam Smith and Death in the Life of the Universal," *Radical Philosophy* 134 (2005): 16.

72. Maurice Blanchot, *The Infinite Conversation*, trans. Susan Hanson (Minneapolis: University of Minnesota Press, 1993), 81.

73. Foucault, *Courage of the Truth*, 183.

74. Ibid., 183–84.

75. See Robert Evans and Jason Wilson, "The Boogaloo Movement Is Not What You Think," *bellingcat*, May 27, 2020, https://www.bellingcat.com/news/2020/05/27/the-boogaloo-movement-is-not-what-you-think; Mehdi Hasan, "How the Far-Right Boogaloo Movement Is Trying to Hijack Anti-Racist Protests for a Race War," *The Intercept*, June 10, 2020, https://theintercept.com/2020/06/10/boogaloo-boys-george-floyd-protests.

76. Foucault, *Courage of the Truth*, 36–37.

77. Ibid., 185.

78. Daniele Lorenzini, *La force du vrai: De Foucault à Austin* (Lormont: Le Bord de L'eau éditions, 2017), 148–49, translation mine.

79. See Michael Hardt, "Militant Life," *New Left Review* 64 (2010): 151–60.

80. Michel Foucault, *The Government of Self and Others: Lectures at the Collège de France, 1982–1983* (New York: Palgrave Macmillan, 2010), 61, 68.

81. See Daniele Lorenzini, "Performative, Passionate, and Parrhesiastic Utterance: On Cavell, Foucault, and Truth as an Ethical Force," *Critical Inquiry* 41, no. 2 (2015): 254–68.

82. Stanley Cavell goes so far as to say that the perlocutionary expression "is not only not to *do* anything, it is in an obvious sense not so much as to *say* anything (yet)." Even so, for Cavell the perlocution produces an emotional state, which is not quite the same as the manifestation of *ēthos*. Stanley Cavell, *Philosophy the Day After Tomorrow* (Cambridge, MA: Harvard University Press, 2005), 171.

83. Foucault, *Courage of the Truth*, 283.

84. Ibid., 270, 287, 184.

# Index

Printed in the United States
by Baker & Taylor Publisher Services